PRACTICE THESE PRINCIPLES

Practice

These

Principles

Living the Spiritual Disciplines and Virtues
in 12-Step Recovery
to Achieve Spiritual Growth,
Character Development, and Emotional Sobriety

Steps 1, 2, 3

Ray A.

Practice
These
Principles

PUBLISHERS

Grateful acknowledgment is made for permission to reprint the following:

The Twelve Steps and the Twelve Traditions and excerpts from *Alcoholics Anonymous, Twelve Steps and Twelve Traditions, As Bill Sees It* and *A.A. Comes of Age* are reprinted with permission of Alcoholics Anonymous World Services, Inc. ("AAWS"). Permission to reprint these excerpts does not mean that AAWS has reviewed or approved the contents of this publication, or that AAWS necessarily agrees with the views expressed herein. A.A. is a program of recovery from alcoholism <u>only</u>. Use of these excerpts in connection with programs and activities which are patterned after A.A., but which address other problems, or in any other non-A.A. context, does not imply otherwise.

Acceptance: The Way to Serenity and Peace of Mind, by Vincent Paul Collins, copyright © 2011. Reprinted by permission of Abbey Press. *Belief in God in an Age of Science,* by John Polkinghorne, copyright © 1998. Reprinted by permission of Yale University Press. *How to Be Good in a World Gone Bad: Living a Life of Christian Virtue,* by James S. Spiegel, copyright © 2004 by James S. Spiegel, Published by Kregel Publications, Grand Rapids, MI. Used by permission of the publisher. All rights reserved. *Humility: The Journey Toward Holiness,* by Andrew Murray. Reprinted with permission of Bethany House Publishers. *Mere Christianity,* by C. S. Lewis, copyright © C. S. Lewis Pte. Ltd. 1942, 1943, 1944, 1952. *Spiritual Emotions: A Psychology of Christian Virtues,* by Robert C. Roberts, copyright © 2007 by Robert C. Roberts. Reprinted by permission of Eerdmans Publishing Co. *The Problem of Pain,* C. S. Lewis, copyright © C. S. Lewis Pte. Ltd. 1940. *Total Truth: Liberating Christianity from Its Cultural Captivity,* by Nancy Pearcey, copyright © 2004 by Nancy R. Pearcey. Used by permission of Crossway, a publishing ministry of Good News Publishers, Wheaton, IL 60187, www.crossway.org. *What's So Great About Christianity,* by Dinesh D'Souza, copyright © by Dinesh D'Souza. Reprinted by permission of Regnery Publishing.

Scriptures marked KJV and NIV are from King James Version and New International Version of the Bible, respectively.

Cataloguing Data: 1. Twelve-Step Programs 2. Spiritual life 3. Emotions 4. Virtue.

Practice These Principles: Living the Spiritual Disciplines and Virtues in 12-Step Recovery to Achieve Spiritual Growth, Character Development, and Emotional Sobriety – Steps 1, 2, 3

This book contains general information about alcoholism, recovery from alcoholism, and related matters. The information is not medical advice. The book is not an alternative to medical advice from your doctor or other professional healthcare provider.

Practice These Principles Publishers

ISBN: 978-1-7370410-3-0 (paperback)

ISBN: 978-1-7370410-5-4 (hardback)

The PTP Publishers and book cover logos are registered trademarks owned by Ray A.

Cover Design by Berge Design.

In Gratitude

To my daughter Tana, my friend Pat,
my sponsor Bob M., and the men and women of
the "If Nothing Changes, Nothing Changes"
Group of Alcoholics Anonymous
in Anonymousville.

CONTENTS

PREFACE

Most of us in long-term recovery know the Steps so well that we could easily rattle them off from memory, wrapping up our recitation with the familiar "and to practice these principles in all our affairs."

But what *are* "these principles?" Exactly what principles are the Steps calling us to practice? Which principles do we practice when working a particular Step? Faced with any number of situations in our daily lives, how readily do we discern the principles that apply, and how well then do we live them out?

In AA practicing "these principles" in all aspects of our lives is the very fulfillment of the 12 Steps. It is the program of action at its best, proof-positive of our spiritual awakening and the most convincing way to carry "this" message. As presented in Step 12 of the *Twelve Steps and Twelve Traditions*, practicing "these principles" is in fact nothing less than AA's prescription for the good and happy life, a life of emotional sobriety and spiritual growth that we share with others as we help to bring healing to all those about us, alcoholic and non-alcoholic alike.

Yet, though crucial to recovery, many of us are not really sure what these principles are. We know there is a connection between Steps and principles, but exactly what this connection is remains a gray area for most of us in AA, and probably for those in other fellowships as well.

This uncertainty is reflected in the recovery literature, which, though extensive, lacks any work that makes a cogent distinction between Steps and principles and that offers a coherent and comprehensive understanding of what the principles are and how they are practiced beyond our problem with alcohol and beyond physical sobriety.

This is what *Practice These Principles* attempts to do. Its purpose is to bring clarity to the relationship between Steps and principles so that we may be able to work the Steps more effectively and practice the principles more fully.

In so doing, the book also seeks to shed light on another and related gray area in recovery: the relationship between the moral, the emotional, and the spiritual, and how these are tied to the development of character.

Because these links too remain unclear, emotional sobriety continues to be the "next frontier" for those in long-term recovery, a distant and elusive goal for many alcoholics in AA and sufferers in other rooms. A clearer understanding of how practicing the principles in our daily lives builds character and brings about spiritual *and* emotional healing will help us to work better toward achieving these three key goals of recovery and seeing the promises in the Steps come to their full fruition.

The book's foundational thesis is that contrary to the widespread idea that the principles are the same as the Steps, the principles are distinct practices and qualities that are *embedded, embodied,* or *contained* in the Steps.

Among these, it distinguishes two large groups long seen as essential to the spiritual life and traditionally known as disciplines and virtues. Disciplines include such practical activities as self-examination, confession, and restitution; virtues such character traits as honesty, open-mindedness, and willingness. Virtues are seen as the ends, the good qualities that through repeated practice become rooted in us and gradually displace our character defects; disciplines as the means to their attainment, the channels through which they are systematically practiced.

The book seeks to show how understanding the principles as disciplines and virtues substantially affects their practice. It elaborates on the distinction between the two and shows how they work together, what makes them spiritual, which particular ones are foundational to each Step, and how they are practiced in each of the Steps to foster spiritual, character, and emotional growth.

This understanding of the principles extends beyond the Steps to the Traditions. These are shown to embody principles that are similar but which have distinct applications in them. Contrary to the conventional view, the Traditions can be practiced not only with regard to our participation in the Fellowship, but in concert with the Steps, with regard to all areas of our lives.

Practice These Principles is built on a close reading of the basic texts in which the Steps and the principles were originally laid out: AA's *Alcoholics Anonymous* (the "Big Book") and the *Twelve Steps and Twelve Traditions* (the "12&12"). As such, it focuses on alcoholics and the AA program. Nevertheless, it is hoped that those in recovery from drug and other addictions may also find help in these pages. As we go from working the Steps with regard to our respective dependencies to practicing the principles in all facets of our lives, the differences between us diminish. We may not suffer from the same dependencies, but we share the same character defects and emotional liabilities, as well as the same challenges in daily living.

In this connection, it should be noted that the book draws as well on the wider AA, recovery, and spiritual literature and on works of psychology that probe the relationship between virtue and emotion in character building, primarily from a spiritual perspective.

Because so many of us wrestle intellectually with the spiritual part of the 12 Steps, the book also draws on the contributions of thinkers in the sciences and other fields who probe the relationship between faith and reason. This is done in the hope that they might help us reconcile the two in our own lives and thus come to a full acceptance of all the Steps and all of their principles.

There are no doubt countless of us in AA and other fellowships who long for continuing and consistent growth in our recovery, in terms of our character as well as spiritually and emotionally. Somewhere along the way we stopped growing and settled into a shallow and joyless recovery hobbled by unresolved issues and often marked by internal struggle and conflict.

Many of us have experienced significant setbacks in various areas, sometimes a physical or emotional relapse. We now have come to a point where we want to move forward, but we just don't know what to do. We may sincerely believe that we have worked all the Steps, or that we did the best we could with those we could get a handle on. In either case, we often feel like we have exhausted the tools of the program. But we haven't. As some of us are beginning to find out, we have barely begun to use them. We are going back, re-examining those Steps and those principles, and re-discovering the path to a life that is "happy, joyous, and free."

What follows is the story of one such experience and how it led to the writing of this book.

Introduction

Like most alcoholics, I came to AA because I was desperate and had nowhere else to turn. Twenty-five years of drinking had closed all the other doors. They had been tumultuous years, as willpower and the bottle enabled me to overcome one obstacle after another only to raise more and still greater obstacles in their place. It seemed I had tried everything in what was a succession of peaks and valleys, with crisis following upon crisis and one bottom following upon another.

After a brief stint with religion, I had turned my back on God and taken other, more traveled roads, turning first to agnosticism and then to atheism in my search for things that I can articulate now only in retrospect, elusive things like purpose and direction, meaning and fulfillment, a sense of identity and self-worth.

There would be more college programs, new jobs and careers, an infatuation with music, art, literature, and culture, commitments to philosophies and social causes, and, of course, the allure of romance. Like religion, all of these things would crumble. Every dream realized, every plan met, every goal reached, and every achievement attained would sooner or later lose its initial glitter and allure. Nothing would satisfy. I would always want more.

In the end, I lost it all. Homeless, broke, unemployable, alone, gripped by fear and depression and consumed with self-pity, I was beaten and humiliated. In all my striving, I had never seen that I was self-destructing. Nor had I paid any attention to the collateral damage I was causing. It all came back to haunt me now. I was tormented by guilt and shame, regret and remorse. The drive and energy were gone. I was literally in the gutter and couldn't pick myself up again. My will was finally broken.

This "low bottom" effectively crushed my rebellion. Coming to the rooms, I offered no resistance to AA. There were no reservations about the "spiritual angle," God, or anything else. I took to the program with the same zeal and intensity that had characterized everything I had done as an active alcoholic.

I found a sponsor the first ninety days and for the next ten years we met practically every week. I went through the Steps with him early on and did what the program said to do. I took an inventory of myself and made amends to those I had hurt. I did service and tried to help another alcoholic. I continued to go to meetings and to work the Steps.

The results were substantial. I grew as a person and made considerable progress in my relations with people. There was some business and material success as well.

Yet all along there was a great deal of unmanageability in my life, particularly in a long-term love relationship and in my work. I tried very hard with both, but it seemed nothing could bring peace and stability, much less happiness, to either. As for the joy the program promised, I didn't have the slightest idea of what that meant.

By my 12th year of sobriety, my life began to unravel. I lost my business and my home and seemed to be on the verge of losing the woman I loved. I tried to start all over again in another city, but nothing seemed to work. The new business I opened failed. I couldn't find a job. With all my funds exhausted, I was facing homelessness again.

This was all too familiar, a reprise of the closing chapter of my drinking story. Except that I didn't drink. I had what I would eventually come to understand as an emotional relapse. For the next six years, I revisited all the dark precincts of my mind. Back were the gnawing anxiety and the swooning depression, accompanied this time by a fear bordering on terror. I sank to depths of despair that rivaled any I had known while drinking.

What about AA? Well, I went to meetings, but that didn't help. I was an embarrassment to myself and the program, an alcoholic in double-digit recovery oozing pain and negativity from every pore. AA didn't seem to work, and that was the message I was carrying. I was living in the problem and nobody was showing me the solution. Or at least I couldn't see it.

I came to the conclusion that my ailment went beyond AA, that I had an emotional illness of the clinical variety. So I tried to get "professional" help again. But therapy and antidepressants had failed before and they would fail again.

Still, I was convinced my problem was emotional. What else could it be? I was obviously an emotional cripple. Searching for an answer, I took the *Twelve Steps and Twelve Traditions* off the shelf and read through Step 12. There it was: "emotional sobriety." Years earlier AA had introduced me to this concept, and somewhere in the back of my mind I suspected that, whatever it was, I didn't have it.

Oh, I had always been an emotional fellow, but I wasn't sure there was anything wrong with that. Besides, I couldn't see what that had to do with all my troubles. But now, for the first time, I saw that I was in fact a bundle of uncontrollable emotions and that my feelings actually ran my life. The solution, the 12th Step seemed to be saying, was to "practice these principles" in all my affairs. If I lived my life according to those principles, I wouldn't be beaten about by all those feelings. I would be emotionally sober. But what principles were they talking about? Hadn't I worked the Steps? Where had I gone wrong?

With these questions in mind, I set out to re-examine the basic AA texts. I also delved into self-help books and even some religious literature. It was like a search for the Holy Grail. Whatever the principles were, I couldn't find them. I lost all hope that there was an answer, that there was any help for this alcoholic.

My mental condition continued to deteriorate and thoughts of suicide started to resurface. Then one day, when I couldn't bear the pain anymore and the world seemed to be closing in on me again, I fell to my knees and cried out to God from some primal place deep down inside of me. I asked God to come into my life and save me from whatever it was that was killing me, and I offered to give my life to him. At that moment, the fear and depression lifted. A sense of peace came over me and with it the assurance that all would be well. Somehow, I knew that he was there and that he had heard me. I was safe.

Though I couldn't explain why, I now felt completely confident that God would show me the way to a better life. I knew now in my own heart that the good life, the sober life, was simply the spiritual life. This is what AA had said all along, but I hadn't understood what that meant any more than I had understood what the principles were. And I still didn't. But what I understood now was that the spiritual life was somehow grounded in those principles, that God was their source, and that if I truly wanted to live them out, he would help me do it.

Having drifted from AA, I started my renewed search through religion. I read a lot and started attending various types of religious services. Little by little, I began to glimpse some of the principles of the spiritual life. But I had no place to work through them with other people. Feeling the need for such fellowship, I drifted back into the rooms. It was then that I came upon a little group meeting in a rural area in what seemed to be the middle of nowhere. This group was focused on working the spiritual program of recovery as originally laid out in the Big Book and the 12&12.

This proved to be another turning point. Apparently, this was the AA group of last resort for many in the area, seemingly hopeless alcoholics who hadn't quite "gotten the program" in other rooms, even if they had stopped drinking and had double-digit sobriety. Many were drunks for whom AA didn't seem to work, here to take a second, a third, maybe the last look. Sticking closely to the text of the book and sharing from the heart, they were re-examining the spiritual solution and doing so with a passion that was contagious.

It was here that the spiritual solution came alive for me. The principles had been in those basic texts all the time, but it took this particular bunch of drunks to breathe life into them. I regained the faith I had lost in the AA program and with it a new hope. This was the hope that, by the grace of God, I would come to understand "these principles" and practice them in all my affairs, and that I would then grow in emotional sobriety and be able to live a full life in recovery.

These pages represent one step in that journey of faith.

PRACTICE THESE PRINCIPLES

"Having had a spiritual awakening as the result of these steps, we tried to carry this message to alcoholics, and to practice these principles in all our affairs."

–Step 12

PRACTICE THESE PRINCIPLES

1

THESE PRINCIPLES

When we first come to AA, few if any of us are terribly interested in having a spiritual awakening, carrying any message, or practicing any principles. We just want to stop drinking and have a normal life.

We go to meetings, admit we are alcoholics, and get sober. Yet our problems are not over. Our lives are still unmanageable. We are said to have been like "a tornado, roaring [our] way through the lives of others" (Big Book, p. 82), and we have left a long trail of destruction behind. The wreckage of the past lies everywhere. We have to clean up and build anew, sometimes from scratch. And that is just the exterior damage. There is havoc inside as well. We are emotional wrecks, and though we may be loath to admit it, morally and spiritually bankrupt as well.

We soon find that not drinking is hardly a panacea. There is work to be done. At some point, the message gets through that our problem is bigger than the bottle. Physical sobriety is not enough. We have a disease that is also emotional and spiritual. To heal in all three areas, we have to take certain Steps.

It is a message most of us don't want to hear. We balk at some of those Steps, in the beginning and often long thereafter. Understandably, we wish there was "an easier, softer way." Experience says there isn't, that "half measures" won't do, and that we have to be willing to go "to any length" if we are to recover fully. We are told that we have to give ourselves completely to a program of action which requires that we "let go absolutely." We have to commit to a way of living that demands "rigorous honesty" (ibid., pp. 58–59).

Before long, it dawns on us that the 12 Steps are not about how to stop drinking. They are not intended to teach us alcoholics how to quit—a futile enterprise if there was ever one—but to show us how to live. For that in the final analysis is our larger problem: we just don't know how to live. And this is what AA has to offer us, a different "manner of living," a new way of life.

We are incapable of living this new way unless we undergo a radical change internally. To effect this change is the purpose of the Steps. And yes, the change is spiritual. If we thoroughly follow the path that the Steps lay out, we cannot fail. We will reach a stage in our recovery when we will experience a spiritual awakening. Healed in spirit, we will be healed in heart and mind. Having had a spiritual awakening, we will try to carry this message to alcoholics and to practice these principles in all our affairs.

It is not what we wanted, but it is what we need. In time, many of us will fall in love with the entire pattern of living we come to find in AA.

Carrying the message and practicing the principles is how we live our new life in recovery. There is nothing ordinary about either undertaking. *This* message is that, as *the* result of these Steps, we have had a spiritual awakening that transformed our very being, "which revolutionized our whole attitude toward life, toward our fellows and toward God's universe" (Big Book, p. 25). *These* principles are the foundational precepts that guide our path as we try to "live usefully and walk humbly under the grace of God" (12&12, S12, p. 125). This, we recognize at last, is our true and authentic ambition.

Practicing these principles in all our affairs is the culmination of the 12 Steps of AA. We work *all* of the 12 Steps, and we work them in *all* areas of our lives on an ongoing basis. In doing this we seek more than physical sobriety, and we seek to do more than carry a message of such sobriety to other alcoholics. We practice these principles in all our affairs "so that we and those about us may find emotional sobriety" (ibid., p. 106). That is what will enable us to live a useful, happy, and joyous life and share it with our fellows everywhere.

At times we have seen the whole AA scheme as a tall order, other times as a noble but impossible ideal. It is neither. It is totally realistic. And it works.

It is true that even the most committed among us fail to practice the principles of the program on a consistent basis. But that is not necessarily a problem, so long as such practice is our goal and we continue to make progress toward it.

The difficulty lies elsewhere. It is a fact of AA life that physical sobriety alone will do a great deal for the alcoholic, at least for a while. The happy fact of this partial solution can have sad consequences. It is the source of the trouble many of us have in recovery.

Once we are sober and our lives begin to improve, there is a tendency to become lax about the program. We feel satisfied with our progress and we become complacent. Our "true ambition" wanes, or we never find it to begin with.

We react in various ways to this common temptation to rest on our laurels. One is to question the need to work the whole program. If things are going so well, why do we need to do all of the 12 Steps? That is when "two-stepping" sets in. We practice that part of Step 1 that says we are powerless over alcohol and that part of Step 12 that calls on us to carry the message, a message now reduced to the fact that we have stopped drinking. We subsist on the baby formula of "don't drink and go to meetings." We stop growing.

Others take a different tack. We are the AAs who acknowledge a problem with the spiritual part of the program. We are sober, aren't we? What do we need all that spiritual stuff for? We avoid the more obviously spiritual Steps, the so-called God Steps: 2, 3, 5, 6, 7, and 11. We try to cobble together some sort of inventory, not getting too moral about it to be sure, and steering clear of the deity. Then we make some general apologies here and there and say how sorry we are. Some of us try to be a little more thorough, while still keeping the deity at bay. We are the "self-helpers," and we are bent on keeping God out of "our" program.

Still other of us have a less discernible problem. We don't object to any of the Steps or to God. We may even be sincere in our religious or spiritual beliefs. We have tried hard and we honestly believe we have done all the Steps. We might even feel that we have had a spiritual awakening, at least of the gradual variety. We certainly don't see ourselves as being lax. Yet, there comes a time when we realize there is something wrong. Things are not going as we expected. We feel that we are working the program, but somehow the program is not working for us. We are baffled and discouraged. We may cut down on meetings or stop going altogether.

Our difficulty lies with that last phrase of Step 12. We may have "taken" the Steps, but we are not *working* them, at least not fully and consistently. Despite our best intentions, and without necessarily being conscious of it, we are not practicing *all* of the principles, nor are we practicing them in *all* our affairs.

This failure to practice all the principles in all areas of life is what the well-meaning, usually one-time "step-taker" has in common with the self-helper and the two-stepper. The result is uniform: not growing spiritually, we fall short of attaining emotional sobriety. We remain far from living the life that AA promises and that we long for. Some of us pay a steep price. Sooner or later, reality catches up with us and we are not ready to handle it. Unresolved issues flare up again. Things we have been struggling with all along at home or work get totally out of hand. Our marriage or romantic relationship falls apart. We lose our job or our business fails. Suddenly, we face a severe financial crisis, can't pay our mortgage or rent, and are in danger of losing our home. Or else, a loved one is unexpectedly diagnosed with a serious illness. Or a tragic accident takes place and death strikes a blow.

When these things happen, many of us find ourselves in an eerily familiar situation. Unmanageability creeps back into our lives. We can't cope.

Many of us relapse. Sometimes we drink; sometimes our relapse is emotional and we do everything but drink. Some of us make it back to the rooms; others don't.

Those of us who do return to AA and try again often discover that the solution to our problem was there all along. We are reminded that we simply have to turn away from half measures. We are assured that whatever calamities may befall us can be transformed into assets that will bring comfort and help us to grow if we turn to the spiritual solution, and working all the Steps, "are willing to receive that grace of God which can sustain and strengthen us in any catastrophe" (12&12, S12, p. 113).

This is AA's message of hope. Forced again by circumstance, many of us return to the rooms with a renewed sense of purpose. We decide to take a second look, to probe deeper. We change meetings and find a new home group. We start going back to Big Book and 12&12 meetings, a practice abandoned perhaps years earlier or maybe never started. We want to revisit the experience of those early alcoholics, study what those books have to say, and come to a full understanding of the Steps. We want to know how it really works and where we went astray. With God's grace, we begin to see that there is a wealth of spiritual wisdom in the Steps and that we have not even begun to scratch the surface of what they have to offer. We realize that we never got past our "spiritual kindergarten" (*As Bill Sees It*, p. 95), and that we were hardly putting the principles to work in our daily lives.

STEPS AND PRINCIPLES

If we are going to "practice these principles in all our affairs," which we reiterate is the loftiest goal of the 12 Steps and our highest aspiration—indeed AA's prescription for the good life—we need to know what this part of Step 12 is calling us to do. When we consider this phrase, most of us tend to focus on the word "all." We know what the principles are and we know what affairs means. The idea is to practice the principles in *all* areas of our lives, not just in the rooms and not just as regards our drinking problem.

This is of course true. But what, exactly, are these principles? Well, at first sight, they appear to be the Steps. Many, if not most of us, think of "these principles" as being synonymous with "these Steps." That is after all how it comes across in the text of Step 12: "these Steps . . . these principles." In addition, in the "How It Works" chapter of the Big Book, "these principles" refers directly to the 12 Steps just outlined (p. 60). Such equivalence between Step and principle is common in the foundational AA literature.

The reason for this is plain: as a rule, we practice the principles by working the Steps, and hence we tend to identify the ones with the others. There are a number of problems with this, not least of which is the fact that the Big Book and the 12&12 use the word principle in relation to terms and expressions that don't seem to correspond to any particular Step. Some of these actually involve the Traditions.

As we explore the matter further, we discover that there is a functional relationship between Steps and principles such that these terms cannot properly be considered identical or interchangeable. Admitting powerlessness, taking inventory, admitting our wrongs, making amends, carrying the message—these acts are not principles in and of themselves. Rather, the principles lie at the root of these acts, informing, motivating, and directing them. The acts are predicated and follow upon these underlying principles. What the Steps do is *embody* the principles. The Steps are guides to action, and the action is based on certain animating principles *embedded* in them.

That the Steps are not equivalent to principles but rather contain and channel them becomes clearer when we consider a number of other factors. We will see, for instance, that each Step involves the practice of not just one but of multiple interrelated principles. Furthermore, we will see that some of the same principles are operational in more than one Step, though in ways that are distinctive and consonant with the specific objectives of the Step. In addition, we will find that when it comes to applying these principles to our various endeavors, we will at times practice some without necessarily linking them directly or immediately to any one Step. That is, we will not be working a particular Step, so much as practicing a principle encompassing several Steps.

The conflation of Steps and principles arises because what distinction AA may draw between the two is made in an ad hoc rather than systematic manner. Nowhere are the principles clearly identified, grouped, and correlated with the Steps. This reflects the experiential origins and development of AA, which is primarily concerned with narrating and describing experience, drawing lessons as it goes. Attempts to systematize or "codify" the principles flowing from AA experience were fiercely resisted by alcoholics from the very start. This was the case with the drafting of the 12 Steps and later the 12 Traditions, and with the publication of the Big Book and the 12&12 subsequently.[1]

The result is that many of us are left with a general and vague impression of the principles and their association with the Steps. This may suffice for early sobriety, but it produces diminishing returns as time goes on and we are faced with the need to grow in emotional sobriety and apply those principles beyond our drinking to issues affecting the ordinary course of our lives.

Over the long haul—and it is a long haul—how well we work the Steps depends on how well we practice the principles inherent in them. To work a Step fully is to practice *all* of the principles it embodies. To practice these principles in all our affairs is to practice *all* of the principles in *all* of the Steps.

If we are to do this, we need clarity. "Understanding is the key to right principles and attitudes," we are told, "and right action is the key to good living" (12&12, S12, p. 125). Right action depends on right principles. We need to be clear on what these are if we are to practice them effectively.

Before proceeding with a preliminary discussion of the principles, however, we might do well to refresh our memory as to what constitutes a principle. Because of its conflation with the Steps, and despite the central place that the concept holds in recovery, "principle" is a term that seldom comes up in the rooms. We talk about working the Steps, rarely about practicing the principles. When the term does come up, the tendency is to use it so loosely and so broadly that the word loses its distinctive meaning and hence its usefulness.

"Principle" derives from a Latin word meaning "first" and denotes a basic truth, law, rule, or standard that forms the foundation on which other things are built or which governs their operation. Principles are first things, that which comes before, that on which other things rest.

The concept is captured in one of the slogans on display in many AA rooms: "First Things First." Applied to our alcohol problem, this says that our sobriety takes precedence over everything because everything else depends on it. If we drink, we are likely to do serious damage to and perhaps even lose everything we have: family, home, job, friends, and in some cases even our freedom and our lives. If we put work first and sobriety second, we run the risk of losing both.

Note that this is not just a question of setting priorities. Priorities are important, and we need to set them to order our goals and activities. But while important, priorities usually respond to considerations of utility within a limited chronological framework. They are generally relative, circumstantial, temporary, arbitrary, preferential, and subjective. Principles are instead objective, permanent, and universal. They come first, before other things, not just because of sequential, order-of-importance considerations, but because they are foundational. They order not just transient activity but life foundations.

Priorities are ordinarily matters of expedience. But expedience and principle are antithetical. If not drinking is no more than a priority, even the most urgent priority at a given stage of my recovery, the day will surely come when an even more important priority will arise and I will put that ahead of recovery, compromising my sobriety.

The 12th Tradition's maxim of "principles before personalities" also encapsulates the concept. It tells us that the Fellowship, like the program, is based on principles. Its survival and growth depend on not allowing personality issues, which are marginal and ephemeral, to trump those principles, which are central and enduring.

Like program and Fellowship, every field of endeavor has its basic foundational and operational principles. This is true of the arts, the sciences, sports, and the lowliest trade. Bridges are built and airplanes constructed according to certain principles of engineering and aeronautics, for instance. If these principles are not followed, the bridge will not stand and the plane will not fly.

The same is true of human life. It too has its principles. If not followed, life doesn't work, and it may even collapse or crash. While we may acknowledge this about those aspects of our lives that have to do with our physical health, we are less likely to do so when it comes to our emotional and spiritual condition.

That there is an order to life and that there are principles governing that order are ideas largely foreign to the mind of the active alcoholic. Chaos marked our lives. We lived in reaction to instincts, feelings, desires, obsessions, compulsions, and impulses—all ignited and fueled by self-will.

Our parents may have tried to instill certain principles in us when we were young. They did not succeed: we rejected or could not put those principles into practice. In some cases, of course, they may have been false principles that did not work in the real world. At various junctures, too, we may have subscribed to different ideas and ideals that we thought would give direction to our lives. Some of these may have been drawn from philosophy, religion, the social sciences, the arts, or literature. These didn't work either, or we wouldn't be where we are.

AA offers us the principles we lacked. If we practice these principles as a way of life, the obsession to drink will be removed and we will be able to live whole, useful, and happy lives. This is no empty promise. The experience of countless alcoholics proves that these principles work. We are reminded of this fact at the end of practically every meeting we attend: "it works if you work it," we declare, sure that we have the goods to prove it.

What is the nature of these principles, which work where everything else failed? The Foreword to the 12&12 is explicit: the 12 Steps are a set of principles "spiritual in their nature" (p. 15). This claim, that the principles of the program are fundamentally spiritual, is repeated and sustained through-out the Big Book and the 12&12. Yet it is not readily apparent why this is so. This gives some of us reason, particularly if we have trouble with the spiritual part of the program, to look for alternative, i.e., secular, accounts of the principles.

If we are to practice *these* principles, and not some other principles, and if we are to practice them in their full scope, it helps to know in what sense AA says they are spiritual. Several things, all closely related, come to mind.

First, these principles have a spiritual purpose: to lead us to a spiritual awakening, to lay our spirit open to a relationship with God as the Power who can restore us to sanity. Second, they have a spiritual application: they represent practical expressions of God's will for how we are to live a life of sobriety in all its dimensions, as it affects our character, our emotions, and all our God-given faculties. Third, these principles are guides to continued spiritual progress; they give us direction as we grow along spiritual lines in our relationship with God and our fellows. Fourth, these principles cannot be practiced on our own power, but by the power of God granted through grace. It is the Spirit of God, working within our spirit, who enables us to live these principles out in the real world.

As we come to accept the spiritual nature of the principles of our pro-gram, we find ourselves changing in unexpected ways. We start to shed our old attitudes and begin to see things in a different light, drawing more of our inspiration from the things of the spirit. We grow more conscious of God's presence and of his power working in us. We become aware that we are do-ing things that we could not possibly do by ourselves.

DISCIPLINES AND VIRTUES

Taking a closer look at the principles now, we will see that they can be classified into two broad, predominant groups. In the Western or Ju-deo-Christian spiritual tradition, these have come to be known as disciplines and virtues. Together, they comprise principles of the spiritual life governing our relationship with God, and principles of the moral life governing our relationship with our fellows. We can look at the virtues as the goals or ends, the spiritual qualities, character traits, and mental and emotional dispositions we aspire to attain; at the disciplines as the means through which we strive toward them.

This is not to say that disciplines and virtues are the only principles at work in AA as laid out in its basic texts. There are others, and we shall have occasion to see what they are and how they work. One of these we have briefly alluded to, for "First Things First" is not just a slogan but itself a key principle of the spiritual life. Yet these other principles do not coalesce into distinct and significant groups. Moreover, they are functionally related to the disciplines and virtues as the core principles through which the Steps work. "First Things First," for instance, is a function of the virtue of wisdom, and it works through such disciplines as prayer and meditation.

Their centrality notwithstanding, discipline and virtue are not part of the vocabulary of AA experience. The terms are used in the literature, but no systematic attempt is made to identify and discuss the principles under these classifications. Instead, we will find that the principles overall are accorded a variety of labels which, while good, are nevertheless general and indistinct. This includes such names as assets, concepts, precepts, qualities, standards, tenets, themes, strengths, tools, traits, values, or even just practices.

This is not surprising, given the aversion to systematization already alluded to. This aversion persists. Many of us prefer generalization, vagueness, and imprecision when it comes to the Steps, the principles, and how AA works. We see this as safeguarding our individuality and leaving us free to choose how to work the program. The more generic or malleable a term, the more we can give it our own personal meaning. AA bends over backwards to accommodate us, even as it pointedly declares that the main purpose of the Big Book is "To show other alcoholics *precisely how we have recovered*" (p. xiii, italics in the original).

Yet words matter. They are the tools that enable us to think. If they are general and imprecise, so will be our thinking. We will fall short of the needed clarity and understanding, the principles will remain amorphous, and our practice will lack substance, consistency, and direction.

Disciplines and virtues are concepts that have developed over the course of more than two millennia within a variety of secular and religious traditions as people have tried to understand the principles underlying human behavior, thought, and emotion, and to apply that understanding to the question of what constitutes a good life and how to pursue it. More than just words, the terms embody a rich tradition of thought and practice that underlies much of the AA program and from which we can continue to benefit as we seek to understand and work those principles in our recovery.

First Set

THE DISCIPLINES

Looking first at what is meant by a discipline, we will find that the term comes from a Latin word from which we get our word disciple, meaning a pupil or student, that is, one who follows or adheres to a given set of teach-

course of learning or training. Attaining mastery or excellence in any field of endeavor requires following a particular discipline, a set of methods, exercises, or practices peculiar to that field.

Recovery in AA is no different. It too has its own set of disciplines. These disciplines apply to two fundamental aspects of our lives: the spiritual and the moral, that is, our relationship with God and our relationship with others.

In the moral life, a discipline refers to a course of training or a set of practices that aims to promote a specific pattern of behavior and character traits in an individual's relations with his neighbor. In the spiritual life, a discipline refers to training and practice designed to bring about a specific pattern of behavior and character traits in an individual's relations with God. The aim is to know God's will for us, especially as it affects our relations with others, and to receive the grace by which to do it. Because of this, because our relationship with God is the basis for our relationship with neighbor, all the disciplines, including the moral, are rightly judged to be spiritual.

The more familiar word "program" by which we refer to the 12 Steps contains some of the same basic ideas as discipline, primarily the idea of an objectively ordered, methodical, and purposeful sequence of actions aimed at attaining a set of skills necessary to achieve a desired goal. What it lacks is the subjective connotations discipline carries of high motivation, deliberate intention, commitment, diligence, and perseverance.

The disciplines form the backbone of the 12 Steps. In AA these consist of surrender, self-examination, confession, restitution, prayer, meditation, service, witness, and fellowship. All of these are of course ancient religious or spiritual practices, though their names and how they are understood and applied may vary from one tradition to another. We learn in AA history that they come to us through the Judeo-Christian tradition via the Oxford Group, the evangelical movement modeled on first-century Christianity that influenced AA in its formative stages.[2]

Of these, surrender is the foundational discipline. This is so in two ways. First, it is the core discipline of the first three Steps (often called the "surrender Steps"), which lay the foundation for the other nine. Second, it is the discipline at the root of each of the other disciplines. We will find that without surrender, no other discipline can be fully practiced and no Step fully worked. Rebellion blocks our way at every turn. Surrender is the requisite spiritual discipline, the discipline that opens the door to a right relationship with God, which in turn makes a right relationship with neighbor possible. Thus our journey through the Steps and the disciplines is first and foremost a continuing and deepening process of self-surrender.

I surrender to the pain on how the "Universe" is trying to teach one something — *self-surrender*

This may come as a surprise to many AAs, since the word is not found anywhere in the Big Book or the 12&12. However, its absence is due to pragmatic and historical rather than conceptual considerations. That is, AA did not object to the principle itself, but to the way it was applied and the overtones it took on at a certain point in time. Of the principles borrowed from the Oxford Group, it was the only one that, ironically, was avoided precisely because of its association with it.

There were three reasons for this. First, the Group had a membership requirement where one had to "make a surrender" on one's knees in front of other members. The act was coerced, and to many alcoholics, it represented one of the most objectionable aspects of religion. This is one of the factors that eventually led to the break with the Group and the formation of AA (and the writing of Tradition 3).

The second reason was that at the time the Big Book was being written, the OG had gotten caught up in a huge political controversy involving Europe and the Second World War. Using a well-known OG term in the book might have drawn AA into that controversy and damage the Fellowship (this aversion to controversy was later codified in Tradition 10).

And the third reason was that at a time of war—which within a few months would engulf the U.S. as well—the idea of surrender seemed to be totally out of place.

As the war and the OG faded into memory, however, it became safe to use the term again. Thus we will find as many as 21 pages of entries indexed under "surrender" in *As Bill Sees It*, published in 1967. In *Daily Reflections*, published in 1990, we will find eight such pages.

These later changes notwithstanding, surrender never became a familiar word in AA and is seldom used in the rooms. Moreover, it became confused with acceptance, which was sometimes used to supplant it. The case is different in the other fellowships inspired by AA, which openly used the word surrender from their inception.

Of all the entries on surrender in *As Bill Sees It* (most from the Big Book and the 12&12), only one (from *A.A. Today*), mentions the word directly. Yet, they clearly show how central the idea of surrender is to the Steps and the whole program of recovery. Indeed, as we read in one of those entries (p. 242) and as we shall discuss shortly, AA was *founded* on the idea of surrender.

The first step in surrender is our admission of powerlessness to control our drinking and manage our lives. At first, this admission doesn't rise to the level of a discipline, which is inherently a product of choice. Instead, it is forced on us by circumstance. But as we continue in recovery, our admission of powerlessness begins to transcend our problem with alcohol and extends to all our affairs. It is then that we start to practice surrender as a discipline and Step 1 becomes, at all times and in all situations, the first and indispensable Step. In Step 2 we continue to yield power and control by surrendering unbelief, which separates us from the greater Power who can restore us to sanity. In Step 3 we make a decision to surrender all to God, our will and our very lives.

The other disciplines grow out of and in their own distinctive ways continue this process of surrender. They become operational through one or more specific Steps.

Self-examination (self-appraisal, self-survey, self-searching) is the discipline we practice when we make an inventory of ourselves in Step 4 and draw a list of character defects and of persons we have harmed; when in Step 6 we review our list of defects and prepare ourselves to have them removed; when in Step 8 we build on the list of those we have hurt, and preparing to make restitution, consider more closely the actual harm we did and the defects in us that caused it; and when in Step 10 we repeat the whole process as we continue to take inventory.

We engage in confession when we admit the exact nature of our wrongs in Step 5, when we acknowledge to others in Step 9 the harm we caused them when we drank, and when, having fallen again into wrongdoing in sobriety, we promptly admit it in Step 10 to God, to ourselves, and to the person we hurt. Confession simply means to admit (in the original Latin) and is synonymous with acknowledging or disclosing our wrongs. It has no religious or denominational connotations in AA, where it is practiced in its own characteristic ways.

Besides confession, Steps 9 and 10 also involve the discipline of restitution, so that we seek not only to admit but also to amend, giving back or restoring what we have taken from others (things tangible and intangible) and repairing our relations with them in acts of reconciliation.

Prayer as a discipline is the business of Step 3, where we offer ourselves to God; of Step 7, where we ask for the removal of our shortcomings; and of Step 11, where we petition for the knowledge of God's will for us and the power to do it.

But we may work prayer into other Steps as well. There will be times when we will ask God to help us accept our powerlessness in Step 1, to help us come to believe in 2, to help us become willing in 3. When prayer guides our self-examination in Step 4, it is more likely to be searching and fearless, for it is conscious contact with God that makes inventory-taking a spiritual practice and not just an intellectual exercise in self-analysis or a morbid introspection driven by guilt. The same applies to confession in Steps 5, 9, and 10, where prayer can help us let go of fear so we can be totally straightforward in our admission of wrongs. In restitution, making it a habit to pray—for ourselves and for the person we are making amends to—can enhance our efforts at healing wounds and division.

Meditation, while sequentially first appearing in Step 11, is a companion to prayer, and as we grow spiritually, we learn to practice this discipline in any Step whenever we seek God's counsel. As with prayer, conscious contact through reflection, contemplation, or meditation can help us get in the proper spiritual frame of mind so that we can look at our shortcomings, the harm we have done, and the restitutions that we need to make free from fear, anger, resentment, and other emotional obstacles that arise when we try to operate without God's guidance.

Service is the discipline we practice in Step 12, where we give freely of ourselves. We share the message of recovery with other alcoholics, and through our conduct in all our affairs, we bear witness to the power of God's love to change lives, helping to bring healing and hope to non-alcoholics as well.

As this suggests, there are two other disciplines closely allied with service in this Step, and we think it useful to distinguish them. These are the disciplines of witness and fellowship. Service is a broad category in AA, and witness is generally subsumed under it. There is logic to this, for as a spiritual principle we can view service as what we do for others for God's sake, because of what he has done for us in restoring us to sanity, and in this sense it does include witness.

But witness has its own distinct characteristics as a discipline. In its essence, witness (Old English for personal knowledge) is primarily concerned with testifying to the truth of something, providing evidence or proof that something is in fact the case. This is what we do when we carry the message by sharing, whether through the spoken or the written word. It is also what we do when we carry the message by example, by applying the principles to the way we live. In one case we are saying and in the other showing that what the program says about the spiritual path to recovery is true, that it works.

Whether by word or deed, our witness grows out of direct personal experience and is a message of strength and hope. Such is the testimony we seek to give when, in the 3rd Step Prayer (Big Book, p. 63), we ask God to take away our difficulties, that in our victory over them we may "bear witness" to those we would help that it is indeed God's "Power, Love, and Way of life" that is at work in us.

We practice the discipline of fellowship when we come together as a group to share. Such sharing of course commonly involves witnessing and may also involve service if, let us say, we are leading or qualifying at the meeting. But fellowship as a discipline aims at more than giving our testimony or volunteering to help. Its goal is to help build a certain kind of relationship among the members of the group, a spiritual kinship or friendship, we might say.

In building this relationship another discipline, already linked to Steps 5, 9, and 10 comes into play, and this is the discipline of confession. We share our weaknesses or shortcomings and our hopes for healing and growth, and as others identify and share in the same spirit, our fellowship deepens. It is in these moments of candid confession, often punctuated by undisguised pain, that many of us sense the presence of God in the rooms of AA.

As we saw earlier with prayer and meditation, we can see also with service and the associated disciplines of witnessing and fellowship that it is characteristic of the disciplines to interact with and build on each other throughout the Steps.

A confession of the exact nature of our wrongs can be only as thorough as the self-examination and inventory upon which it is based. We cannot surrender our shortcomings in Step 7 if we have not laid the groundwork through surrender in the preceding Steps, and coming to Step 6, abandoned all resistance to God's will. And only as we are entirely ready to surrender the wrongs in us are we truly prepared to make restitution for the wrongs we have done others in Steps 8, 9, and 10. In Step 12, all the Steps and all the disciplines come together as we seek to live a life of spiritual wholeness and practice the principles in all we do.

These various practices exhibit all the characteristics of a discipline outlined earlier. As disciplines, they account for the fact that none of the Steps of AA is a one-time or a one-issue proposition, meant to be taken only once or just occasionally or haphazardly. The disciplines that lie behind them are intended to be practiced regularly and applied to all aspects of our lives with purpose and commitment.

In the process of our doing so, the Steps gradually become less of a tall order, and in time the disciplines grow into spiritual habits, a progressively natural way of life. We surrender and yield with greater ease and grace. We examine our conscience daily and are quick to admit wrongs and make amends. We seek conscious contact and God's will consistently, taking to our knees morning and night in prayer and meditation and reconnecting at regular intervals during the course of the day. We give of ourselves and share freely. We engage with others and participate with pleasure in the things that bring us together for the common good.

Second set

THE VIRTUES

But the disciplines will not accomplish these things on their own. The disciplines are means or channels. They are the agency through which we practice the second set of principles embedded in the Steps. These are the virtues.

Like principles and Steps, disciplines and virtues are also sometimes conflated in AA. This results in part from the fact that the practice of a virtue requires discipline in the sense of consistent and repeated effort. More generally, the confusion stems from the fact that disciplines and virtues are closely connected and interdependent. They share common ends. Both are ordered to our relationship with God and neighbor. Both seek to further a spiritual transformation that brings about a change in character and in emotional and behavioral patterns.

But while the disciplines aim to effect this change, we might say, indirectly, through the practice of certain acts (self-examination, confession, restitution) that remain external to us, the virtues aim to do so directly, through the practice of certain acts that ingrain specific inner qualities in us to which the acts correspond and of which they are the outward expression.

Examining, admitting, and making amends for our wrongs are activities that require certain inner qualities in us if we are to carry them out to good purpose and maximum effect. When driven by these qualities, repeated practice of the activities has the effect of etching the qualities deep into the self so that, over time, they become the kinds of interior habits we call character traits.

While complementary, then, disciplines and virtues are not equivalent. Disciplines are activities, virtues their motivating traits. Disciplines involve external acts, virtues include internal qualities. Disciplines are what we do, virtues how we do them.

Virtues are interior habits or traits of character, and in recovery we acquire them in the process of practicing them within the framework of the disciplines. We practice the virtues that they may take root in us, that they may become an ingrained and integral part of our character, disposing us to think, to feel, and to act in certain ways.

As they do, our practice of the disciplines becomes progressively better and, in time, virtuous, that is, fully in tune with their worthy objectives and fully capable of realizing them. The dynamic is one where virtuous action generates virtuous traits, which in turn generate more virtuous action and do so more naturally, with greater consistency, and within a greater range of situations.

The virtues encompass a group of activities that in early recovery are geared to the immediate tasks of staying sober, cleaning house, and helping another alcoholic, but which in later recovery can be extended to a greater array of tasks as we try to practice the principles in all areas of life.

The virtues reflect the fact that as human beings we have innate capacities for a multiplicity of activities. At the broadest level, we have the capacity to perceive, care, think, imagine, believe, feel, and act. From these derive larger groups of capacities, such as a potential to learn, teach, work, create, communicate, make decisions, relate to others and to God. These capacities are exercised in different situations and under varying circumstances. From a spiritual perspective, which is the primary AA concern, they have as their ultimate purpose the flourishing and happiness of the human person.

We have the freedom to use these capacities well to bring about their intended good, or to use them poorly and thus fall short of their goal and bring about harm. The habitual ways in which we use these capacities for good are denominated virtues and accorded specific names that identify them in relation to the activities in which they are exercised. The habitual ways in which we fall short of their intended purpose and use them for ill are denominated vices or, in AA parlance, shortcomings or character defects, and they too bear distinctive names connected with their respective activities.

We come across these names throughout the Big Book and the 12&12, but though we recognize those which designate shortcomings or defects of character, we seldom recognize those which designate virtues as such, for as we have noted, virtue is not part of AA's vocabulary. But virtues are properly speaking what those other names designate, and we need to attend to them as much as we need to attend to character defects, for they are two sides of the same coin.

It may help our discussion at this point if we look at a list of the principal virtues that are named in the two basic texts of AA. In alphabetical order, these are **acceptance**, compassion, consideration, **courage**, courtesy, discretion, **faith**, **forgiveness**, fortitude, frankness, generosity, gentleness, **gratitude**, harmony, **honesty**, **hope**, **humility**, integrity, **joy**, justice, **kindness**, **love**, mercy, moderation, modesty, **open-mindedness**, patience, peace, perseverance, prudence, responsibility, restraint, **serenity**, **simplicity**, sincerity, tactfulness, temperance, **tolerance**, trust, understanding, **willingness**, and **wisdom**.[3]

These virtues are variously embedded in different Steps. Those in boldface are the ones that will ring a bell with most of us. We may easily link many of them with specific Steps. We may associate humility with Steps 1 and 7; open-mindedness and hope with Step 2; willingness, acceptance, serenity,

commitment

courage, and wisdom with Step 3. Faith we may connect with Steps 2, 3, 6, 7, and 11; forgiveness with Steps 8, 9, and 10. And we may associate honesty, one of the most frequently mentioned virtues in the program, with several Steps, including Steps 1, 2, 4, 5, 6, 8, 9, and 10. Gratitude, joy, and love we may link with Step 12.

Connecting the virtues to the disciplines that are also embedded in those Steps may not be as easy, but it isn't hard to see that surrender calls for humility; self-examination, confession, and restitution for honesty; and prayer for faith.

The disciplines and the virtues are respectively the "what" and the "how" of the Steps. This is reflected in a familiar acronym that stands for three of the virtues on our list, virtues generally considered indispensable for recovery: Honesty, Open-mindedness, Willingness (HOW). If we don't have these three even in their most rudimentary form, our chances of getting sober are practically nil. If we don't grow in these and the rest of the virtues, our chances for emotional sobriety are similarly negligible.

To grow in them and be able to work the Steps and practice the principles fully in all we do, we need to attend to the virtues, know what they are, how they are acquired, and how they work in tandem with the disciplines to further our recovery.

When we specify that honesty, open-mindedness, and willingness are principles, we are saying that they are more than just qualities, or whatever other label we may conventionally attach to them. We are saying that they are first things, things that form the foundation of the program of recovery and govern the operation of the actions we take through the Steps. The Steps rest on these principles and will not properly work without them.

When we further define those three principles as virtues, we are also talking about more than qualities, values, strengths, or assets, even though they are all of these things. We are talking about interior habits of mind and heart, about character traits that are essential to the practice of the disciplines, which in turn facilitate their acquisition by providing a spiritual framework for their consistent practice. The disciplines depend on the virtues and will not bear fruit without them.

Without growing in the virtue of honesty beyond the minimum required to admit that we are powerless over alcohol, we cannot make progress in our practice of the discipline of self-examination in Step 4, confession in Step 5, or restitution in Steps 9 and 10. And without such growth and progress, we cannot continue to change and achieve full sobriety.

The virtues make it possible for us to continue to grow along spiritual lines toward full sobriety because they shape how we think and feel and therefore how we act. They give form both to our character and to our emotions. In this chapter we will concentrate on the first, on their effect on character. In the next, we will focus on their effect on emotions and the goal of emotional sobriety.

As principles of recovery, the virtues govern the best use of our capacities for a wide range of human activity. They are constitutive of the good life, what we call in AA a life that is happy, joyous, and free. Derived from the Latin for "strength," virtue denotes, more than strength, "excellence," its meaning in the Greek where the concept originally arose in the Western tradition. We can therefore look at a virtue as a human and, in our context, a specifically moral excellence, a specific trait constitutive of good character that is lived out in specific acts.

Character and morality are sometimes problematic terms, and so it may help to take a closer look at what they mean. Character got its name to describe a person's habitual ways of being because it was understood to reflect a distinctive pattern of "characters" (from the Greek for "stamping tool") or marks that are stamped in the person and distinguish or identify that person. (All of the marks on this page are characters that, organized into certain patterns, convey certain meanings.)

As a trait of character, a virtue is a quality that is engraved in the self, a distinctive mark that is inscribed or imprinted in us through repeated action in given situations until the action becomes habitual and is performed spontaneously and automatically whenever those situations arise. It is an abiding and stable disposition that inclines the person to the good in the particular activity that it governs.

As moral traits, we are specifying those virtues which concern the way we live our lives, as opposed to, say, how well we might play the piano, write poetry, or paint a landscape, all of which involve their own virtuous or excellent qualities. Hence Step 4 calls for a moral (from Latin *mores* for "custom") inventory, an examination of those qualities in us that through customary patterns or habit governed the way we lived when we drank.

Morality is a word we alcoholics don't particularly care very much about. We tend to associate it with self-righteousness and proscriptions on sexual conduct. Yet as humans we are intrinsically moral beings. We are built to distinguish right from wrong as a necessary condition of our survival and thriving. We instinctively seek what we perceive to be right, though we may err in our perception. Even if unconsciously, we all follow moral tenets in our pursuit of what we understand to be a good life.

When we talk in AA about living a sober life, we are talking not only about living a life free from alcohol, or about being successful in the various worthy if worldly objectives we may set for ourselves. We are talking about living a *moral* life, about avoiding harm to ourselves and others, about doing good and shunning evil, about pursuing the best and the highest standards in our relationships and in all we do.

What we really object to about the notion of morality is more its prescriptive than its descriptive sense, the implication that there is a right way and a wrong way to conduct our lives. Yet we alcoholics know better than most that this is the plain and simple truth. After all, we tried our way, and it didn't work.

Driven to excess by the bottle, we often insisted on an absolute right to determine right and wrong for ourselves. It is how we played God. When we admit we are powerless over alcohol, we are taking the first step toward making an infinitely more consequential admission: that we are *not* God. This opens the way to making the ultimate decision on which our recovery hinges: to surrender totally to the God that is.

Out of that surrender grows the desire to seek and do God's will. This accords with AA's understanding that, as our creator, God knows what works and what doesn't work for us human beings. When we pray for knowledge of God's will for us, we are praying for God to make known, first and foremost, his *moral* will for us, how we are to comport ourselves, how we are to live if we are to thrive and find happiness. And because we can't do his will on our own, we pray to be given the power to carry it out.

This is the reason why in AA the virtues, like the disciplines, are fundamentally spiritual in nature, as is the solution to our drinking problem and the entire program of recovery. The moral virtues that animate the Steps are attributes or qualities that mark the human character as it is conformed to the will of God. To be virtuous is to embody God's will for me in my being and to live it out in my conduct day by day. As I grow in virtue, so do I grow in spirit, in character, and in the good and happy life.

This process doesn't work unless I am a willing participant. Hence in AA we focus not on the prescriptive but the descriptive sense of morality. We don't dwell on the "ought" part, on what we "ought" to do and how we "ought" to live. That sounds like preaching and invites resistance and rebellion. That is why AA shuns what is called "musty" language, talking about how we "must" do this and how we "must" do that. We are not given to exhortation. We practice what has been called "a morality of happiness" rather than "a morality of obligation."[4] We focus on what works, on what enables us to live well in recovery, as shown by the experience distilled in the principles and evident in the rooms.

Our character is the product of our moral choices, the choices that we make for good or ill over the course of our lives: as we act time and again, so do we become. Virtuous character requires virtuous choices. To acquire a virtue, we need to practice, cultivate, and nurture it.

We can perform random acts of kindness—to take one virtue—without becoming kind people. To gain this virtue, our acts of kindness cannot be haphazard or occasional but pursued consistently and persistently over a sustained period. Kindness grows into a virtue when we practice it repeatedly until it becomes impressed in us as an abiding habit, a fixed part of our character, a stable or settled disposition to be kind. We are then kind toward others as a matter of course, even when circumstances may not be propitious or when others may be unkind to us.

Virtues are good moral habits. We sometimes talk about acquiring good or healthy habits in AA in place of the bad or unhealthy habits of our drinking days. But good and healthy can describe brushing my teeth and taking a bath every day, or eating properly, exercising regularly, and getting enough sleep. No doubt some of us didn't acquire these laudable habits until we came to the rooms, but their absence when we drank was symptomatic of the emotional and spiritual condition to which we had reduced ourselves. It is this condition that the principles of the program address. It is what new spiritual, moral, and emotional habits we develop through the practice of the virtues and of the disciplines, that ultimately make a lasting difference in our lives, even in its ordinary and prosaic dimensions.

As we acquire these moral habits called virtues and they come to reside in the self, they shape and change who we are. We think, feel, and act differently.

We have so far stressed the repetitive nature of habit formation. But the acquisition of virtue requires more than mere repetition. As *moral* habits, virtues involve not only morally right acts but morally right intentions. Virtue is a unity of act and purpose. A virtuous act is an outward reflection of an inward virtuous intention. If the intention is not there, neither is the virtuous quality. What the repeated act does is to work an intent-bearing trait deep into the fabric of our character so that it becomes a virtuous habit.

This should give added meaning to the AA saying that "it's an inside job." We don't change by going through the motions and performing a series of prescribed mechanical procedures. We are not computers to be programmed by following a set of predetermined instructions. We are intentional, purposeful human beings, and we practice spiritual principles that reach deep into the soul and engage all our faculties.

Among our many capacities to act is the capacity to give of ourselves, to use our resources (spiritual, emotional, intellectual, material) to promote the wellbeing of others. Exercising that capacity well, for its intended purpose, is accorded the name of generosity. Giving money, for instance, is an authentic act of generosity that can instill that virtue in our character if our motive in giving is really to help those in need. If we give money to be seen, to please or impress others, to look good, or to play the big shot, then we are not practicing generosity and that virtue will not become a habitual part of our character no matter how much and how often we give.

Our intentions guide our actions and reflect how we see things. When we repeatedly act on those intentions and ways of seeing, we are impressing them into our character and habituating ourselves to act the same way when similar situations arise.

The person who in giving sees his financial resources as a means to help others and shares them with that intention in mind is ingraining generosity into his character and growing into a generous person. The person who in giving sees his resources as a means to help himself and parts with them for the sake of appearance, in order to varnish his image and reputation, is ingraining the traits that accompany such self-centered intentions. These traits are not virtues but reflect instead such ordinary flaws as vanity and hypocrisy.

We gain virtue by doing the right thing for the right reason and with the right grasp of a situation, in this case, the spiritually and objectively ordered purpose of giving, namely, to help our fellows in need.

Right intention speaks of desire or want. This suggests a third factor that is involved in the acquisition of virtue and which we mentioned is the focus of the next chapter. This factor is right emotion. No virtue is fully acquired until it is accompanied by a right emotional disposition. If we give reluctantly, in response to pressure or guilt, or out of a sense of duty or obligation rather than out of a real desire to give because we care about those we are giving to, then our heart is not in the giving and generosity cannot be fully implanted in us.

The virtues motivate, guide, direct, and give meaning to the activities we engage in out of the various faculties and capacities with which we are endowed as human beings. That is why the Western tradition, both secular and religious, historically has grouped the virtues according to these activities as it has tried to understand how they work.

AA is part of this tradition, in its case grouping the virtues around those 12-Step activities we have called disciplines. Before we probe further into this arrangement and explore in greater detail how virtues and disciplines interrelate and interact with each other in the Steps, it may be instructive to have a quick overview of the way the virtues have been organized and systematically thought about in the spiritual tradition closest to the program, best represented perhaps by Thomas Aquinas, who built on the more secular Aristotle.

In this tradition, activities are grouped in the first place according to whether they govern our moral life in the way we act in the world and relate to others, or whether they govern our spiritual life directly related to God.

The moral virtues are then grouped under four broad categories that are considered to encompass much of what we do in life. Each of these is headed by a virtue that is considered "cardinal" (Latin for "hinge") or pivotal because it is the central, core virtue informing the other virtues that govern the multiple activities within the group.

Thus there are virtues that incline us to well-ordered relations with those around us, where we give each person his due as a fellow human being, and they are headed by the cardinal virtue justice. Under it are such virtues as gratitude, harmony, honesty (and corollaries like frankness and sincerity), and consideration (and corollaries like courtesy, respect, and loyalty).

There are virtues that order our desires and passions, restrain our instinctual drives, and moderate our enjoyment of pleasures so that we avoid excess in the activities that are concerned, and they come under the cardinal virtue temperance (sometimes called self-restraint or moderation).

There are virtues that enable us to face difficulties well and remain constant in the pursuit of the good despite internal or external obstacles, and these are grouped under the cardinal virtue fortitude. From it derive such virtues as perseverance, patience, acceptance, serenity, and courage.

And there are virtues that enable us to grasp situations accurately, make right decisions, and choose well. These come under the cardinal virtue prudence, which is also known as practical wisdom and more popularly as good judgment and common sense. They include such virtues as willingness, open-mindedness, and discretion. Prudence or wisdom enables us to discern how the other moral virtues apply to particular circumstances so that we can practice them in the right situation and at the right time.

Some of the above virtues may also be organized under different types of activities where they perform distinct functions. Thus humility, open-mindedness, generosity, courage, and wisdom work in certain situations as intellectual virtues or traits of intellectual character, in that they govern the right exercise of such activities as learning and teaching, or acquiring and imparting knowledge and understanding. This of course doesn't make them any less moral, since they impact the way we live.

The spiritual (or "theological," that is, pertaining to God) virtues are three: faith, hope, and love. They form the foundation of our moral activity, the spiritual ground for our practice of justice, temperance, fortitude, and prudence, and the many virtues that revolve around these four.

The secular part of the Western tradition holds that the virtues can be practiced by our own efforts, through our own power alone, that we can live a moral life without any need for God ("Good without God," as the title of one book has it). That is not the AA experience. Personal powerlessness and the need for a higher Power are the cornerstones of the program. We can't do the right thing even when we know what the right thing is and we want to do it, and half the time we either don't know or don't want to.

There is a what, a how, and a who to recovery, and the who is where the power comes from. "That one is God," says the Big Book in introducing the 12 Steps (p. 59). "May you find Him now," it immediately adds, for those Steps and their disciplines and virtues won't work without him. The 12&12 gives the reason why in Step 5 when it notes that all of the 12 Steps "go contrary to our natural desires" (p. 55). Or as we might hear a newcomer put it sometimes, they are "unrealistic." And that they are, absent God. Hence the need for supernatural help. Faith, hope, and love lead us to the spiritual source of the right intention and emotion without which it is simply impossible to give each person her due, avoid excess, face difficulties well, and make right choices with any degree of consistency in the multiple activities that routinely occupy us day in and day out.

If we take work as an example, we can easily see that our capacities in this general type of activity play themselves out differently in different occupations, trades, and professions, each with its own set of tools and skills, and within each a specific tool for each particular task.

It is like that with all of life. Its multiple moral activities coalesce into distinct groups, each with its own set of tools. These tools are the virtues, and just as there is a right tool for every job, so there is a virtue for every activity. To use the right tool, we need to know the job we are doing. To be able to do this, we need to correlate the task with the virtues which can best help us to perform it.

We get the necessary training through the practice of the disciplines. As we get better at making these connections, we will enter situations equipped with the right tools: the attitudes or spiritual and emotional dispositions that are required to bring the best out of any situation.

Disciplines and Virtues: Interaction

We have noted that in the West the concept of virtue reaches back to classical Greece and is present in various secular and religious traditions. These do not necessarily agree on what character traits constitute virtues, or assign the same weight to or share the same understanding or practice of a given virtue. As we find them in the 12 Steps, the virtues, like the disciplines, come to us through the Judeo-Christian tradition, and most immediately through the Oxford Group.

AA has taken these principles and done something entirely new with them. First, AA brings these disciplines and virtues into an effective working relationship and orders them into a unique program of action—the 12 Steps—that is simple, practical, and accessible to everyone. We don't need to be philosophers or theologians to understand them. Nor do we need to be ascetics, monks, or saints to practice them.

It is enough to be drunks. And this is the second unique feature of AA: the principles are reformulated and tailored to the alcoholic. Unlike the Oxford Group, which wanted to reach everyone and whose stated ambition was nothing less than to save the world, AA's primary purpose is simply for us to stay sober and help other alcoholics to achieve sobriety.

This brings us to the third unique feature of AA, and this is the Fellowship. Taking many of the principles of the program and forging them into a set of 12 Traditions, AA has given rise to a unique vehicle through which we alcoholics can put the disciplines and virtues to work.

The Fellowship provides us with a real-life community in which we can do two things: a) practice those principles within the community itself, and b) share with each other how we are applying them outside in our everyday lives, thereby benefiting from our collective experience. This is the soil in which we cultivate and nurture the virtues, for their growth can be enhanced and their practice sustained only in community. In this manner, the process that originally gave rise to Step and Tradition, program and Fellowship—one alcoholic working with another alcoholic—continues to bear fruit in the microcosm of the group and in the larger arena of life.

We have suggested that we gain virtue by doing virtue, and that the disciplines provide us with a structured set of practices for doing this. Thus, to gain in humility, we practice specific and repeated acts of surrender as we work through the 12 Steps, putting God first and declining to elevate ourselves above others. Through surrender we also grow in willingness, open-mindedness, acceptance, and serenity, as we admit our limitations and let go of power and control. We grow in honesty as we practice self-examination and confession, taking inventory of ourselves and admitting the exact nature of our wrongs. We become more just and forgiving as we proceed to make restitution to those we have harmed. Through prayer and meditation we grow in faith, hope, and gratitude as we become more aware of the power of God's grace in our lives. And we grow in love through acts of selfless giving in service to our fellows, manifesting this love in patience, compassion, generosity, kindness, and other virtues that are the fruits of charity, the love of God in us.

There is as well a two-way interaction between virtue and discipline. As we continue to practice the discipline of self-examination and continue to take inventory, we grow in the virtues of honesty and humility, and conversely, as we grow in these virtues, we become better at looking at ourselves and discerning our shortcomings. Promptly admitting our wrongs to those we have harmed will become a habit with time, disposing us to justice, and the more just we become, the more readily and openly will we admit to such wrongs.

There is a unity to the virtues and they also interact among themselves, so that growth in one effects progress in another. Faith and trust in a loving God who cares for our wellbeing will help us to let go of fear and gain in courage. Gratitude for being forgiven will in turn make us more forgiving and help us to let go of anger and resentment, and as we give thanks for what has been given us so freely, we will become more generous and desire to give in equal measure. When we consistently seek to bring peace to relationships and situations and thus practice peace as a virtue, we will also grow in patience and tolerance.

The virtues are what animate the disciplines, their spiritual substance, if you will. It is not hard to see how without the virtues the disciplines can become hollow practices. For the spiritually averse, they can easily turn into mere formalities, mechanical acts, methods, techniques, and gimmicks, the kinds of exercises found in many self-help books which follow the letter of the Steps while abandoning their spirit.

Those inclined to a certain kind of secular psychology may reduce the disciplines to those which allow for repeated forays into the childhood past, never-ending probes of the unconscious, and exhaustive analyses of motives, moods, and feelings. The religious may be tempted to focus especially on those disciplines that afford an occasion for private piety and devotion directed to God, while neglecting the action-oriented practices directed to neighbor. Those who consider themselves "spiritual but not religious" may see some of the disciplines as nearly magic formulas for uncovering "secrets" or "laws," connecting with mysterious or esoteric "forces" in the universe, or harnessing unknown mystical powers in nature, none of which may have anything to do with the business of how we can live with others in the real world.

Some of these tendencies seek to skirt the spiritual altogether, others to decouple it from the moral, and all to detach it from practical, painstaking, and persistent God-directed work.

The disciplines cannot stand on their own. They are ordered to the virtues, which ground them and provide their just motivation and goal. We surrender to God because humility demands it. We look at who we are and admit what we have done as honesty demands. We make amends and restitution to satisfy the demands of justice. We pray because it is what faith demands. We serve others because love demands it in us. Ultimately, we are called to practice these virtues and instill them in our character because their source is God's own character and will. It is who God wants us to be as full human beings: humble, truthful, just, faithful, loving. That is what makes them spiritual. It is also what makes them practical, for life doesn't seem to work well without them.

Taken together, disciplines and virtues present a clear and proven path to a transformed relationship with God, neighbor, and self. Taken apart, the principles lose their cohesion and the Steps their compass, and we drift and dither.

If I am having trouble with a Step, the likelihood is that I am having trouble practicing one or more principles underlying that Step. Upon closer examination, I may discover that I am having trouble practicing a particular discipline because I am not practicing the virtues that make that discipline work.

If I am having trouble making a fearless and searching moral inventory, I just may not be willing to take the necessary action. Or I may have a problem being honest with myself. Or I may lack in perseverance, short-circuiting the process and acquiescing in sloth or indifference instead. Or that spiritual awakening I thought I had never got beyond Step 1, and I am lacking in the faith that grows through Steps 2 and 3, with the result that fear still blocks my way. Or I may not be willing to humble myself and accept that I am a deeply flawed human being and that only by surrendering to that truth will God turn my weakness into strength.

If I keep putting off those amends I need to make, my reluctance to forgive may be holding me back. Or I may be allowing self-centered fear to get in the way of doing the right thing, and I may need to grow in courage by trusting God and turning any negative expectations over to his care. I may also have a self-servingly myopic view of justice, still seeing the concept in legal or social but not in spiritual terms, the province of the courts and the concern of political movements. I may fail to see that justice is very much at the core of the very spiritual and very personal discipline of restitution, and that it always begins with me.

Virtue and Character Development

This consideration of the relationship between virtue and discipline in the working of the Steps can help us gain a better understanding of the process of character development in the program. We practice the principles in all our affairs to *do* good and, by *doing* good, to *become* good, so that we can do still more good. This doing and becoming is how we grow in virtue and thus in good character; it is the seed and the fruit of our spiritual growth.

The same process of habit formation that is at work in the acquisition of good character traits is at work in the acquisition of defective ones. Defects of character are deeply ingrained bad habits acquired through repeated action over long periods of time. These traits are the very opposite of virtues. They fill our character with the attitudes, tendencies, and propensities to ill which are the cause of our discontent and at times our ruin. Whereas virtues are ways of living life well, vices or character defects are ways of living life poorly.

We can see character development then, as a process of replacing vices with virtues, character defects with character strengths, deeply ingrained bad habits with equally deeply ingrained good habits. This is why the saying that AA stands for "Attitude Adjustment" makes perfect sense. Like choice, attitude is a buzzword in our culture. So much of what we do seems to hinge on our attitude and the choices we make. But attitude as currently used is just a more popular word for an older and richer term that forms part of the virtue tradition, and this is disposition. And this, our attitude or disposition, the way that we tend to lean spiritually, morally, and emotionally, is precisely what the program seeks to affect and fundamentally alter.

In AA this change commences with the virtue of willingness. This is the key that opens the door to all the other virtues for the alcoholic. Its connection with attitude adjustment or change in disposition is readily apparent. To dispose is defined as "to put into a willing or receptive frame of mind." That is, as regards virtue, to be willing is to have our will disposed or inclined to the good, to be well- rather than ill-disposed. The initial adjustment and turning point take place in Step 1, where we experience an internal shift from willfulness to willingness. We yield and let go of resistance and defiance. We become ready to do the simplest and yet for us the hardest thing to do: to ask for help and accept direction.

As we grow in recovery and we practice the spiritual principles of the program—disciplines and virtues—these attitude adjustments multiply and accumulate until our spiritual orientation and prevailing frame of mind have undergone a radical transformation and we have developed a habitual inclination toward the good in all we do. The virtues take hold in our character. We now live in the solution. Doing the right thing for the right reason and with the right emotion becomes almost second nature. We have entered a new spiritual dimension. Yet it all begins with nothing more than a simple willingness to give the program an honest try.

Starting with the virtue of willingness, character development becomes an interactive two-way process of letting go of defects and acquiring their missing counterparts in the virtues. In our first journey through the Steps, much of the letting-go part involves practicing in varying degrees the disciplines in Steps 4 through 10: examine and confess our shortcomings, become ready to release them and pray for their removal, admit them and make amends.

The acquisition part naturally involves the actual practice of the virtues themselves as we work the Steps through the disciplines. With time this becomes a deliberate, intentional, and purposeful process of choosing right over wrong, exercising virtue where we would otherwise exhibit defect.

We understand letting go as not holding on to our character defects, whether through defiance, justification, or rationalization (themselves underpinned by defects of character), but instead turning them over to God. We also understand that acquiring virtue is receiving virtue. As Bill W. suggests in the 12&12 (S12, p. 107), virtue is a gift from God. We make ourselves ready to receive it precisely by letting go, emptying ourselves, making space inside, and consciously desiring and seeking it. We turn a defect over to God, and God grants us the grace to practice a virtue in its place.

Without the principles we call virtues as a lens, trying to understand and act on our character flaws can become pretty disconcerting at times. Step 5 talks about admitting "the exact nature" of our wrongs. This is one of those expressions in AA that, like "these principles" we tend to skip over. Our tendency is to zero in on "wrongs." Even then, we don't always appreciate the double meaning of the word. The "wrongs" are both what we do to others (our wrongdoing) and the wrongs in us (our defects) that cause us to do it. Still, this begs the question. What are the wrongs we do to others? What are our defects of character? What their exact nature?

Understanding the relationship between virtue and character defect can help us to answer these questions. We read in Step 5 that a defect cannot be corrected unless we can see clearly what it is and act on it accordingly.

That is, we need to see its "exact nature." Bill W. suggests how we do this when he writes that in doing our inventory we saw "we lacked honesty and tolerance" in our relations with others, and that, lacking in humility, we were seized sometimes by "self-pity and delusions of personal grandeur" (12&12, p. 58) which caused us to act out in hurtful ways. That is, we do the harm we do because we lack in those virtues and practice instead the contrary defects and related defective emotions.

We see the exact nature of our wrongs when we recognize behind our wrongdoing their root causes, the moral deficiencies that make up our character flaws and produce wrong action and emotion.

We need to discern where pride, intolerance, and dishonesty govern our attitudes and actions if we are to treat not just the symptom or outward manifestation in what we do, but the underlying cause in what we are. We cannot let go of a defect that we don't recognize in us and therefore cannot admit to.

Where we can see pride at work, there we can take steps to humble ourselves and surrender it. As we do, pride diminishes and humility grows. With increased humility comes an increased sensitivity to pride, with the result that we are quicker to detect its myriad manifestations in our daily lives and to let go of it. In this way defect gives way to virtue.

This idea is not developed systematically anywhere in the basic AA literature. But it is the underlying concept in Step 4 of the Big Book, where we searched for those defects in our character "which caused our failure" (p. 64).

We found then that much of our wrongdoing when we drank was fueled by anger, resentment, and fear, and that behind these lay specific character defects like intolerance and unforgiveness. These constitute the exact nature of our wrongs, what generates harmful actions and, by implication, the emotions associated with them. Identifying these specific defects is a necessary step in surrendering them. Only then can we practice the corresponding virtues in their place.

In the 12&12 version of Step 4, Bill W. takes a more direct and somewhat more extended look at character defects within the virtue-vice paradigm when he looks at the Seven Deadly Sins. These are called deadly not only because they are especially harmful in and of themselves, but also because they lead to still more sins or character defects.

Pride heads the list, for it is "the basic breeder" of most of our problems and the "chief block" to real progress. Pride leads us to pervert and misuse our "God-given instincts" and is the engine of fear and still more character defects (p. 49). Foremost among these are the other deadly sins of greed, lust, anger, gluttony, envy, and sloth. Such ills constitute the exact nature of

our wrongs, the character defects and related emotions driving the harm that
we cause.

All of these defects have their countervailing virtues. Earlier, we identified the principal ones at work in the 12 Steps of the program. First among
these is humility. If pride is the chief vice, humility is the chief virtue. Andrew
Murray explains why when he writes: "Humility is the only soil in which
virtue takes root; a lack of humility is the explanation of every defect and
failure. Humility is not so much a virtue along with the others, but is the root
of all, because it alone takes the right attitude before God and allows Him"
to be God.[5]

In the practice of the principles that lead us to God and a new life in recovery, no virtue is of greater significance than humility. Not only is humility
the quintessential virtue, but as we shall see it is the principle that underlies
all the other principles in AA. At the heart of each and every Step in the program and of all the Traditions in the Fellowship, lies this virtue of humility.
Working through surrender, the touchstone of the disciplines, humility leads
the way to a spiritual awakening and a right relationship with God and our
fellows.

The primary cause of our drinking and failure in life, we read in the
12&12, is our character defects (S4, p. 50). And these, we read in the Big
Book, proceed from "self, manifested in various ways" (p. 64). Our character defects are that, various manifestations of self, "instincts gone astray"
(12&12, ibid.) under the relentless drive of self-seeking pride. However many
its manifestations, be they subtle or obvious, one thing is always true of self:
it only wants to take.

The virtues are the perfect antidote to self and the selfish imperative, ·
for in all instances they represent ways of giving. We grow in virtue by doing
virtue, and to do virtue is to give of ourselves such good as, by the grace of
God, starts to take root in us. As we grow in character, we desire to give the
best of who we are. We become interested in what we can add to the good in
"the stream of life" (Big Book, p. 86).

We carry the message of our spiritual awakening to other alcoholics.
And we go further. We carry the message to all "those about us," including
the non-alcoholic (12&12, S12, p. 106). The message that we carry is of a
loving God who restored us and who can restore others, if they will but seek
him. Sometimes we try to do this with words. But as St. Francis would say,
most convincingly we try to carry the message by example, through what
we do, through the ways in which we embody in our character and display
in our conduct the virtues that God would have us live out. By trying even
in our limited and imperfect ways to show to others the grace that God has

shown to us, we become channels of his peace and of his love. We can give no greater service.

Disciplines, Virtues, and Traditions

We have focused so far on examining the principles underlying the 12 Steps and how our understanding of them affects their practice and the nature of the message we carry. We have tried to sketch a general outline of how an understanding of these principles as spiritual disciplines and virtues can help us work the Steps in all their fullness, practicing all the principles in all of our affairs and carrying the liberating message of a spiritual rebirth to all.

Thus understood and thus practiced, the principles of the program can lead us to continued spiritual progress as we grow in character and move beyond physical to emotional sobriety and the fulfillment of the Promises in our lives.

Specifically how this process works to bring about emotional sobriety bears closer scrutiny. But first, we need to complete our overview of the principles embedded in the Steps by considering how they extend to the Traditions.

Applying the same understanding of the principles as disciplines and virtues, we need to look at how these are present in the Traditions governing our lives in the Fellowship and how Traditions and Fellowship affect practice and message outside in our everyday lives.

Traditions meetings are perhaps the least popular of regular (non-business) meetings in the Fellowship. Some AAs avoid them completely and many have little or nothing to say if caught in one. This arises in part from a limited view of the Traditions as applying only to the life of the group.

Many of us don't see the Traditions as being particularly relevant to working the Steps outside the rooms. We fail to see the connection between Traditions and Steps, and we fail to do this because, just as we confuse Steps and principles, we also fail to distinguish between principles and Traditions.

We don't see that the Traditions, like the Steps, have certain conceptual and operating principles embedded in them, and that these principles connect the two. Steps and Traditions share common spiritual principles because the problems they address are the same, originating in our individual hearts, manifesting themselves variously in the AA group, at home, at work, at church, among friends, and in other areas of our lives.

The Traditions exist to safeguard the existence and the unity of the Fellowship in order that, by working the program together, we may pursue our common purpose of staying sober and helping other alcoholics to achieve sobriety. Tradition 1 posits the goal of unity, attained by the grace of God through individual and voluntary adherence to spiritual principles. The rest of the Traditions lay out what these principles are and how they led to the formulation of the concrete policies through which they are practiced. But these principles, we insist, directly affect our practice of the Steps as well and extend beyond the rooms.

We can identify five key spiritual disciplines in the Traditions. These are surrender, anonymity, service, witness, and fellowship. As with the Steps, the discipline of surrender underlies all the Traditions, for putting self aside in favor of the common good is what makes AA unity, and hence personal recovery, possible.

Putting our common welfare first (Tradition 1); yielding to group conscience and seeking to serve rather than control (Tradition 2); welcoming any and all alcoholics to membership and granting individual groups autonomy (Traditions 3 and 4); sticking to our primary purpose (Traditions 5 and 6); supporting ourselves through our own contributions (Tradition 7); shunning professionalism and organization (Traditions 8 and 9); avoiding outside issues and eschewing controversy (Tradition 10); stressing attraction rather than promotion (Tradition 11), and placing principles before personalities (Tradition 12) all call on the individual alcoholic to subordinate self-centered considerations and give something up for the general welfare.[6]

Closely linked to surrender is the distinctly AA discipline of anonymity. Originating in the Greek term for "nameless," anonymity is made explicit only in Traditions 11 and 12. It nevertheless forms "the spiritual foundation of all the Traditions, ever reminding us to place principles before personalities" (12&12, T12, p. 184). Anonymity shares with surrender the goal of abandoning personal ambition and subordinating personal considerations to the common good.

Practicing anonymity in diverse ways in and out of the rooms, we seek to attract others to AA and the spiritual way by showing through our conduct how the principles work for good in our lives, rather than by promoting or highlighting aspects of our own or another member's identity, broadly construed. In the same manner, we make AA principles the focus of our work with others in the Fellowship, not allowing personality differences to take precedence.

More than not revealing our last name in the rooms or our AA affiliation outside, anonymity is a way to strip the self of all the superfluous marks of identity by which we seek to set ourselves apart from or above our fellows, alcoholic or not. Thus we downplay or leave unmentioned things

that would be highlighted in other groups or situations: educational credentials, professional, trade, or business occupation, financial and social status,
achievements and accomplishments of various sorts, and other badges of
merit, distinction, and differentiation.

We come next to the discipline of service, considered the lifeline of the
Fellowship. Without it, the Fellowship dries up and dies. Tradition 2 tells
us that in practicing this discipline we alcoholics seek to grow into trusted
servants and yield all pretensions to authority, power, or control (whatever
form such pretensions may take), whether in making coffee, leading or sharing at regular or business meetings, doing 12th Step work, or serving in committees or special boards. In this spirit of service, we recognize a loving God
as the sole authority in AA, governing group as well as individual conscience.

Witness, as noted in connection with the Steps, is in AA generally subsumed under the discipline of service. But witness has long been viewed as
a spiritual discipline in its own right, and it is no less so in AA. In the Fellowship it is closely associated with Tradition 5, which makes carrying the
message the group's primary purpose, and Tradition 11, which informs the
spirit in which we AAs are to carry that message: by attraction, rather than
promotion.

This means that our witness focuses on the spiritual principles of the
program and not on our person. Yet this doesn't mean that we promote
the principles as opposed to the person. We promote nothing, sell nothing.
Rather, we witness by sharing our experience, strength, and hope, showing
by word and deed how the principles are working in our lives and helping us
grow and serve others. Take what you want (or can, or are ready to receive)
and leave the rest: that's the attitude which, formed in surrender and humility, marks our witness.

Fellowship as a discipline is at the heart of the Fellowship as a collective
entity. Broadly defined, fellowship is a friendly association of people who
share and meet to pursue a common interest or objective. Organizations and
groups of all sorts may include fellowship as part of their activities. But in
AA, fellowship is not a part, but central. Nor is fellowship in AA founded
on secular interests, whether social, professional or otherwise. It is instead
markedly spiritual, as is also the goal that brings us together. "A Vision for
You" in the Big Book refers to it as a "Fellowship of the Spirit" (p. 164),
while Tradition 5 describes each group as "a spiritual entity" (p. 563).

When we say of AA that it is "a *we* program," we mean that it is practiced in fellowship. I can stay home and study the Big Book and the 12&12
all I want, but if I neglect to go to meetings and participate in the life of the
group, my ability to help and be helped is going to be severely limited. My

spiritual growth may be stunted and I may even drink, for giving my sobriety away is key to my keeping it.

I can't give service and witness in isolation, nor can I practice the other principles of the program in their full dimension without the shared experience, strength, and hope of fellow alcoholics. While some Traditions address the practice of fellowship more than others, all of them are suffused with this discipline. All Traditions exist to make our Society possible so that we can get sober and grow in recovery together with other alcoholics.

Through their distinct disciplines and policies, the Traditions aim to create a corporate or communal environment in which certain individual virtues can be cultivated, nurtured, and practiced. These virtues are necessary if the practice of discipline and the implementation of policy are to be sustained. Interacting with each other, disciplines and virtues enable personal recovery and make the survival and success of the group possible.

The Traditions are conduits for a set of virtues that overlap with those in the Steps but which under the Traditions are practiced in their own particular ways. Two factors account for the unique expression of these virtues in the Traditions. One, the virtues are informed by a discipline that is particular to the Traditions, that of anonymity. Two, the virtues are specifically geared to the individual's participation in a defined community.

Principal among these virtues are humility, simplicity, faith (trust), tolerance, patience, love, wisdom, prudence, generosity, integrity, and peace (harmony).

As with the Steps, the virtue of humility is the soil in which all the Traditions take root and grow. Humility begins with accepting who I am, and in the context of the Fellowship specifically who I am as an alcoholic, no different from any other, no better and no worse, not unique and not special. I don't put myself first, or elevate another AA above myself or others. I humbly admit that I am not self-sufficient and accept my dependence on the group as a tested vehicle for God's restoring grace. I humbly acknowledge that I am "but a small part of a great whole" (T1, p. 130) through which God works to bring recovery to all who will receive him.

Closely allied with humility is the virtue of simplicity, which also informs all the Traditions. With humility and the disciplines of surrender and anonymity, simplicity is fundamental to AA unity. Indeed, simplifying and unifying work in tandem, sharing as they do a core meaning of oneness.

Simplicity works by fostering certain specific attitudes and practices in the life of the Fellowship: putting our common good first; acknowledging God as the sole authority governing the group; reducing all membership requirements to a single, plain, and unqualified desire to stop drinking; granting complete autonomy to each group, except where it would affect other groups or the Fellowship as a whole; adhering to one primary purpose; avoiding any affiliations or entanglements that would divert us from that purpose, including financial dependence on outside contributions, professionalizing 12th Step work, or expressing opinions on outside issues; forging a spiritual community of equals rather than building a hierarchical organization of leaders and led; and adopting anonymity as the great spiritual leveler of the individual ego so that, whatever he may be outside, in the rooms the alcoholic is just another drunk.

No doubt the personal attitudes and practical policies flowing from these four principles of surrender, anonymity, humility, and simplicity have helped AA to avoid falling victim to the forces of division and dissension at work in the individual alcoholic and society at large. They account to a great extent for AA's ability to unite, prosper, and grow, where preceding movements like the Washingtonians and the Oxford Group fractured and failed.

Looking now at the other virtues, we find that faith is the virtue we practice through Tradition 2, where we trust God as our ultimate authority as he may express himself in the group conscience. We are called to practice patience and tolerance through Tradition 3, where we welcome to AA anyone who has a desire to stop drinking. Trust and again tolerance are at work in Tradition 4, which grants autonomy to each group in most things. In Tradition 5 we respond to the love of God as we try to carry the message to the alcoholic who still suffers, and to the counsel of wisdom as we make that our primary purpose. The virtue of prudence underlies the policies of no-endorsement and self-support in Traditions 6 and 7. With Tradition 8 we practice generosity and integrity as we give back what we have been given, seeking neither remuneration nor reward for 12th Step work. Peace or harmony is the virtue behind the no-controversy policy of Tradition 10. And with Traditions 11 and 12 we are brought back to the virtue of humility, working through the self-effacing discipline of anonymity.

Anonymity, we are told in the 12th Tradition, is "real humility at work" (12&12, p. 187). As is evident from the brief survey above, the virtues work with each other and in concert with the disciplines in the Traditions too, as they do in the Steps. These two, anonymity and humility, are the locus of their interaction, informing surrender and faith, fellowship and peace, service and love.

And these two, service and love, are in turn the sum and object of all the disciplines and virtues, in the Steps as well as in the Traditions. Love in action is the essence of Step 12. It is here that "we experience the kind of giving that asks no rewards," for "When the Twelfth Step is seen in its full implication, it is really talking about the kind of love that has no price tag on it" (ibid., p. 106). It is a free gift which, through the practice of the principles, we have in some measure made ourselves ready to receive and are now ready to freely give to others.

If the virtues that we practice are in all instances ways of giving the best of who we are becoming (forgiving, compassionate, generous), love is their highest expression. To which the memorable words: "And now these three remain: faith, hope, and love. But the greatest of these is love."[7] Love is "the more excellent way," for it contains faith and hope and all the virtues and blessings, giving them form, inspiring, and animating them.

This is where we experience a way of giving that expects no reward, says the 12&12. For like all the virtues but more than any other, love is its own reward, growing in us and fostering our own wellbeing even as we foster the wellbeing of others. It is in this selfless giving of ourselves that we experience "the joy of living," the theme of AA's 12th Step and proof positive of our spiritual and emotional recovery.

It is in light of this understanding that we can rightly say that to practice these principles in all our affairs is our highest calling in AA, the culmination of the 12 Steps, and the greatest service we can render. It is the clearest evidence of our spiritual awakening. It is how we can most truthfully carry this message to alcoholics. And it is the unmistakable mark of our spiritual progress as we continue to grow in character, achieve emotional sobriety, and help those around us to heal.

IN ALL OUR AFFAIRS: EMOTIONAL SOBRIETY

A A is a spiritual program. It is designed to help us experience a spiritual awakening in a growing relationship with God. This is fostered through the practice of certain spiritual principles that we have characterized as being embedded in the Steps and identified as disciplines and virtues. Applied to our alcoholic problem, the practice of these principles, though necessarily limited at first, can open us to receive the grace of God by which our obsession to drink is removed. As we practice these principles more fully in all areas of life, we are gradually restored to sanity emotionally and in all parts of our being. Our spiritual recovery encompasses all of who we are.

We have tried to sketch how this process works, particularly as it affects our moral growth in character development. In so doing, we have suggested that the same process is at work in our moral growth in emotional development, in the development of emotional sobriety. We now take a closer look at this aspect of our recovery.

EMOTIONS, SPIRITUALLY SPEAKING

The relationship between spiritual recovery and emotional sobriety is probably a gray area for most of us. There may be three reasons for this, all closely related. One, we are not clear about what, practically speaking, a spiritual awakening is. The very idea of the spiritual being practical sounds like a contradiction in terms. Two, we are not certain what the principles are and in what specific ways they can be said to be spiritual and practiced as such, with the result that our practice, and hence our awakening, is inhibited. These two reasons we have already touched upon. The third we have not, and this is that we are mostly in the dark about what, from a spiritual point of view, emotions are and how they function. The result is that our practice of the principles is not consciously directed to a specifically spiritual shaping and transformation of our emotional life.

These various uncertainties proceed in no small part from a false dichotomy that we have created in our minds between the spiritual and the emotional. Absorbed from modern secular culture, this considers emotions the proper and exclusive province of psychology and the spiritual (whatever that is) the province of religion. AA does not subscribe to this division, following rather in the footsteps of William James, Carl Jung, and other psychologists who, in their own way, were also men of faith and discerned that the two are inextricably connected.

Once the emotional is divorced from the spiritual, the natural tendency is to reduce it to the material. This is of course the trend in neuroscience and several other disciplines, and these are exerting a growing influence on many who write about recovery. On this view, our emotions are nothing more than the product of a physical organ, the brain. Recovery and emotional sobriety become largely a matter of brain management as we learn about the brain's evolution, how it is structured and wired, which of its parts govern which functions, and how neurological events determine how we feel.

Armed with all this information, which is grafted to the traditional concepts of secular psychology and psychiatry from which this view emerges, we can then supposedly apply various therapies and techniques to exercise control over our emotions.

Whatever merit these self-help approaches may have, they tend to be based on a view of emotions that discounts if not entirely dismisses the reality of mind or spirit. As such, they bear little or no relation to the spiritual principles AA says can lead us to emotional sobriety when practiced in all our affairs.

The findings of neuroscience and brain research may very well contribute to a better understanding of emotions and help our recovery, but only to the extent that they are employed to complement rather than supplant the spiritual, taking into account our full humanity as both biological and spiritual creatures.

Indeed, some key findings of brain science lend empirical support to the process by which 12-Step principles can bring about character and emotional growth, particularly when those principles are understood and practiced specifically as spiritual disciplines and virtues.

The phenomenon of neuroplasticity, for instance, helps to explain the process of habit formation that is at work in the acquisition of character virtues and defects, and the emotional states these can generate.

The concept was first introduced by William James, who referred to it simply as plasticity. Succinctly, this says that repeated activity engaging specific neuronal circuits will deepen, widen and strengthen those pathways in the brain so that like activity will then tend to repeat itself more or less automatically. This is the same process we have described—with broad reference to the self rather than narrowly to the brain—to explain how certain traits can become rooted, ingrained, imprinted, or impressed in us to form our character, disposing us thereby to habitual patterns of behavior.

Neuroplasticity would lead us to conclude that the way we live shapes the brain we have. This is good as far as it goes. But of course, we are not our brain. We can't be reduced to three pounds of gelatinous tissue. The brain, as James saw it, is rather like a receiver, a conduit for a transmission whose source is the mind. It is the physical substrate of mental activity. Research now supports this view, showing how mental activity can have an activating effect on the brain and bring about lasting changes in its neural circuitry.

In the context of recovery, we could therefore say that there is such a thing as mind over matter. But it is not a question of willpower nullifying or overriding neurological circuits in the brain. It is a question of spiritual practice reshaping them.

We cannot ignore the mind and pretend to reduce our emotions to the activity of dendrites, axons, and neurotransmitters in the amygdala and limbic system, as the materialist would have it. After reading a neuroscientist's book, observes Robert C. Roberts, a person may infer that his amygdala is active when he feels strong anxiety or fear. "But nobody feels his amygdala being active," he adds. "Instead, he feels afraid."[1]

If we cannot ignore the mind, however, neither can we ignore the brain, not if we are to practice a spirituality that accounts for reality and the true nature of things. We are composite beings, mind and matter, physical and spiritual.

How then does AA understand specifically moral emotions, that is, the kinds of emotions that bear upon the way we live, and how is it that a spiritual awakening and the practice of the principles work to reshape and transform them so that we can achieve emotional sobriety?

In looking at the emotions spiritually, our first consideration is of necessity the understanding we have of their origin. The same applies to the understanding we have of the brain. The spiritual perspective of AA holds that our ability to experience emotions is a faculty that has its source in God as our Creator. This capacity is his gift to us, as are also our rational, imaginative, creative, and other powers. With mind and will, feelings are a constituent part of the human spirit. As such, emotions are not a simple function of matter, a chance evolutionary product of our animal nature having little but survival value. They are not just physiological sensations, neurological phenomena, and biochemical reactions, though these may be detected, identified, measured, and analyzed by the neuroscientist and other specialists.

Second, as part of our spiritual endowment, emotions cannot be properly regarded as psychological liabilities or burdens. They serve God's purpose for our lives in the natural and human environments in which they are intended to function. Hence our goal is not to suppress or escape the emotions, to "manage" them so as to limit their negative impact, or to try to transcend them into a supposedly detached, enlightened, or pure spiritual state where we can be impervious to them. They are an integral part of our spiritual identity. What we seek is their redemption and wholesome restoration, their spiritual reordering and renewal.

Third, as an endowment of our spiritual and not only of our animal nature, emotions are not simply spontaneous or instinctive reactions to natural or environmental stimuli. Such a deterministic view is widespread and is mirrored in the typical dictionary definition of an emotion. This assumes that we can exercise little influence or gain any mastery over our emotions.

If this were the case, it would be pointless to talk about achieving emotional sobriety. We would be hapless victims of our feelings. But a spiritual view of things tells us this is not the case, for God granted us free will, and if we are to be free moral agents—able to choose how to act out of our God-given capacities, whether for good or for ill—then we have to be capable of emotional freedom. Common sense and ordinary experience tell us that we are.

This connection between free moral agency and emotional freedom is the reason why character development and emotional sobriety are two aspects of the same process of recovery. Our growth in one affects our growth in the other. Character development is a gradual process of acquiring virtue through repeated practice of right action, right intention, and right emotion. We cannot grow in character without an accompanying growth in our emotional disposition, for virtuous character and virtuous emotion work off each other, just as character defects and defective emotions do.

We recall that our spiritual awakening and the character growth that accompanies it can be seen simply but accurately as a process of "attitude adjustment." Beginning with the most elementary virtue— willingness—and continuing with the gradual but growing practice of the other virtues and the disciplines that make up the spiritual principles, these attitude adjustments multiply and accumulate, displacing our old ideas and awakening in us an increasingly spiritual view of things.

This in turn enables us to carry our practice of the principles to new levels and areas of our life. As we persevere in their pursuit, over time the virtues become engrained in us as permanent character traits, weeding out the character defects long rooted in us, defects that we now willingly surrender. We develop a habitual, settled disposition to the good in all we do.

Even as we do this, however, most of us find that emotional growth lags behind character building, so that our moral disposition to *do* right is often limited by our emotional inability to *feel* right. Anger, fear, resentment, and a variety of other negative emotions, while less damaging than when we drank, continue nevertheless to undermine and sabotage our moral effort. Our moral and our emotional dispositions are at odds. We are still unable to do that which we now know to be right and which we very much want to do. We need to add to moral, emotional virtue, to right character, right emotion. We can do this if we tie character and emotion to a rightly spiritual view and practice of the virtues.

NEW OUTLOOK, DIFFERENT MOTIVATION

To explore this, let us look at a snippet of one alcoholic's story. Abandoned by his parents as an infant, this man had migrated to this country still a child and risen from poverty and homelessness to become a college teacher. He had dreams of a successful career as a tenured university professor. The bottle, however, led him down a different path. When the end finally came, he had lost his family, friends, job, and self-respect, and found himself homeless again, broke, and unemployable. Reduced as he saw it to driving a taxicab, he was drunk, depressed, and overcome with self-pity, a danger to himself and others as he plied his nightly trade through the streets of New York.

He came to AA an emotional wreck. But before long, his cab-driving experience had undergone a complete overhaul. As he shared at meetings, he had become "a grateful cabbie." He drove safely and was friendly and appreciative of his fares. He didn't decline any destination and was thankful for even the smallest tip. Where he had cursed God before, he now thanked him that he had a job and might soon afford to put a roof over his head. Gone were the shame and regret, the depression and self-pity.

What happened to this man? He had experienced the first stirrings of a spiritual awakening. AA had begun to change the way he saw himself, others, and God. He was no longer a failure but a sick alcoholic. He was no longer fighting the world to survive or succeed but seeking help to recover. What most mattered to him now was to stay sober, and the experience of his fellow alcoholics showed that he could if he took certain steps. He began to view things through this new lens. Seeing God now as a benevolent Higher Power working for good in his life, he became grateful. Same job, same circumstances, a different cabbie.

When he did find his first apartment in sobriety, a wretched hole-in-the-wall no one would rent, the man was very grateful to have a home. He had undergone an emotional change.

The basic ingredients of this change were twofold: a new outlook, and a different motivation. His desire to stop drinking began to color the way he saw things and with that his emotional reactions to them.

These two factors, outlook and motivation, are central to the understanding of emotions that is at work in AA, an understanding that is implicit in the concept of a spiritual awakening at the heart of the AA message.

We may trace its earliest expression to the words of Carl Jung to Rowland H. Here was a man in the throes of desperation, unable to find relief for his alcoholism anywhere. Religion had failed him and now so had psychiatry. Chronic alcoholics like him were hopeless, Jung told Rowland. But, he added, "Here and there, once in a while, alcoholics have had what are called vital spiritual experiences . . . They appear to be in the nature of *huge emotional displacements and rearrangements. Ideas, emotions, and attitudes which were once the guiding forces of the lives of these men are suddenly cast to one side, and a completely new set of conceptions and motives begin to dominate them*" (Big Book, p. 27, our emphasis).

On Jung's suggestion, Rowland looked for a favorable spiritual environment to situate himself in, found it in the Oxford Group in New York, and delivered from the alcoholic obsession at last, passed the message of his spiritual experience to Ebby T., who then passed the message of his own experience to Bill W.

William James, who through extensive research had reached the same conclusion about the ability of a religious experience to transform the outlook and motivation—and with that, the lives—of variously troubled individuals, gave Bill W. the idea that in most persons this process took place as a gradual awakening (which could still build up in some cases to a sudden and dramatic change). This opened the possibility that, through the practice of spiritual principles over time, the desired awakening, *with its perceptual and motivational transformation,* could take place.

The italics are crucial, for this radical reshaping or trans-formation of outlook and motivation, issuing from a spiritual awakening, constitutes the essential internal shift that eventually translates into a changed life. We tend to lose sight of this, with the result that we miss the connection between the goal of experiencing a spiritual awakening and the goal of attaining emotional sobriety, for outlook and motivation are the twin pillars upon which our emotions are built.

This transformation is central to the view of a spiritual awakening that we find throughout the Big Book and the 12&2. "There's a Solution" says of the spiritual experiences of early alcoholics that they have "*revolutionized our whole attitude toward life, toward our fellows and toward God's* universe" (ibid., p. 25). The Promises assure us that "Our *whole attitude and outlook* upon life will change" (ibid., p. 84). The 12th Step in the 12&12 explains that "the most important meaning" of a spiritual awakening is that we have "now become able to *do, feel and believe*" that which we could not on our "unaided strength and resources alone" (pp. 106–107, our emphasis in all citations).

A radical change in perception and orientation that God brings about in us, enabling us to see, think, feel, and act in distinct spiritual ways that transform our lives and can significantly impact the lives of others, is the essence of a spiritual awakening and what makes it an eminently practical proposition, playing itself out as it does in our ordinary, everyday affairs.

Robert C. Roberts, who writes on the psychology of the virtues and the spiritual emotions, helps to shed light on how motivation and outlook can give shape and expression to the emotions. He uses the terms "concern" and "construal" to designate their two fundamental components, defining an emotion as a "concern-based construal."[2]

A concern is something that matters to me, that I consider important or significant, something that I value, something that orients my heart and moves or motivates me. A construal is a way of construing, interpreting, or perceiving things, how I see, take, or understand them. That to which I attach significant value and motivates me is an emotion-disposition, a concern that inclines me to a range of emotional responses. Which particular emotions arise depends on how I see those situations impinge on my concerns, how they affect or have a bearing on what I care about. My construal is the trigger that activates one or more of those emotions.

This view of emotions reflects common sense and ordinary experience. We don't get exercised over things we don't care about, and we routinely speak of people we think shouldn't have gotten upset with us in a given situation as having misconstrued what we said, or as having misunderstood or taken what we said the wrong way. A Yankees victory over the Red Sox is obviously a source of joy for ardent fans of the New York team and of despondency for those of the Boston, while a reversal of fortunes for the two teams would elicit a corresponding reversal of emotions for their respective fans. Meanwhile, people who are not "into" baseball couldn't care less either way. Plainly, we respond emotionally to things only as they impact what we value. That is why it was said long ago that "Where your treasure is, there will your heart be also."[3]

By his own account, our cabbie cared a great deal about achievement and success, to such an extent in fact that much of his identity was built around it. He construed driving a taxicab as an inferior occupation, and himself therefore a failure. The emotions he experienced were the natural outflow of this, his "concern-based construal."

What a spiritual awakening does is to reconstruct my "concerns" and my "construals," to give me a new perspective on what really matters and a new way of looking at the big picture of life, and within that larger context, at the little picture in the circumstances of my everyday experience. With this, my emotions are laid on a new, spiritual foundation.

Starting with a desire to stop drinking as a motivation that is first induced in me by the emotional debacle of my bottom, I become willing to listen to the experience of alcoholics in the rooms and open myself up to a different, spiritual view of life to which they credit their recovery. As the AA narrative begins to take hold in me, my desire to stay sober deepens and I begin to see myself and my immediate situation within that narrative. I come to view myself as an alcoholic, just like the others, and I identify myself as such when I share. I admit I am powerless. Gradually anger, fear, depression, self-pity, and other harmful emotions recede. I feel a little grateful here, a little hopeful there. Without realizing it, I have started on the road to recovery.

This is the basic paradigm. I bring the desire and the willingness and AA gives me the blueprint and the tools to build a whole new spiritual *and emotional* foundation to my life. How far I get in this project depends on the lengths to which I am willing to go to practice the principles that will result in a spiritual awakening that revolutionizes my *whole* outlook and attitude, that radically changes in a spiritual direction my concerns, the things that really matter to me, and the way that I look at "God's universe" (Big Book, p. 25).

That last phrase contains the seeds of what we might call a master construal. It is planted with my admission of powerlessness in Step 1, germinates with my coming to believe in Step 2, and begins to sprout into a new life with Step 3. When I come to see this world as God's universe and surrender to the fact, that becomes the prism through which I begin to look at God, at myself, at my fellows, and at all of life.

There is a center, and God, not me, occupies it. Not me and not any other person or thing. I am like the rest derivative, contingent, and utterly dependent on him. Gradually, I come to understand God as "the Great Reality" (ibid., p. 55), the ultimate source of all that is true and all that is good. A desire grows in me to see things the way he wants me to see them, to live the way he wants me to live. In the fullness of time, doing his will and growing into the person he wants me to be becomes my overarching, master concern, the passion or desire that motivates me above all other concerns and orders and gives them form, what gives meaning, purpose, and direction to my life.

CHARACTER AND EMOTIONS

As an abiding master concern, this passion for God and his will for me becomes deeply imprinted in my character and gives shape to my psychological identity. It is what now drives and informs my practice of the principles in all my affairs, for that is how his way of life is fulfilled and becomes manifest in me. The virtues themselves become concerns and construals, shaping what matters to me and how I see things in the course of everyday events. I am moved by and see through the eyes of faith, hope, love, compassion, and gratitude.

Virtues and emotions are inextricably linked in this process. As moral and spiritual dispositions, they share the same perceptual and motivational foundations that are built through the process of a spiritual awakening. Yet emotions are episodic states, they ebb and flow with varying degrees of duration and intensity. It is the virtues that, through repeated practice, can become etched in our character and become firm and settled dispositions. It is the virtues that, through character building, can provide a stable spiritual and moral foundation for the emotions. By practicing them in all our affairs, the virtues can give shape not only to our moral but to our emotional life, disposing us to right action and right feeling.

To the extent that they are moral then, emotions have an identifiable source in our character. They are affective expressions of character traits. Healthy or wholesome emotions are manifestations of virtue and good character; unhealthy or unwholesome emotions of character defects. Said differently, character defects will tend to show up in warped emotions that are out of line with the true nature of a given situation, while character virtues will tend to manifest in emotions that are appropriate to a particular circumstance. By practicing the virtues, we cultivate the soil from which healthy emotions sprout; by letting go of our character defects, we drain the swamp in which diseased emotions breed.

This connection between character and emotion is not a fully conscious part of our understanding or practice in AA. But it is clearly what underlies Step 4, as noted in our earlier discussion of the "exact nature of our wrongs."

Our moral inventory as laid out in the Big Book (p. 65) is an examination of our *character* flaws as they relate to three *emotions*: anger, resentment, and fear. We make a list of the people we are angry at and note next to each the "cause" of our resentments (our perception of what they said or did, how we construed their words or actions). Next to that, we list the areas of concern that were "affected." These are things we saw at stake in the situation, that we considered to have been "hurt," "threatened," or "interfered with." The book lists such things as our "sex relations," "security," "self-esteem," and "pride." Following each of these, we affix in parenthesis the word "fear," the third emotion issuing from our perception of how they were affected.

Reversing the habit of a lifetime, we focus on finding the cause of these emotions, not in the other person, but in ourselves. It is then that we can make the connection between emotion and character. As we take inventory and examine our resentments, issuing from hurts real or imagined, we begin to see the exact nature of these resentments in the character defects that lie behind and account for them.

But this doesn't happen automatically. We need to consciously look for these defects. The "Cause" column of the Big Book's "grudge list" will reveal—if we look hard enough—such flaws as jealousy, dishonesty, disloyalty, competitive pride, intolerance, and self-righteousness. We will find these and more "common manifestations" of self in us, if we dig deep enough when we look for the real cause. They are what feed the unforgiveness eating away at us, and the chronic anger we call resentment.

Our character defects generally rest on a perception of others as being deficient in some manner, that is, on a perception of *their* character defects. What this does of course is blind us to our own. Anger, resentment, and fear recede when we ask God to help us see people, especially those who have actually hurt us, as being no different from us. They too are "spiritually sick" (Big Book, p. 66).

This view or "construal" helps us to identify with people's weaknesses—even when they affect us. Intolerance and the other character defects lose their perceptual justification and so we can more readily surrender them. Honestly seeing our defects for what they are instead of trying to rationalize them, we can then focus on letting them go and practicing their virtuous counterparts, rather than responding to wrong with wrong.

Motivated by a desire to do God's will, to be of service and of help, we ask "each morning in meditation that our Creator show us the way of patience, tolerance, kindliness and love" (ibid., p. 83), for when we practice these and the other virtues *as reflections of a spiritually transformed character*, anger loses its triggers and resentment its fuel.

When we reflect on that part of our 4th Step list that pertains to our fears and inquire as to their cause, we find that they also spring from our defects of character. The Big Book suggests that our fears—and here we can add related emotions like worry and anxiety—often arise on the heels of a prideful self-reliance which invariably ends in failure, for it is motivated by a false understanding of ourselves, dependence on God being intrinsic to our nature.

We try to gain self-esteem and security by making demands of ourselves and others that neither they nor we can meet. With failure come anger and resentment and concomitant emotions like depression and self-pity. These diseased emotions lose their power over us when we consistently practice the virtues of faith and humility through a trusting reliance on the power and goodness of God. As we progressively surrender pride in its many forms, serenity emerges as a stable state of mind.

We have seen that AA considers pride the chief motivator of our character defects and humility the chief corrective virtue. Pride and humility are master self-construals, how we see ourselves in relation to the world, our fellows, and God. Pride puts self at the center, and everything is seen in terms of it, what it lends to it and what it takes away, what it promises and what it threatens. All of our diseased emotions flow ultimately from that attitude and perspective. Humility acknowledges the center belongs to God and selves exist to serve him and one another for the love of him. From that place proceed all the virtues and through them all the good and healthy emotions.

If anger, resentment, fear, and the other diseased emotions that plague our recovery are to lose their hold on us, we need to work Step 4 and the rest of the housecleaning Steps in the context of a spiritual awakening, practicing the disciplines and the virtues as distinctly spiritual principles.

This will help us to see how specific defective emotions in specific situations are attached to specific self-centered concerns and construals, so that we can reorient ourselves spiritually. It will help us to identify the character defects that generate these diseased emotions and the virtues that counteract them. We can then practice these virtues and let go of those defects. The virtues we practice gain increasing traction in our mind, our character, and our brain, while the defects we surrender grow weaker from lack of use. So do the corresponding emotions gain or lose strength. As with much else we do consistently, these practices develop into habits over time, so that we become increasingly adept at monitoring, shaping, and channeling our emotions toward the good.

Emotion-Virtues

While all the virtues, practiced from a spiritual perspective, can have a positive impact on our emotional life, there is a set of them that has a special relationship to the emotions. They are what Robert C. Roberts calls emotion-virtues. They are both moral character traits *and* expressions of emotion. In addition to fostering the healthy emotions they name, these virtues are a direct counterweight to the opposite defective emotions and counteract directly or indirectly other diseased emotions as well, sometimes in interaction with other virtues. Among these are five we practice in AA: gratitude, hope, compassion, peace, and joy. We will consider gratitude as a paradigmatic example.

Gratitude is considered a moral virtue because it is the proper and just response to a gift freely given, what is due to the person who so favors us (hence placed under the cardinal virtue justice). We have a capacity for receiving goods from others and giving thanks is how we exercise that capacity well, expressing our gratitude through a gracious response to the grace that is shown to us. But gratitude is also (or the word also denominates) an emotion, a capacity to experience a certain feeling that accompanies the receipt of the good. We not only give thanks, we *feel* grateful. As an emotion-virtue, gratitude disposes us morally to act right and emotionally to feel right, to do good as regards others and to do well as regards our mental condition.

Gratitude promotes feelings of wellbeing because it is a perception of good. It is a perception in terms of a benefit, a beneficiary, and a benefactor, what Roberts calls the three interlocking B's (*bene* is Latin for "good" or "well") that make up the framework of gratitude.

Gratitude becomes spiritual, a spiritual virtue and a spiritual emotion, when we are moved in our response by a God-centered view of the three: gift, gifted, and giver. This is the view we gain in AA. The AA understanding is that we are sober by the grace of God. Our gratitude is a response to grace, freely given.

We grow in this gratitude as we come to see not only our sobriety, but every proper good we have as gifts from a loving God, and ourselves as blessed. We grow still further as we come to see the blessings of our fellows and of the natural order from the same perspective. Gratitude is our just and loving and distinctly human response to God's providence, for as the Big Book and the 12&12 repeatedly affirm, we are his creatures and his children, equally made in his image and equally dependent on his grace.

We know from our experience when we drank that gratitude, even of the garden variety that leaves God out of the picture, was one emotion that seldom arose spontaneously in us. Gratitude was not in our repertoire, as some might say. More likely, we still had the capacity, but it was greatly impaired. We took whatever good we had for granted, feeling entitled to or giving ourselves credit for it. Rather than look for the good and give thanks, we tended to look for the bad and complain. Dissatisfaction was our default mode, creating a psychological climate in us that was hostile to gratitude and fed our power-driven obsession with changing everything. This naturally made for unsettled lives and unstable emotions.

This begins to change when we come to AA, as we saw with the grateful cabbie. But if our practice is to be spiritual and if it is to result in emotional sobriety, gratitude needs to be firmly grounded in an understanding of God as ultimately the giver of all good gifts and us as his favored and blessed recipients.

If we consciously practice it as such, time and again, through such disciplines as prayer, meditation, and service, and in matters big and small, gratitude will over the long term become embedded in us as a habitual, settled part of our character. We will be morally *and emotionally* disposed to gratitude, looking for a reason to give thanks even in the most difficult of circumstances. In Step 11 we will then come to the knowledge that giving thanks "in all things"[4] is God's will for us. Saying that "I am a grateful alcoholic" will then reflect the truth about who we have become in our person, having understood deeply and intimately that God in his grace can turn any evil, any pain we have suffered or inflicted, to good purpose.

Practiced as a response to grace, we will find that gratitude the virtue can give shape not only to gratitude the emotion, but to other emotions as well, and even that it can be consciously elicited to do so. This is the idea behind the slogan "Put some gratitude in your attitude," which sees gratitude as an attitude that can be cultivated and bear fruit in a healthy mental state. It is also the idea behind the suggestion that we make a "gratitude list," the opposite of our "grudge list" and AA's way of saying "count your blessings." For when we lose our gratitude and thanklessness prevails, we lose our emotional bearings all around and become prey to discontent and dissatisfaction, at times even to depression and despair.

Gratitude can counter these and other hurtful emotions. It can temper sorrow, when sorrow is the appropriate response to a loss, helping us to see something to be thankful for even in our grief. It can mitigate anger because when we are grateful for being forgiven our many wrongs, we can more willingly forgive the wrongs in others. It can be an antidote to greed and various emotions associated with our lust or excessive desire for more and better and different, for it helps us to appreciate and be content with what we have. And it can displace envy and jealousy, from which also issue resentment, for it helps us to see others' blessings as such, not as objects of comparison and competition.

If my deeply held view of the goods I have—physical attributes, skills, abilities, talents, accomplishments, wealth, possessions—is that they are God's blessings, then I have in this construal the emotional basis for feeling grateful rather than proud, rightly seeing God as the giver and myself the receiver.

My motivation is equally altered. I am not concerned with what these things say about me or with getting recognition or credit for them. My view of myself and of my worth does not rest on such things or on people's validation of me on account of them. Instead of using them to build up my ego and image, I become interested in being a good steward of these gifts, using them generously in service to others out of gratitude to God, for his glory rather than mine. Where false pride would make me emotionally dependent, gratitude, based on a true grasp of how things really are, sets me free.

As with gratitude, so with the other emotion-virtues. As they become rooted in me as spiritual character traits, I become a hopeful person, compassionate, peaceful, and joyful, and my tendency to react to difficulties and obstacles with a host of contrary unhealthy and unproductive feelings loses its hold on me. My ability to feel these virtuous emotions is not dependent on fallible people and changing circumstances, but rests entirely in God and his will for me. Hope, compassion, peace, and joy become habits of the heart and stable dispositions. I can experience them even under conditions that might appear unfavorable.

AA tells us that our character defects are the source of most of our difficulties in life. They proceed from a self-centered outlook and are motivated by self-serving attitudes and selfish interests that drive us to excess and disordered or broken relations.

A spiritual awakening that wholly reorients our heart and makes God and his will for us the ground of our view of life and of the things that we value makes it possible for us to practice the disciplines and the virtues as distinctly spiritual principles. As we practice them in all our affairs, we are progressively freed from the defects of character and emotion that dominated us when we drank and that continue to rob us of the joy of living well into our recovery.

Right Principles, Right Practice

In 1958 the AA Grapevine published a letter Bill W. had written a friend in which he confesses that, like many alcoholics with long-term sobriety, the joy of living had eluded him. Like them, he had failed to grow spiritually and emotionally and still lacked emotional sobriety. For Bill, this expressed itself most dramatically in chronic spells of a deep depression that had bedeviled him for much of his recovery. One such spell had lasted eleven years, and at the time of writing, he had recently emerged from what he feared was another long relapse.

The published piece was an effort to re-examine the question of emotional sobriety and find an answer for the failure of many old-timers like him to attain it. This issue had been first raised with the publication of the 12&12

in 1953, when many AAs had achieved double-digit sobriety and found that not drinking wasn't enough. The book was written with the express purpose of applying the 12 Steps to the business of living, and not just getting, sober.

The earlier Big Book had of necessity focused on the urgent and immediate task of not drinking and helping others to stop (the chapter on Step 12 deals exclusively with carrying the message, as reflected in its title, "Working with Others"). Though it implied the goal of emotional sobriety, it did not articulate it, and the concept remained undeveloped.

With the 12&12, as we have seen, emotional sobriety becomes a central goal of Step 12 and the ultimate goal of all the Steps, and practicing the principles in all our affairs the path to its attainment and transmission as we share it with others. But as we have also seen, the goal is not necessarily central for all alcoholics, and it remains out of reach even for many for whom it is. There are those, too, who want the emotional benefits without the spiritual work and are unwilling to go through the spiritual process that the 12 Steps lay out. For many of us, practicing the principles in all our affairs remains the road less traveled.

Revisiting the issue in what the Grapevine titled "The Next Frontier: Emotional Sobriety,"[5] Bill attempts to probe deeper into the question of why emotional sobriety remains out of reach even for those of us who really want it and are willing to work for it. If our 12 Steps are right and we are convinced of the fact, and if we are earnestly trying to practice their principles in all our affairs, why are we still not able to achieve emotional sobriety even after many years in recovery? Why is it that the peace and the joy that the program promises still elude us? This, writes Bill, is the predicament, the real quandary, that many of us in long-term recovery face.

Like many of us who have walked in his shoes, Bill kept asking himself why the 12 Steps hadn't worked on his emotions, in his case to effectuate a release from depression.

After much soul-searching and long periods of meditation on the St. Francis Prayer, the answer finally dawned on him. He realized that his main character defect had always been his dependence on people and circumstances to provide him with security, recognition, prestige, and similar emotional satisfactions. When he didn't get these things the way he wanted, he would fight for them. And when he still failed to get them, depression would predictably follow.

Bill had focused on the Prayer of St. Francis because he believed that it held the answer to his problem. If he could practice the kind of love expressed in the prayer, he thought, he would be relieved of his depression and the other emotional handicaps that afflicted him. What he was able to see now was that his dependence had denied him the freedom to love this way. Rather than giving of himself selflessly, he had always expected and often even demanded something in return. In effect, he had been trying to control people and circumstances even as he gave.

To Bill, the lesson was clear. Every emotional disturbance, he concluded, could probably be traced to an unhealthy dependence and the unhealthy expectations and demands that usually come with it. If we could surrender these dependencies and demands, then we would be free to live and love. Emotional sobriety would be ours.

Bill acknowledges that he is not really presenting a new idea. As we quoted earlier, he had written in Step 12 of the 12&12 that emotional sobriety is a product of practicing "the kind of love that has no price tag on it," and "the kind of giving that asks no rewards." We also read there that "our desires for emotional security and wealth, for personal prestige and power, for romance, and for family satisfactions" all had to be "tempered and redirected," so as to "place spiritual growth first" (p. 114). All character defects breed wrong dependence on others. Recognizing this, he had also written that right dependence on God was "the best possible source of emotional stability" (ibid., p. 116). It was the answer to the dependence-domination syndrome from which we suffered in our relations with others and which kept us from giving and loving and living freely.

What is apparent, however, is that until the experience which led to the writing of the letter published by the Grapevine some five years later, Bill had not been able to see how these things applied to himself, in key areas of his own life and in specific, down-to-earth, practical terms. They don't seem to have gone beyond beliefs and intellectual convictions, until a recurrence of intense emotional pain forced him to probe further and more deeply into his character and his heart.

Since becoming sober, Bill had given and given richly, and God was able to work through him to give us AA and through it the gift of our own recoveries. But by his own account, he had remained under the sway of the self-centered motivations and ways of looking at things of his drinking days. He still gave expecting to be given in return the approval, validation, and other emotional satisfactions that continued to hold a significant place in his heart. His emotional wellbeing depended on getting these things and on the people and circumstances he expected to give them to him. He was therefore not free to give and hence not free to love, for there was always a price tag attached. Love and service, the spiritual goal of the 12 Steps so beautifully expressed in St. Francis, remained an impossible ideal.

His depression, Bill now acknowledges, came on the heels of his failure to get from people and circumstances what he desperately thought he needed and misguidedly believed they could give him.

Why hadn't he seen this before? Bill wondered. This led him to raise a question that goes to the heart of the problem of emotional sobriety. How, he asks, can we translate right belief, right mental or intellectual conviction, into right feelings or healthy emotional results, and therefore into healthy and happy living? This, he recognizes, is the problem that faces not only the alcoholic but anyone willing to live by right principles. To Bill, the problem seemed to stem from the unconscious. That, he says, is where our old fears, compulsions, and false aspirations continue to stream from long into sobriety. Our main task, he adds, becomes one of bringing our unconscious into conformity and harmony with what we actually believe, know, and want now.

Apparently, Bill planned to pursue this question further in a later work. However, he was never able to. Nevertheless, the experience he recounts in the Grapevine reaffirms his original understanding in Step 12 of the 12&12: the key to emotional sobriety is practicing the principles of the program in all our affairs. If that is so, then the answer to Bill's question is clear. How can we translate right principles into right emotions? By right practice. The issue is what we understand by right principles, right emotions, and right practice.

His story shows that Bill was able at some point to practice the principles of prayer, meditation, self-examination, surrender, and humility in ways that resulted in a spiritual and emotional breakthrough. Character defects and emotional liabilities were revealed to him that he had never seen before. Things long latent in his unconscious were now brought to his conscious mind and he was able to act on them. He was then able to reach a new level of emotional stability and serenity which he continued to build on by giving of himself unconditionally, practicing the principles of love and service as Francis did.

Bill raises the right question and he gives us the results of his experience. However, he does not extrapolate from that experience an explicit and comprehensive account of how the process of achieving emotional sobriety might work. That is exactly what we have tried to outline in this chapter.

When, through right action, right beliefs and convictions are integrated deeply into our emotional constitution, then living them out becomes natural and is no longer a struggle. Our moral and emotional dispositions are no longer at odds. We are no longer divided between what we believe, what we feel, and what we do. Seeing the problem of the unconscious from the perspective of a spiritually-informed neuroscience, we could say that the renewal of our mind begins to effect a rewiring of our brain. Our biological life is progressively brought into conformity with the spiritual life in us. We become whole and harmonious human beings.

According to the understanding of emotions that we have presented here, how we react emotionally to situations depends on how we see those situations affect the things we care about. If status is important to us and we hanker after recognition and prestige, that desire comes with an emotion-disposition intrinsic to it that inclines us to a corresponding range of emotional responses. When our acts are motivated by that desire and they fulfill it, we may respond with, say, pleasure, pride, "elation," or "grandiosity" (Bill's words), depending on the intensity of the desire and effort. When they don't fulfill it, we may react with, say, disappointment, frustration, or anger. Or, as in Bill's case, with depression, when we "fight" for our heart's desire and we lose.

This process (identified earlier as a "concern-based construal") describes how an emotion like depression can arise on a given occasion. How the same emotion arises consistently time and time again is described by the process of habit formation. Every time we act on our desire to promote our image and reputation and we fail, an adverse emotional reaction will follow. Repeated action and reaction will habituate us to that emotional response to the point where the response is unconscious, lying deeply engraved in the brain and beyond our mind's awareness and control. We lose the freedom to think, feel, and act differently in those situations. The brain goes on automatic pilot and we keep thinking, acting, and feeling the same way over and over again. This is how we develop our dependencies, or if you will, our addictions.

It is also how our character is formed, and how it shapes our emotions. Through repetition these defective ways become impressed in the self as character traits, disposing us to still more flawed intention, flawed action, and flawed emotion. And because these things are habitual and unconscious, we are not aware of what we are doing to bring on the unhealthy emotion, such as depression. Instead, we blame people and circumstances, which is just another way of expressing our unhealthy dependence on them.

This literally vicious cycle is broken when something happens (invariably involving pain, sometimes inducing a bottom) that awakens us to the real nature of what we are doing and enables us to view and value things in starkly different terms, as apparently happened to Bill. We stop looking to people to provide us with what we need and start looking to God instead. At the same time, those needs are less and less worldly and socially centered things like status, recognition, and prestige, and more and more the things of the spirit. This is Jung's "displacements and rearrangements" at work, with their new set of "conceptions and motives," or in the terms of AA, another instance of our spiritual awakening.

We say another instance because our spiritual awakening is not one long, seamless, uniform process. It is more like a series of awakenings, slow incremental changes marked by sudden qualitative leaps, breakthroughs and turning points, recurring internal shifts that progressively reveal more of our liabilities in more areas of our lives.

A spiritual shift reverses the previous process of unhealthy habit formation in a given area and initiates a healthy one. We begin to act out of these spiritual ways of seeing and caring about particular things and out of the intentions and desires that accompany them. We begin to practice virtue in situations where we had instinctively practiced character defects.

When we intentionally use our skills, talents, and any other good we have out of an understanding that they are God's gifts to us and that they bless us in proportion as we use them for their intended purpose of blessing others, we are with every act and in every situation ingraining those views of ourselves, of God, and of others in our character and in our heart. As we do, we are also ingraining their corresponding virtues and emotions: humility, gratitude, generosity, compassion.

When we put first things first and we see our spiritual needs as preceding and informing all other needs and seek to fulfill them in concrete action through right dependence on God, we will be engraving in us the virtue of faith and with it a deep sense of security that no amount of striving after some spurious self-esteem and social recognition can ever bring.

Virtues are ways of giving because in practicing them we are giving others the best of ourselves. For the same reason, they are also their own reward. In practicing them we are further reinforcing in us those qualities that make for our spiritual, moral, and emotional health. Practicing the virtues is therefore how we can give and love, live freely, and flourish in all of our humanity.

This is the process by which, practiced in all our affairs, the principles work to bring about emotional sobriety. If we are not growing along those lines, it is probably because we are not practicing them.

This may be because physical sobriety is all we want out of the program and we have no desire to grow further, in which case nothing will happen until we develop that desire. Or it may be because we are not willing, in which case we are not practicing the first principle, the indispensable virtue without which the other principles don't work. Or if willing, it may be that we don't understand the principles well enough to practice them in all their fullness, in which case we are not working with a full set of spiritual tools. Desire and willingness are necessary, but they are not sufficient. They need to be directed to right principles and right practice. Otherwise, they are thwarted and frustrated and our actions come to naught, leaving us in the predicament of wanting, but not being able.

In AA emotional sobriety proceeds from spiritual growth. Our emotional illness is a reflection of our spiritual disease. We are selfish and self-centered not simply because we have failed to mature and grow up from a developmental condition peculiar to childhood and adolescence, but because that is our nature, that is who we really are. We naturally hanker after and expect the world to supply us with the things we want and mistake them for the things we need. We want what we want when we want it, and more often than not what we want will not bring us the happiness we seek.

Nor is our problem just the result of inadequate nurture. The rooms represent alcoholics of widely divergent backgrounds and experiences in all categories (familial, social, cultural, economic, educational). We have had the best and the worst of parents and upbringings and opportunities. Yet in our spiritual condition, as in our physical and mental addiction, we share the same malady.

Though no longer under the influence of alcohol, we remain under the influence of our "ism." Our problem is not just developmental or circumstantial, but spiritual. When we straighten out spiritually, says the Big Book (p. 64), we straighten out mentally. That is why when Bill talks about maturity and balance in his Grapevine article, he defines these in terms of the fundamental spiritual principle that, together with surrender, underlies all of the Steps and all of the other principles. This is the virtue of humility, the virtue that puts things in their proper perspective and tempers our excessive drives and desires, the disordering and destabilizing claims that proceed from placing ourselves at the center of the universe and playing God.

If emotional sobriety is to become a practical reality in our recovery then, we need to see how a continuing spiritual awakening and the practice of the principles that bring that awakening about can work to re-shape our emotions. We need to see how the principles, understood as spiritual disciplines and virtues, can be practiced in all our affairs to build our character as the spiritual bedrock of our emotions, so that we become naturally inclined to the good and the healthy, morally and emotionally, in the things that we do and the things that we feel.

It is through the steady assimilation and integration of these transformative spiritual, moral, and emotional habits that a right mental conviction can be translated into a right emotional result, and, by the grace of God, emotional sobriety achieved. How this works in the Steps is the business of the chapters that follow.

STEP 1

*"We admitted that we were powerless over alcohol—
that our lives had become unmanageable."*

"We know that little good can come to any
alcoholic who joins A.A. unless he has first
accepted his devastating weakness and all its
consequences. Until he so humbles himself,
his sobriety—if any—will be precarious. Of
real happiness he will find none at all."

–12&12, pp. 21–22

Step One

LACK OF POWER: OUR DILEMMA

As Bill W. prepared to travel to Akron after repeated failures to sober up anyone through the Oxford Group in New York, Dr. Silkworth reminded him of William James's observation that "truly transforming spiritual experiences are nearly always founded on calamity and collapse." He urged him to "Stop preaching at them, and give them the hard medical facts first. This may soften them up at depth so that they will be willing to do anything to get well. Then they may accept those spiritual ideas of yours, and even a Higher Power" (Big Book, p. 13).

BILL W. MEETS DR. BOB

The "hard medical facts" were the then-novel concept that alcoholism is a disease, or as we say nowadays, an addiction. We suffer from a mental state that compels us to drink and from a physical condition that makes us crave for more and renders us helpless to stop. The disease is progressive. It can only get worse. There is no cure for it. We can never drink safely.

Up to that point, Bill had been giving the "spiritual angle" first, setting forth the treatment before presenting a full diagnosis of the illness. He would stress the need for a spiritual experience such as he had had, leading to a relationship with God, as the solution to the alcoholic's problem. Predictably, he had been coming up against the fierce resistance of the average drunk to anything that smells of religion.

Of course, what Dr. Silkworth was telling Bill was to apply the lesson of his own experience. Hadn't he resisted Ebby's "I got religion" approach at that kitchen table in Brooklyn Heights? Hadn't his epiphany at Towns Hospital been founded on his own "calamity and collapse?"

Dr. Silkworth wasn't telling him to skip the spiritual and stick just to the physiological and psychological facts of the illness. The idea was to address the underlying cause of the alcoholic's resistance first. This was his self-centered pride, or in the language of psychology, his bloated ego.

Though he might not have realized it himself, Dr. Silkworth's counsel was not merely a matter of "using psychology" in a tactical sense, though it was that. Its objective was fundamentally spiritual: to chip away at the wall of denial erected by pride. It involved an early application of what would become a key AA principle: the virtue of simplicity. Embodied in the maxim

"First Things First," it meant getting to the spiritual end through immediately practical means.

Indeed, bringing the spiritual down to earth and tying it to the practical would become a hallmark of AA simplicity. In things of the spirit as in everything else, we learn and grow by steps. AA's task became one of breaking up the spiritual path the alcoholic had to travel into a series of progressive and concrete steps that would gradually lead him to the desired spiritual experience or awakening, thus putting him firmly on the road to recovery.

The first step was to "deflate" the alcoholic, an apt image for lowering his pride and humbling him. He had to be shown that, objectively speaking, in the medical or "scientific" view, his was a hopeless case. Only then would he be open to a spiritual solution he might otherwise instinctively reject. For this to be accomplished, the alcoholic's circumstances had to be dire. Under such conditions, being confronted with the fatal nature of his disease had the effect of sucking any remaining air out of the alcoholic's "prideful balloon" (12&12, S2, p. 29). Any vestige of the illusion that he could handle things on his own would be gone. He would be forced down to a hard landing, hit bottom, and admit defeat.

When he met Dr. Bob, Bill W. followed Dr. Silkworth's advice, and the rest is history. We follow in their footsteps. Defeat, despair, and collapse force us to surrender and admit what we would not willingly admit, that we are powerless over alcohol and that our lives have become unmanageable.

Admitting Powerlessness

The admission of powerlessness is a distinctly AA way of practicing certain spiritual principles that are key to recovery. Chief among these are the discipline of surrender and the virtue of humility. We have characterized these two principles as being foundational to the entire program, underlying all the Steps and extending through all stages of recovery. In Step 1, surrender and humility interact with four other virtues that help pave the way to the admission of powerlessness. These are the virtues of honesty, acceptance, willingness, and open-mindedness.

Surrender

Of course, when we first "take" Step 1 and admit we are powerless to control our drinking and our lives, we can hardly be said to be practicing any disciplines or virtues. Discipline and virtue involve choice, and our very first surrender over alcohol is not exactly a product of choice. At the point of this capitulation, we are generally in a physical, emotional, and spiritual state that precludes the ability to choose. In fact, it can be said that we surrender precisely because we have no choice. We have truly run out of options.

Few of us will surrender unless our backs are up against the wall. We do only because we are in trouble, very serious trouble in many cases. We have made a mess of our lives and we can't cope anymore. We have tried everything and nothing has worked. We have played our last card and we have lost. We are desperate and exhausted and have no fight left in us. Our willpower, in which we took so much pride, is useless. We can't stop drinking and we can't fix ourselves. Alcohol has beaten and humiliated us.

Defeat and humiliation drive us to the rooms and there we learn the true nature of our condition. For us alcoholics, willful in the extreme, defeat is a necessary condition for surrender, humiliation a prerequisite for humility. Our admission of powerlessness is *forced* on us by the consequences of what we have done as active alcoholics. We surrender only because we have been defeated in our attempt to live by our own power. Through "calamity and collapse" we actually *experience* powerlessness. Admitting and accepting it is the next step. If we can scrape up enough honesty and humility to do so, that's only because pain and suffering have rendered us "as open-minded to conviction and as willing to listen as the dying can be" (12&12, S1, p. 24).

Admitting powerlessness is the first and fundamental step in surrender. The reason is that the whole issue of power is central to the alcoholic's problem, and therefore to its solution. The acquisition and accumulation of power in its varied forms is a natural part of our development as human beings. The problem arises when we disconnect from the source of that power, misuse that power, and reach for powers that are not ours to have. We try to center power on ourselves, on our own will, and we overreach. Power becomes self-serving and corrupting.

In this we alcoholics are no different from anyone else. But alcohol plays a peculiar role. "First I took a drink, then the drink took me," we say in AA. At first, the bottle is a source of power. It fuels our imagination and emboldens our will. Under its influence, we think there is nothing we can't achieve. And so we push, and invariably we push too hard and too far. With time, the bottle becomes a power unto itself. It controls us and pushes us even further afield. It dissolves all natural restraints and silences our conscience. It brooks no limits. All is permissible. We cross lines we never dreamed we would cross.

Warping our instincts and driving us to excess, alcohol eventually brings about our downfall. We sometimes say we drank to medicate our pain, but for many of us that came later. We first fell in love with the bottle for the sense of power it gave us. In the early stages, this power was benign: we felt more sociable, less inhibited, less self-conscious. With time the power became destructive. We acted in ways that caused us and others untold damage. We then medicated the resulting pain with more alcohol, which drove us to still more excess and more pain, and so on in an endless cycle of self-defeat. The bottle was in control, and we became powerless.

Lack of power is the alcoholic's "dilemma" (Big Book, p. 45). We don't have the power to break alcohol's dominion over us. We need another Power. We are loath to admit to this. In our eyes, powerlessness is tantamount to helplessness. Paradoxically, the opposite is true. The alcoholic who cannot admit to her own powerlessness remains closed to the Power that can deliver her. Insisting on self-reliance when self-reliance is of no use, she will neither ask for nor accept help. She can't help herself, nor can anyone help her. Clinging to the illusion of power and unable to admit her fatal weakness, she remains in a state of total helplessness.

HONESTY

"Admitted" is a word closely associated with various principles we practice as we work through some of the Steps. Most obvious among these is the virtue of honesty. In Step 1 our admission of powerlessness and hence our practice of surrender, honesty, and the other principles is incipient and limited in scope, applying to alcohol and taking place under duress. In Step 5, "admitted" takes on a broader significance as an expression of honesty and humility, and becomes operative through the discipline of confession, both of character defects and of past wrongdoing. In Step 10 to admit is again to confess humbly and honestly, but not only to ourselves, God, and another human being as we do in 5, but also to those we have harmed, as we do in 9 when we make restitution.

Honesty is arguably the most widely recognized virtue in AA, with gratitude perhaps a close second. The "How It Works" chapter of the Big Book—the first three pages of which preface meetings in rooms everywhere—declares flat out that the least likely to recover are "men and women who are constitutionally incapable of being honest with themselves." These people "are naturally incapable of grasping and developing a manner of living which demands rigorous honesty" (p. 58).

The need for honesty is most evident with the housecleaning Steps, where we take a probing look at ourselves and openly admit what is wrong with us and what harm we have done. But honesty is required from the very outset, with our admission of powerlessness and unmanageability. Such admission lays the foundation for our growth in this virtue as we progress through the other Steps. If we are less than honest with Step 1, we are going to be less than honest with the other Steps as well.

In Step 1, our inability to be honest takes the form of self-deception or denial. What keeps me from coming to AA is my denial that I have a problem with alcohol. The denial starts when I become aware on some level that I do in fact have a problem, for I can't deny what I don't know or at least suspect to be the case. Perhaps I have done something under the influence of alcohol that I realize I wouldn't have done otherwise. Or perhaps someone in a position to observe my drinking and behavior has expressed some concern.

Yet, I deny that whatever problems I am having have anything to do with alcohol. I rationalize that I have other "issues." Or employing another technique of self-deception, I minimize the problem, conceding that maybe I am drinking a little too much and may need to slow down. I may then try various controlled-drinking strategies. In a case of what psychologists sometimes call motivated irrationality, I am so biased against the thought of my being an alcoholic that I will find every conceivable alternative explanation to avoid facing up to the truth. I won't admit that I can't stop drinking, that I can't handle alcohol. I can't acknowledge that the bottle has taken center stage in my life and governs much of what I do.

My inability to be honest with myself spills over into dishonesty with everybody else, for as we read in *As Bill Sees It*, if I deceive myself I will of necessity try to deceive others (p. 17). I live a double life, rife with deceitfulness, dissembling, and duplicity. When we look back from the vantage point of sobriety, many of us realize that when drinking we often felt like a fake, a fraud, and a phony. That's probably because we were.

For the alcoholic, dishonesty is a function of a more encompassing vice. What enables my denial and blinds me to the fact of my alcoholism is my pride. This brings us to the link between humility and honesty. To be humble is to know who I really am. My lack of humility keeps me from seeing the truth about myself. If I am full of pride, I live of necessity in self-deception, pretending to be what I am not and presuming to know what I don't. I know what an alcoholic is, I assure myself, and I am not like that. I am different, meaning of course better. I conjure up all sorts of stereotypes about AA.

One of the first things we realize when we finally come to the rooms is how little we did know about alcoholism, alcoholics, and AA. But to be honest with myself about my drinking, I have to be willing to admit to the possibility of a weakness in me that my pride won't let me acknowledge.

To honestly acknowledge my condition and admit that I am powerless also means to recognize I need help, and here too my lack of humility gets in the way. Asking for help is an admission that I fall short, that I need something or someone, that I am not self-sufficient. It puts me in someone else's debt and makes me dependent, and that rubs against my pride.

That is why many alcoholics would rather invest a considerable amount of money on psychoanalysis than go to AA. It is easier to camouflage my need when I pay to see a shrink, for my money still affords me a certain amount of self-importance and control. Tradition 7 does nothing for my pride. My ego gets no bang for the buck I drop in the basket.

That such character defects as pride and dishonesty are behind the alcoholic's denial is not an understanding always shared outside of AA, even in programs using the 12 Steps. Instead, denial is often seen in the terms of pop psychology as an expression of insecurity and lack of self-esteem. The alcoholic is already feeling pretty bad about himself, and having to admit that he is an alcoholic can only make him feel worse. The prescribed treatment, therefore, is therapy or self-help strategies that can improve his self-image and make him feel better. The general effect of this, however, is to enable his denial and prolong his condition. We don't admit we are powerless because we are feeling good and brimming with self-confidence.

ADMISSION OF HOPELESSNESS

Dishonesty and pride stand in the way of surrender. These barriers are so high that Step 1 often begins as no more than a partial sort of surrender, a reluctant concession to the fact that our drinking and our lives are out of control. But if our admission remains no more than a concession, we are not likely to stay sober. We will simply go back to business as usual when things brighten up a little.

Hence AA's insistence that before we can truly surrender and admit powerlessness, three things have to happen: we have to admit the hopelessness of our alcoholic condition, accept defeat, and hit bottom. This flows as we have seen from the experience of our founders, and it has been repeatedly confirmed by the experience of early AAs and recovering alcoholics since.

When we come to AA, we discover that our disease is fatal and our condition hopeless. We learn this truth in AA in a way we are not likely to learn it anywhere else—not in therapy, rehab, self-help groups, other recovery programs, or church. It is spoken to us from the heart by fellow alcoholics who have learned the truth through pain and suffering and who are uniquely qualified to transmit this truth to us.

Such was Bill W.'s vision of our Fellowship as conveyed to Carl Jung. As he wrote to the doctor, if each recovering alcoholic could bring to the alcoholic who was still suffering the news that alcoholism was, scientifically

humility

speaking, a hopeless disease, then he might be laid wide open to a transformational spiritual experience (*As Bill Sees It*, p. 217). Others might bring such a message to the alcoholic's mind. But only another alcoholic can imprint it on his heart. Because attached to the message of hopelessness is a message of hope. It is staring the newcomer in the face.

This experience is more than cognitive or psychological. The brutal facts about our condition can shatter our ego and lead to despair. But feelings of hopelessness alone won't accomplish the job. We have to assent to that hopelessness, we have to admit and accept that, on our own resources, there is no hope for us. Only then will we be willing to try the spiritual solution the program offers. So long as we cling to any hope that we can drink normally, or that there is an alternative answer to our drinking problem, we will not surrender. Here too the AA message is paradoxical: hope is born out of our admission of hopelessness.

ACCEPTANCE OF DEFEAT

The second condition that AA proposes as necessary to the admission of powerlessness is admitting and accepting defeat. We sometimes tend to focus on *admitting* defeat and overlook *accepting* defeat. In fact, we may not associate the virtue of acceptance with Step 1 at all. But as an expression of humility, acceptance is key to the Step: "unless he has first *accepted* his devastating weakness and all its consequences," and so "humbles himself," the alcoholic can expect little from AA, and "his sobriety—if any—will be precarious" (our emphasis). There is no true humility without acceptance of one's weaknesses—or without gratitude for one's strengths, as suggested earlier.

Acceptance cannot be forced on us. It is an interior act. Circumstances may force me to admit, but not to accept. It is possible to admit that one is powerless over alcohol, that one cannot stop drinking on one's own, yet have attitudes that betray a lack of acceptance. These attitudes get in the way of a complete surrender and block the way to subsequent Steps. They take various forms.

One is resentment. I admit the fact I am powerless, but this makes me angry. I want it to be different. Why can't I drink like everybody else? Why do I have to be an alcoholic? I'm still lacking the necessary humility to accept the reality of who, in fact, I am. I don't want to accept my condition and the insufficiency that goes with it. I may even resent God for my predicament, blaming him for supposedly creating me with such an awful handicap. Or if an unbeliever, I will blame somebody else, my parents perhaps, or society. Blaming and resenting keep me from accepting.

Another form a lack of acceptance may take is a sort of residual denial, the harboring of the illusion that, while I may be powerless now in my present circumstances, this is a temporary condition and I will regain control once my situation improves. Sometimes this lingering doubt as to whether I really am an alcoholic will lie dormant and not surface until after a long period of sobriety. The result is always the same. Once an alcoholic, always an alcoholic.

Still another form that not accepting powerlessness may take is the idea that I am in charge of my recovery. I reserve the power to choose which tools I will use to abstain from drinking and manage my life. I may no longer be trying to do it all on my own, but my Higher Power is no more than an accessory to my individually determined efforts, an upper-case Tool. This is the conceit that recovery comes by choice and not by grace. What AA has given me is not a way to God but the power to choose. I don't believe the obsession to drink is removed because I do not acknowledge a divine Power that can perform such a miracle. Not drinking is a choice I make. I may concede I need the help of other alcoholics, but I see that as no more than group therapy, self-help pure and simple.

This attitude reflects the view of choice prevalent in our culture, where choice is associated with a self-centered understanding of freedom. Not grounded in God, choice is often no more than a thinly veiled cover for self-will and self-determination.

Those who subscribe to this view take pride in their reasoning powers. But to admit powerlessness over alcohol and simultaneously claim the power to choose is hardly rational. It is patently illogical, a contradiction in terms. Choice connotes power. If I have the power to choose whether or not to drink, then I cannot possibly say at the same time that I don't have that power, that I am powerless. Choice also involves rational motivation, but there is no rationality in drinking alcoholically. Obsession, compulsion, and impulse by their very nature preclude the ability to make a free and rational choice, which requires at least a minimum of deliberation.

AA experience shows that choice is available only in the early stages of the potential alcoholic's drinking. "Whether such a person can quit upon a non-spiritual basis depends upon the extent to which he has already lost the power to choose whether he will drink or not." We may have had plenty of character and even some virtue, and we may have had an enormous desire to stop forever, but we just couldn't do it. "This is the baffling feature of alcoholism as we know it—this utter inability to leave it alone, no matter how great the necessity or the wish" (Big Book, p. 34).

Once the drinker has crossed a certain "invisible line," he loses the power to choose. That is what makes him an alcoholic. As defined by AA, being powerless over alcohol and being an alcoholic are two ways of saying the same thing. The person who can choose whether or not to drink may be a hard drinker or a problem drinker or any other number of things, but he's not an alcoholic.

The idea of choice in AA is generally posited as an alternative to grace, usually by those who have a problem with the spiritual dimensions of the program. But this confuses the object of choice. Freedom from alcohol gives me the freedom to choose in many areas of my life, but not when it comes to the bottle itself. If not drinking is a choice I make, I obviously have control over alcohol. To say that AA has given me that control is to make a claim that AA nowhere makes for itself. The AA experience is that the obsession is removed. At one point it's just gone. My choice lies in the decision to work the Steps and practice the principles. The result is not a choice. It is a gift.

Lack of acceptance, under whatever guise, always implies resistance, and if I am resisting, I am not surrendering. I am still in rebellion. If I am to admit powerlessness over alcohol, I need to reach a point where I can humble myself, accept defeat, and surrender totally and unconditionally, harboring no reservations whatsoever in my heart.

Admitting Unmanageability

Hitting Bottom

The third condition that AA says the surrender of Step 1 requires, is for the alcoholic to hit bottom. We hit bottom when alcohol renders our lives unmanageable and an inner shift takes place. We realize somewhere deep down inside of us that we cannot go on living the same way anymore. We desperately want things to change, but we feel hopeless to bring about the change ourselves.

In effect, we experience the powerlessness to which we will admit when we come to AA. We are inherently limited human beings, but as alcoholics, we often cannot acknowledge that—until we are forced by the painful consequences of our actions to come face to face with those limitations. We literally reach the end of our physical and emotional resources. We call it hitting bottom because we cannot sink any lower.

In Step 1, hitting bottom means specifically hitting bottom over alcohol. There are other bottoms we can hit. Many of our stories contain a series of such bottoms: over school, causes, work, and relationships. In every

department of our lives, we reach a crisis where the edifice we have labo-
riously and willfully built collapses and we go through serious dislocations
and considerable pain. We reach a point where we cannot go on. We quit
school, abandon the cause, leave the job or career, walk out of the marriage,
or end the relationship. Yet we see no connection between these crises and
our drinking. Sooner or later we pick ourselves up and go at it again with
renewed determination. This time it will be different, we tell ourselves. And
we repeat the cycle.

Hitting a series of emotional bottoms over other issues may eventually
get us to come to AA and hit bottom over alcohol, but not necessarily. The
connection with drinking has to be made at some point, and something has
to give inside.

Hitting bottom over alcohol is both an external and internal process.
Externally, it may be precipitated by physical illness or injury. Drunk, we total our car and end up in the hospital. After decades of abuse, we are told our
liver is shot and we need a transplant. Or we may experience an emotional
crisis directly related to our drinking. Our spouse has had it with our drinking
and puts us out. Our employer has had enough and we get a pink slip, or
we have attended to booze more than to our business and we have to close
shop. We end up broke, maybe homeless. Or that car crash that sent us to
the hospital resulted in somebody's death, and we face manslaughter charges
and imprisonment.

But external conditions are not enough. Things may get very bad for us,
yet we may not hit bottom—even when the connection to drinking becomes
all too obvious. Something has to give within. We have to come to the end
of the proverbial rope. We have to be so thoroughly whipped by alcohol and
left in such a state of despair that we are forced to admit defeat.

When we have recognized our hopelessness, admitted defeat, and accepted our condition, we have hit bottom. We are then able to admit our
powerlessness, which is to finally acknowledge reality and surrender the illusion of a power we lost long ago when we crossed the metaphorical threshold and became alcoholic.

This general process obtains whether our bottom over alcohol has been
a "high" or a "low" bottom. As we know, the first edition of *Alcoholics Anonymous* dealt only with low-bottom cases. Alcoholics who were less desperate,
those whose lives had not yet become totally unmanageable, could not admit
that they had been completely defeated by alcohol and that their situation was
hopeless. Later, the less desperate cases had their bottoms "raised" (12&12,
S1, p. 23). That is, by listening to the stories of low-bottom alcoholics, they
were able to see that their problem was not a "mere habit" but the start of a

"fatal progression," that the alcoholic has lost control long before he's able to see it, and that it can only get worse.

Subsequent editions of the Big Book are filled with the stories of these kinds of drunks. These newcomers had to hit bottom emotionally, "But they did not have to hit every possible bottom in order to admit that they were licked" (*As Bill Sees It*, p. 29). Yet the tool that brings them down remains the same: the message that they suffer from a real disease, an obsession and an allergy they cannot treat on their own. This is the "nutcracker" that can shatter their ego and convince them that, on their own resources alone, their chances are nil (ibid., p. 118).

"High" or "low," we all have to hit bottom. We have to be beaten. How badly depends on two factors: the progression of our disease and the extent of our willfulness. The further along in our disease we find ourselves, the more unmanageable our lives become, and the greater the dislocations and pain we are likely to experience. Similarly, the higher we rise in our willfulness, the harder must we fall if our will is to be broken. We may be driven into the dirt and thoroughly humiliated, or simply humbled and knocked off our high horse. But we have to be taken down.

HUMILITY AND HUMILIATION

It may be said that the difference between a high bottom and a low bottom is the difference between being humbled and being humiliated. It is a matter of degree, of the severity of the manner in which we are cut down to size.

This distinction may account for one of the reasons why some of us hit bottom over alcohol more than once. We may come in as a high-bottom alcoholic, with most of our so-called support systems in place. We still have the family and the house, the job, money, friends. We get sober. We regain our confidence. Soon we return to our previous mode of life, minus the bottle. We neglect the program. Lacking any foundation in humility, failing to "develop much more of this precious quality than may be required for sobriety" (12&12, S7, p. 70), we get cocky and we relapse. We haven't been humbled enough. The second time around, if we survive, we may have to be thoroughly humiliated and experience a lower bottom. Of course, the low-bottom alcoholic is not exempt from relapse. The deciding factor is that "precious quality."

The connection between humility on the one hand, and being humbled or humiliated on the other, is not readily apparent. Humiliation has the larger currency, and some newcomers may conflate it with humility, which makes this virtue all the more suspect. In reality, the relationship is one of cause and effect: humiliation is what may happen to me if I fail to live humbly. There is an order to reality and my place in the universe, and when out of pride I think I can make up my own rules and fail to conduct myself in accordance with that order, reality will sooner or later set in and forcibly conform me to itself.

This becomes clearer if we look at the etymology (Greek for study of true meaning) of humility, continuing the practice established in the previous chapter of closely examining certain keywords in recovery. It should be clear by now that this is a practical matter and not at all academic. We all have a natural tendency to think that we know more than we do. This is in itself symptomatic of pride. It enables dishonesty and denial and keeps us from learning the truth about ourselves. Exploring the original or root meaning of a word can be useful because, as language changes, that meaning may become obscure, even as it remains relevant to a full understanding of the word.

Humility originates in a Latin word, *humus*, which shares the same Indo-European root as *human* and signifies ground, soil, earth, dirt, or dust. We find this meaning in "the dust of the ground," the lowly stuff out of which, according to Genesis, our bodies were formed when life was first given to us. We find it again in "dust to dust," our final humbling as that life is taken from us and we return to the earth.

We have a humble beginning and will have a humble end. We are lowly creatures, and so to live humbly is in keeping with our true nature. When we drink, we get high, and like Icarus in the Greek myth, we get carried away with a false sense of freedom. We pretend to ascend to the heavens on the wings of our fantasy, imagination, and will. The sky is the limit. We get full of ourselves, full of an illusory power we don't have. We pretend we are not subject to the laws of nature. That is pride, and being "high" is a fitting description of our state. Inevitably, we are pulled back down by the force of gravity, the pull of the real world, and we crash. We are brought back down to earth. We are humbled—or humiliated.

There is another way in which we don't fully appreciate the relationship between humility and humiliation. A standard dictionary defines "humiliate" as "to lower the pride, dignity, or self-respect" of someone. We have seen that, if we are proud and lack humility, we will create circumstances that will humiliate us and work to forcibly "lower our pride" in the sense we have been discussing pride.

But there may be circumstances that are not of our own creation and which we may yet find humiliating in the second sense of lowering our dignity or sense of worth. We are sober and working the program and we lose our job through no fault of our own. We have to deal with the unemployment office and we find the experience humiliating. Or we are forced to take a less remunerative or rewarding job, perhaps even a menial one. This too, we find humiliating, "beneath" us, as we might say.

But a lack of humility is at work here as well, and what these circumstances are rubbing against is our pride, not our dignity or self-respect. Or to put it differently, "dignity" and "self-respect" have become euphemisms for pride. Not incidentally, the dictionary definition makes these equivalent, almost synonymous, terms. In the modern view the dictionary reflects, pride is no longer a vice but a virtue, a good of a piece with dignity and self-respect. Humility, deemed a weakness, may even be seen as detracting from a sense of worth.

But to be humble is to have a proper estimation of myself. If I am humble, I know who I am, and no person or circumstance can lower my dignity and self-respect, for I know these are given to me by God and it is not within anyone's province to take them away. In the circumstances described, my task is to humble myself and accept things as they are, trusting that God will direct my efforts and work things for my good.

If I feel humiliated, it is a sign that I need to surrender my pride, and either learn, or if I have forgotten remember, who I truly am as a child of God. For if I am a lowly creature fashioned out of the dust of the earth, I am also a special object of God's love, alone of all created things intimately and caringly fashioned by his very hands and bearing the image of his own Spirit, which he directly breathed into mine.[1]

What causes us to feel humiliated then is pride, a lack of humility, which is to seek our worth in something other than its real source. This is a hard and unpalatable truth. But an even harder truth is the fact that no amount of humiliation will of itself render us humble or impart us with humility. Ultimately, humility is an inside job. We have to humble ourselves. "Until he so humbles himself, his sobriety—if any—will be precarious."

A Humble Admission

We can now fully understand the nature of the admission that we make in Step 1: "Every newcomer is told, and soon realizes for himself, that his *humble* admission of powerlessness over alcohol is his first step toward liberation from its paralyzing grip" (12&12, S7, pp. 72–73, our emphasis). Our admission may first be forced by circumstance, and it may begin as a reluctant concession, but sooner or later the external process of being humbled or humiliated has to turn into an internal process of surrendering and humbling ourselves willingly and with time even gladly, for that is our path to freedom.

The Fellowship of AA creates the human environment in which this humble surrender can take place. It is uniquely able to bring together the constructive forces that can break through the wall of denial and break down our willful resistance. Coming to the rooms beaten by alcohol, we find ourselves surrounded by fellow alcoholics who have been through the same ordeal and can speak from deep, personal experience. The stories they tell are our stories. Yet they have come through, and they stand before us as living proof of release. Speaking to us in the language of the heart, they bring hope out of our despair. We stop fighting at last. We surrender.

Humility and fellowship work together in AA, and they start with the opening words of the first Step: We admitted. The language reflects an experiential and spiritual reality. AA was born when it became a "we" program: one alcoholic, Bill W., sharing his experience of recovery with another alcoholic, Dr. Bob. Standing alone in the lobby of the Mayflower Hotel, facing the bar where laughter and merriment beckoned seductively, Bill knew he could not stay sober on his own. This is an early lesson in humility that we learn when we come to AA, though at first we may not be conscious of it: I cannot do it alone; I am not self-sufficient.

This runs counter to our attitude as active alcoholics. It involves a radical reorientation of our perspective, a new way of seeing things. We found it hard to be "one among" (12&12, S4, p. 53). At work, in school, at church, or wherever we had to associate with others, we often tended to compare and compete. We were either too good or not good enough. In either case, we were different.

As our drinking progressed, this led us to cut ourselves off from others and isolate. In the end, many of us ended up alone, alienated from family and friends and withdrawn from life. Even if we still had a home and a job, we didn't feel a part of, but apart from, living mostly in our heads, the bottle our only trusted companion.

Underlying the "we" of the program and Fellowship of AA is the spiritual understanding that human beings are made for relationship. This is not just an echo of the "social animal" or "herd instinct" theories of secularist sociology, which reduce man to the status of a mere beast and deny his spiritual nature. It is a spiritual understanding precisely because it acknowledges that we are made in the image of God and for fellowship with him and one another.

That is why we can truthfully say that AA is not so much about alcohol as it is about relationships. In recovery what we do is to straighten out those relationships: with God, with others, and with ourselves, with the constituent but dissevered parts of our person. We become complete and fully integrated men and women.

I admitted I was powerless over alcohol by the grace of God and in relationship with others because others before me made the same admission and showed me how to do it and what it meant. Though I have to make that admission *for* myself (nobody can make it for me), I cannot make it *by* myself, in isolation from others, or of my own power alone. My humble admission is made in fellowship.

Step 1 is the first step in the surrender of power. Indeed, our admission of powerlessness constitutes the foundational act of surrender. This admission is at first over our inability to stop drinking and restore order to our lives. But as we work the Steps and grow spiritually, it progressively becomes an admission that, ultimately, we are powerless over life itself. Even the ability to surrender, we finally come to recognize, is a gift of grace. The desire to surrender is not natural to us, nor is the power to do so our own. What power we have is derivative. When we accept that all power resides in God, our surrender becomes total, if not always in practice, because we are still this side of heaven, at least in spirit.

This is the journey that we begin with Step 1. As we try to practice the principles of this Step in all our affairs, we will become more willing to admit that we are powerless not only over alcohol but over "people, places, and things." We will accept defeat more quickly in our attempt to control what is beyond our power to control. We will be more ready to acknowledge our need for help and less reluctant to seek and accept such help, whether at meetings, from our sponsor, or in situations beyond the Fellowship of AA. We will become more open-minded as others share their experience with us, more willing to listen and learn, particularly as it relates to spiritual matters. We will become willing and eager participants in the process of deflating our ego and taking an honest measure of who we are.

Admitting powerlessness in later recovery may still come through pain and suffering, but it doesn't have to. If we humble ourselves willingly, we won't have to be humbled forcibly through circumstance. We can admit powerlessness without having to go through defeat, despair, and still another bottom. "We saw we needn't always be bludgeoned and beaten into humility. It could come quite as much from our voluntary reaching for it as it could from unremitting suffering" (12&12, S7, p. 75).

At first, we "reach for a little humility, knowing that we shall perish of alcoholism if we do not. After a time, though we may still rebel somewhat, we commence to practice humility because this is the right thing to do. Then comes the day when, finally freed in large degree from rebellion, we practice humility because we deeply want it as a way of life" (*As Bill Sees It*, p. 211). No longer a response to the force of circumstance, or merely to duty and obligation, humility then becomes a stable disposition, a trait engraved in our character. What we call a virtue.

So can the other virtues embedded in Step 1 become embedded in our character. As they take root in our heart and we begin to desire them deeply as a spiritual way of life, they will also give form to our emotions. We will be invited to practice them in distinct ways again and again, in Step after Step, situation after situation, through a variety of disciplines and in conjunction with other virtues that further their growth. As we do, one weakness after another will turn into strength.

That God brings strength out of weakness is a fact of the spiritual life. In the Jewish and Christian traditions, we see it in the transformation of a frightened fugitive, an uncertain and inarticulate sheep keeper, into the fearless leader who would command mighty Pharaoh to "Let my people go" and deliver them from slavery, a humble shepherd's staff his only visible weapon.

So would a discouraged and frightened band of Apostles huddled in an upper room in Jerusalem become the bearers of another message of deliverance from a different sort of slavery, a bondage to self. Paul tells of other biblical characters who "out of weakness were made strong" and sees this seemingly paradoxical truth in himself, declaring, "when I am weak, then I am strong."[2]

AA grows out of these spiritual traditions. For us alcoholics the miracle materializes time and again when, desisting from our instinctive desire to run the show and control what we cannot possibly control, we humbly repeat those simple words of surrender: I am powerless. It is then that a Power greater than ourselves can work in our lives. Sanity then becomes possible.

STEP 2

"Came to believe that a Power greater than ourselves could restore us to sanity."

"Step Two is the rallying cry for all of us. Whether agnostic, atheist, or former believer, we can stand together on this Step. True humility and an open mind can lead us to faith, and every A.A. meeting is an assurance that God will restore us to sanity if we rightly relate ourselves to Him."

—12&12, p. 33

STEP TWO

4

THE WILL TO DISBELIEVE

In Step 1 we surrender control over alcohol, as we humbly admit our powerlessness to stop drinking and manage our lives. In Step 2 we surrender unbelief, itself a form of control, of a continued clinging to the illusion of power. The will to disbelieve is driven by certain character defects that the principles in this Step are intended to correct. Primary among these principles are the discipline of surrender and the virtues of humility, simplicity, willingness, open-mindedness, and honesty. Through them we are led to faith, and through faith to hope, as we come to believe that a Power greater than ourselves can restore us to sanity.

THE DENIAL OF SPIRITUAL REALITY

Since the advent of AA, much has been made of the concept of denial as a stumbling block to recovery, a subject we broached in the previous chapter. The idea is often understood in psychological terms as a defense mechanism. In the more popular version of this, denial is an attempt to avoid facing and dealing with painful realities simply by refusing to acknowledge them.

But from a spiritual perspective, denial cuts deeper. The "defense mechanism" is a symptom of a larger problem, and that is the denial of reality as comprehending more than just the material universe. At its root, denial is the refusal to acknowledge the spiritual reality underpinning the world of the senses. There is a spiritual order to things that has implications for the way we live. If we are aware of this order at all, we are likely to see it as unjust, as infringing on our will and restricting our freedom. Hence, we ignore or refuse to recognize it. It is this failure to live in accordance with the spiritual order that produces the painful consequences from which the psyche then seeks protection—unsuccessfully.

The denial of spiritual reality, expressed as the rejection of or resistance to a transcendent faith, is the stumbling block many of us come up against in Step 2. Against Step 1 our denial takes the form of refusing to admit, first, that we have a problem with alcohol, and second, that we cannot solve that problem on our own. This is a denial of our condition, that we are alcoholic. Against Step 2, our denial takes the form of refusing to acknowledge the reality of God, and of who we are in relation to him. We deny not only an external but an internal order. Ultimately, we deny our humanity, for we bear God's imprint on us and our identity subsists in him.

Our denial of faith is rooted in character defects that Step 2 brings out into the open. Dishonesty is the most immediate. It is what enables and sustains denial. Many of us deceive ourselves about the reasons for our lack of faith and refuse to see the connection between our rejection of God and our failure in life. Rather than look at ourselves, we focus on others and cast blame, judge, and condemn. We come up with all sorts of rationalizations and fancy theories about why we don't believe, when the truth is that we don't *want* to believe, that our minds are shut tight and we are not willing to take an honest look at the facts about God, religion, and the things of the spirit.

Yet behind dishonesty lies a more fundamental character defect and this is pride. We fancy ourselves too smart, too sophisticated to buy into all that stuff about God. Characteristic of this sort of conceit is the tendency to think that we know more than we do. The more intellectual or more educated among us tend to go further. We make reason the object of faith. Whatever we can't understand through reason simply doesn't exist. We presume to possess reasoning powers we lack and refuse to accept the limits to knowledge that are inherent in the human condition. In short, we want to be our own god, and that is the source of our pride.

The essence of humility is knowing who we are and who God is, and the hallmark of pride confusing the two. In Step 1 we make the barest beginning of knowing who we are. In Step 2 of who God is. The two Steps work together. We cannot do one without the other.

At meetings we sometimes hear an alcoholic laugh at herself as she revels in a new discovery: "I found out there is a God, and it ain't me." We laugh with her, no matter how many times we may have heard the line. It is so ridiculously obvious. And yet, such is the hold of pride on us that we can never remind ourselves of this simple truth too often. For us in AA, it is the beginning of wisdom. To know that *we* are not God, to know that there *is* a God, and to *know* that God, these are the Steps in their essence.

From a spiritual perspective, we cannot know who we are apart from our Creator, for he gave us our being and identity and set the parameters governing our growth and development. Though not ordinarily seen this way, Step 2 is in part a self-examination, a spiritual self-assessment that precedes and sets the foundation for the moral stocktaking that begins with Step 4. In this latter Step we start looking at ourselves in the context of our relationship with others; in Step 2 we start to look at ourselves in the context of our relationship with God.

In the spiritual order of things, our relationship with God comes first and informs our relationship with others. This is the transcendental meaning inherent in our slogan First Things First, which originates in the familiar biblical injunction to seek first the kingdom of God.

In examining our relationship with God through Step 2, the testimony of AAs who have come to believe can help us to "sweep away prejudice" and "think honestly," and it can encourage us to "search diligently" within ourselves (Big Book, "We Agnostics," p. 55). We start to take an honest look at the ideas, biases, resentments, and shortcomings that keep us from God and which prevent him from coming into our hearts and restoring us to sanity, in our inner and outer lives.

A THREEFOLD DISEASE

In Step 2 we are faced with the fact that ours is a *three*-fold disease. Though the term is not used and no explicit mention is made of the spiritual nature of our malady, the spiritual is the issue here. Many of us accept the allergy part and the obsession part (what we now call addiction). We think them more objective and scientific, though we have no rational basis for this. We are not prone to argue with "science."

We also accept this part of the diagnosis because it doesn't require anything of us. It is descriptive. We are simply told why we can't drink and what will happen if we do. It is different with the spiritual part, which is decidedly prescriptive. We are to take "certain steps," which however qualified and sugarcoated at times, are recognizably spiritual. We "balk," we resist. We deny their spiritual character. Some of us do this as newcomers and others persist in our denial even after a long period of dryness.

The two-prong medical diagnosis doesn't ask us to do anything because it doesn't offer a solution. Dr. Silkworth, who in AA is credited with first articulating this diagnosis of the alcoholic, could describe the problem, but he couldn't prescribe a cure. It was rare the alcoholic, among the countless he had treated at Towns Hospital, who would sober up. Dr. Tiebout, the psychiatrist who in his time probably knew more about alcoholism than any other in his profession, fared no better. Nor, by his frank and humble admission, did Carl Jung. They all deferred to the spiritual.

Averse to things spiritual, some of us gloss over this fact of AA history. The medical profession's failure to solve the alcoholic's problem led to the search for a solution elsewhere and the eventual birth of AA. The profession's efforts fare no better today, though we in AA nevertheless remain supportive. For alcoholism, there is still no medical cure, whether of the physiological, psychiatric, or psychological kind. If there were, our condition would not be fatal or hopeless. A procedure or a pill or the couch would fix it. The rooms of AA would be deserted. But they are not. Instead, they are full of people who have stopped drinking and are recovering. They are the evidence, the living proof, that there is a solution.

We know all of this, yet many of us resist drawing the logical conclusion regarding the nature of this solution. Even when cornered into doing so, we are still reluctant to accept it. We try to reduce AA from spiritual fellowship to secular group therapy, whether in theory or in practice. There is many an AA meeting where it is rare even to hear the word God mentioned, except when the Serenity Prayer is recited. There is also a growing number of recovery books that censor the word even in the prayer, and blot it out from the Steps as well.

That alcoholism is a three-pronged disease, that the root is spiritual and so is the solution—this is the problem for many of us in AA, with Step 2 and with the rest of the program. It is a bigger problem than we may realize or are willing to admit. It touches the believer as well as the unbeliever, at the early and throughout all stages of recovery.

The self-help shelves of the major bookstore chains (and their online equivalents) are filled with titles offering alcoholics an alternative to AA, meaning primarily an alternative to the spiritual heart of the program. Many of us gravitate toward those shelves when we stumble in our recovery, looking for "an easier, softer way" (Big Book, p. 58). One typical title promises to teach the alcoholic how to "Get Control of Your Own Recovery." Ultimately, that is what the resistance to the spiritual boils down to, control. The spiritual offers us power, but never control. And the power is on loan, not really ours, subject to conditions we don't set ourselves. The power is given to fulfill, not ours, but God's will. We are empowered to take the action, but the results are not in our hands.

We saw in Step 1 that knowledge about the allergy and the obsession is not what brought us to admit our powerlessness over alcohol and the unmanageability of our lives. Head knowledge never helped us with our drinking. No amount of information by and of itself would cause us to change, no matter how badly we wanted it. We did because we were trapped by circumstances of our own making that we could neither deny nor escape. We took Step 1 because we were defeated and forced to surrender, and by this very act, though we might not realize or wish to recognize it, we were thrust into a spiritual process of recovery.

Three Pertinent Ideas

Step 2 weans us away from a failed faith in ourselves and things human and brings us face to face with the spiritual heart of the program. Having accepted "that we were alcoholic and could not manage our own lives," we are asked to come to terms with two further propositions: "that probably no human power could have relieved our alcoholism," and "that God could and would if He were sought" (Big Book, p. 60).

These "three pertinent ideas" are rightly called the ABCs of the program, for they constitute the basic premises upon which the Steps are built. Central to each, as we have seen, is the issue of power. I don't have it. Nor does any other human agency. God does. The first proposition we accept in Step 1. The second is an extension of the first and a bridge to the third, and it contains a crucial qualifier: probably. Reflecting the modesty which is characteristic of the program, AA makes no absolute claims that the spiritual solution is for everyone, much less that God works through AA alone.

Yet for many of us, like for the early AAs, the spiritual *is* the only solution, for we too have found—the hard way—that there was in fact no human power that could heal us. Information about alcoholism, clinical data, self-knowledge, philosophies, moral codes, religious precepts, and ideas galore could not solve our alcohol problem. No matter how hard we exerted ourselves, none of these things could save us, because "the needed power wasn't there. Our human resources, as marshaled by the will, were not sufficient; they failed utterly" (ibid., p. 45). AA speaks to those of us who share that experience when it assures us that God has the power, and that he will restore us if we seek him through the concrete course of action that the Steps lay out.

Our powerlessness is of a spiritual nature. It is powerlessness not only over alcohol, people, and circumstances, but over ourselves, over our very human nature. This understanding of powerlessness originates in the Judeo-Christian concept of human fallibility. Paul first articulated this concept when, despairing of his inability to do what he *knew* to be right, he confessed that "The good that I would, I do not, but the evil which I would not, that I do."[1]

Such an admission of personal powerlessness over oneself was as counterintuitive and countercultural in Paul's day as it is in our own. The 12&12 rightly point out that we instinctually rebel against this idea (S1, p. 21). A modern writer explains that, "Paul in a single phrase repudiates an entire tradition of classical philosophy founded in Plato. For Plato, the problem of evil is a problem of knowledge. People do wrong because they do not know what is right. If they knew what was right, obviously, they would do it."

This is the idea of human perfectibility that still predominates in secular culture. This says that our basic problem is ignorance and the solution knowledge. "But Paul denies that this is so," continues this writer. "His claim is that even though he knows something is wrong, he still does it. Why? Because the human will is corrupt. The problem of evil is not a problem of knowledge but a problem of will."[2]

We alcoholics would naturally identify with Paul, for as the saying goes, we've been there and done that. Indeed, Paul's cry of powerlessness reverberates in all of us. We all face the same predicament, as Bill W. recognized in the Grapevine article on emotional sobriety we discussed earlier. Right belief, right knowledge, and right desire do not necessarily translate into right action. Powerlessness cuts very deep.

Note that our problem is not that of a *weak* will, but as we will see in Step 3, of a *corrupt* one. In AA we would use the language of finance and call it bankrupt (same root idea: a breaking down or depletion of value or virtue). We don't control our will; our will controls us. Hence the failure of self-knowledge and willpower to deliver us from alcoholism and restore us to sanity.

Though the Big Book repeatedly underscores this failure, it is worth pointing out that there was a pro-psychology and anti-religion faction in the early fellowship that didn't see it that way. This is reflected in an edit made to the following passage in the book's working manuscript: "*The fact is that most alcoholics, for reasons yet obscure, have lost the power of choice in drink. Our so-called will power becomes practically nonexistent. We are unable, at certain times,* no matter how well we understand ourselves, *to bring into our consciousness with sufficient force the memory of the suffering and humiliation of even a week or a month ago. We are without defense against the first drink*" (p. 24, italics in Big Book, underlined on page 43 of the manuscript).[3]

A New Jersey psychiatrist named Dr. Howard objected to the crossed-out text and annotated the manuscript's margin with this comment: "every psychiatrist would argue [against] this, saying 'If we understood ourselves well enough we would never do anything harmful to ourselves.'" Evidently, the doctor subscribed to Plato's view of the power of knowledge, which had filtered down to his secularist-dominated field. A non-alcoholic, he wasn't speaking from experience. His was knowledge of the bookish kind. Though the passage was deleted, his view was nevertheless rejected.

AA is not against knowledge. It is against knowledge as the solution to our alcoholic condition. We can see this with reference to another annotation Dr. Howard makes to the manuscript. Here's the passage; "We do not like to pronounce any individual as alcoholic, but you can quickly diagnose yourself. Step over to the nearest barroom and try some controlled drinking. Try to drink and stop abruptly. Try it more than once. It will not take long for you to decide, if you are honest with yourself about it. It may be worth a bad case of the jitters if you get a full knowledge of your condition" (pp. 31–32 in Big Book; p. 46 in manuscript). The last nine words were the doctor's edit, and they were adopted.

But the context is entirely different. The first passage is addressing the issue of the solution to alcoholism (the chapter is titled, appropriately enough, "There Is a Solution"). The second passage is addressing alcoholism in general (from the chapter "More About Alcoholism"). Some people with a drinking problem may be alcoholics, and some may not. An experiment is suggested to help a person find out. The experiment may lead that person to a knowledge of her condition, but if it turns out she is an alcoholic, the knowledge itself will not relieve her from it. Ideally, it will lead her to AA. That's where she will find the solution. (Today AA publishes a pamphlet—*Is A.A. for You?*— which tries to serve the same purpose.) Again, our problem is not ignorance. It is powerlessness.

The point cannot be emphasized often enough because, to the extent that we cling to our own or any human power for deliverance, to that extent we will not yield to divine power. We will invariably choose the human option. First, because it is easier for us to understand how human power works. Second, and consequently, because where human power is involved, we can always exercise some degree of control. Not so when it comes to God. Before him, our powerlessness is complete.

If we accept the limitations of human power, we are faced with the third proposition. Here we come to the central question of faith that is raised by Step 2: whether we believe God has the power to heal us. This is not an invitation to ponder philosophical or theological abstractions. Instead, it is an invitation to enter into the simplicity of the spiritual life. Here spirituality is linked to utility in what is an intensely practical, down-to-earth issue. This issue is whether God can restore us to sanity. We are not asked first to believe *in* God, with all the religious hurdles that might raise, but to believe *that* God. The spiritual principle is plain: we come to know that God *is* by what God *does*. Ultimately, in AA, by what he does in us as we become able to do what we cannot do for ourselves, as we are told in the Promises (p. 84).

ROADBLOCKS TO FAITH

We are invited in Step 2 to embark upon an experiment in faith. If we take certain actions, we will experience a spiritual awakening as God works in us. The evidence will be a changed heart, a changed character, and a changed life.

Some of us get started on this experiment more smoothly than others, surrendering unbelief and our denial of faith with relative ease. Others struggle. We are weighed down by a lot of old baggage about God and religion that we can't let go of.

Some of us are atheists. We can't see how a God that we don't believe exists can possibly do anything for us. Others of us are agnostics. We feel no compelling desire to choose between belief and unbelief, though in practice we chose long ago, excluding God from our everyday lives. Then there are the ex-believers. We think we tried faith and it failed us. We now straddle the fence between agnosticism and atheism. As for the believers among us, we have a curious problem. When it comes to our alcoholism and the way we live, God might as well not exist. Whether nominal believers who rarely go to church or devout types who attend regularly, there is a disconnect between faith and experience for us. We are, for all practical purposes, functional agnostics, for we don't know the power of God in our personal lives.

Some of us go through all four of these stages before we come to AA. Whatever our old ideas about God, Step 2 is a process of letting them go, for they obviously failed us. As we do, we will acquire new understandings of God that flow from our actual experience of recovery, and with them, a new spiritual outlook and motivation on which to build a life of emotional sobriety.

For most of us, the process is slow and gradual. The Step doesn't say we believed. It says we *came* to believe: process is written into its very language. It unfolds as we let go, listen to the experience of other alcoholics with an open mind, and take an honest look at our own lives. All we need is a little willingness and a little humility.

The roadblocks to faith we encounter in our journey of recovery differ for different alcoholics. The chapters on Step 2 in the Big Book ("We Agnostics") and in the 12&12 look at what some of these obstacles are for the atheist, the agnostic, the ex-believer, and the believer, and how practicing the principles in the Step can lead us to a healing faith. Here we revisit these four groups and, especially as concerns the atheist, consider the historical context of unbelief and how the progress of science since the original AA texts were written may encourage us in our journey of faith.

The Atheist

About half the original Fellowship of AA consisted of alcoholics who thought themselves atheists or agnostics. Practically all recovered and came to believe in God, as recounted in the chapter to the agnostics.

Those of us who come to AA as atheists are mostly of the practical, common-folk variety. We just don't believe in God and we live accordingly, advancing no particular argument to support our view. In this, we are part of a long tradition. There have always been men and women who have lived as if there is no God. AA experience shows that most alcoholics in this category come to believe as they advance in recovery.

A smaller group of us subscribe to a theoretical atheism. We are convinced God doesn't exist, and we claim the support of reason and science. We are the heirs of a more recent tradition that developed among some intellectuals with the rise of materialism in the 18th century Enlightenment.

This is the hard-core atheist that we meet in the 12&12. As in that book, he will be the focus of attention here, for though representing a minority view, the issues that his atheism raises are issues that all of us have to deal with at one time or another in our recovery.

This atheist comes to Step 2 "still smarting" from his admission of powerlessness in Step 1. He is the type of alcoholic who reluctantly conceded, rather than humbly admitted, his powerlessness. He is called the "belligerent one" (p. 25). The description is apt, etymologically designating one who makes war, in this case, one who turns his intellect into a weapon against God.

Some of us were like that. The Big Book describes us as having read a few "wordy books" to convince ourselves that "this universe needs no God to explain it" (p. 49). Yet we didn't reject faith altogether. Instead, we transferred our faith to a pantheon of lesser gods. We became devotees of the "Age of Reason," and even if we never read any of their books, we came under the influence of men like Voltaire, Rousseau, and Diderot. These French philosophers built the intellectual bridge from belief to atheism that many of us would cross as our alcoholism progressed. Deists, they believed in a God of reason and nature that they distinguished from the traditional God of Judaism and Christianity. With time, Reason and Nature became their new religion.

The *philosophes* wanted to change everything, and we identified with that. Many of us were rebels who would not accept things as they were (the "status quo" or "the system") or change ourselves to conform and adapt. We couldn't stand reality, and we sought to escape via the bottle and by trying to change the world to meet our own specifications.

We became idealists and utopians. We romanticized revolution, starting naturally with the French, when atheism first gained historical significance and became entrenched in Western culture. The French revolutionaries rebelled against a ruthlessly oppressive aristocracy allied with a corrupt religious establishment, and identifying God with the church, they decided to overthrow the deity as well. Since then, atheism has been closely identified with a rebellion against religion, and God has been blamed for what people have done in his name. But people are people, and in the name of atheism, the revolutionaries inaugurated a Reign of Terror whose symbol was a blood-spattered blade. It would reach apocalyptic proportions in the 20th century.

The intellectual foundations for the coming holocaust would be laid by Ludwig Feuerbach, Karl Marx, and Friedrich Nietzsche, men whom the radical atheists among us admired. For Feuerbach, God was man's invention, the human mind's projection of his deepest fears, hopes, and longings. Marx recast this philosophy as social science. Historical Materialism claimed that religious beliefs were part of a superstructure of ideas resting on social and economic foundations. Religion was a pathological attempt to compensate for the harshness of life and social injustice. God was, in Marx's famous phrase, the opium of the masses. Take the drug away, and people will rise and change the world. Their target, again, was the God of Jews and Christians.

So was Nietzsche's, who saw Christianity in particular as a religion of the weak, with its supposedly escapist view of the afterlife and effete notions of humility and equality. His notion of the *Übermensch*, coupled with evolution's theory of natural selection and the survival of the fittest, found its way into the philosophy of *Mein Kampf* and informed Hitler's views of racial supremacy. Capturing an era's zeitgeist, Nietzsche declared the death of God, and Dostoevsky predicted that thenceforth there would no longer be any restraints on man. Everything was permitted. We saw the results of this will to power in the mass murders committed by the kindred ideological movements of fascism and communism in the last century: six million Jews exterminated by the Nazis, more than a hundred million starved to death or executed by the communists, and millions more killed as the result of the wars both unleashed upon the world.

Some of us who are atheists sometimes like to highlight the crimes perpetrated in the name of religion and use that as a justification for our unbelief. But the horrors wrought by atheism we would rather ignore. That is not surprising. We have to deny the historical record if we are to accept atheism on a personal level and adopt it as a way of life. That is, after all, the goal of all the theory and intellectualizing, or, as the Big Book puts it, the "windy arguments" (p. 49). Atheism is about power. The will to disbelieve is the will to control. We want to do our own thing, as those of a certain generation put it, and we are not going to let the inconvenient truth about the consequences of atheism get in our way. So we lie to ourselves. Hence the psychology of denial.

With Sigmund Freud, we see a great advance in the secular project of giving a scientific rationale to atheism and fabricating a conflict between faith and reason. Religion is not the result of deliberate self-deception or social conditions, says Freud, but rather a product of the unconscious. God is an illusion and religion "a universal obsessional neurosis."[4] Freud's views greatly influenced the then-budding field of psychology and contributed to a philosophical movement that sought to replace religion with psychology as a way to explain human conduct. The aforementioned Dr. Howard, who wanted to edit every reference to God out of the Big Book, was a faithful representative of that movement.

Freud's historical account of the psychology of religion is now largely discredited, and his characterization of religion as a mental illness is dismissed. Survey after survey has now shown that religious people overall tend to be healthier than the non-religious.

Citing this research, former agnostic and science writer Nancy Pearcey points out that in the medical community "It is now widely accepted that religious people have lower rates of depression, suicide, family instability, drug and alcohol abuse, and other social pathologies." She adds that "religious belief also correlates with better *physical* health—with lower rates of virtually everything from cancer to hypertension to cardiovascular disease . . . All told, people who attend church regularly are happier, healthier, and even live longer" (italics in original).[5] All this supports the conclusion that we are "wired for God." Mind and body function better when we believe in God and try to live accordingly, even if we don't always succeed.

Two other developments point to the waning influence of Freudianism. One is the popular trend away from psychology in general and back to the spiritual, most conspicuous perhaps in the New Age movement that arose starting in the 1960s. The other is the movement within psychology itself away from a radical philosophical materialism and blind empiricism and toward a serious consideration of the spiritual in the life of the person. As part of this latter and more recent movement, we have witnessed a return to the virtues, *qua* character traits or strengths, as constituting a proper subject for psychology.[6]

AA has contributed to this spiritual trend. Bill W. saw psychology as a friend and complement to the spiritual, and AA is indebted to William James, Carl Jung, and more immediately and intimately, to doctors William Silkworth, Harry Tiebout, and Harry Emerson Fosdick. Key to AA's contribution is the concept, foundational to the 12 Steps, that the removal of our mental obsession with alcohol and thence our recovery from our diseased emotions and defects of character is fundamentally a spiritual process.

Nevertheless, Freudian atheism has had an enduring cultural impact. It influenced the way many of us understood ourselves and regarded religion when we drank. Having rejected God, we looked to psychology to deal with our problems with alcohol and life. But the couch and psychology books didn't help. Neither did psychiatry and drug prescriptions.

Today the active alcoholic who seeks therapy will likely be referred to AA, if the therapist is honest. Yet faced again with the God question in AA, the non-believers and skeptics among us often latch on to a failed, materialistic view of psychology. We see this type of psychology as providing a rival, non-spiritual account of how AA works. We want to get better, but we don't want to give God any credit. Denial and dishonesty continue to dog our recovery.

As a materialist and naturalist worldview, atheism rests on three pillars, and after Marx and Freud, Charles Darwin is the third. His influence is greater than that of the other two. It is felt throughout most fields of study and is dominant in many academic and scientific disciplines.

From his theory of evolution has emerged a *philosophical* movement generally known as Darwinism which has caused three seismic changes in the way we view religion and science, changes that have had wide-ranging social and cultural repercussions.

First, it has succeeded in causing a shift "from religion as *knowledge* to religion as *faith*" (italics in original).[7] While religion had been considered heretofore a legitimate way to knowledge of objective reality, it now becomes at best a matter of personal values and subjective preferences. Reason is decoupled from religion and becomes the exclusive province of science. The scientific method becomes the only valid way to know.

Second, it has brought about a redefinition of science so that, in the minds of many, science becomes synonymous with materialism and naturalism. Since Darwinist philosophies are premised on the a priori assumption that nature or the material is all there is, God and the spiritual are automatically excluded from any scientific consideration. Any evidence that might point to the divine is either rejected out of hand or reinterpreted in naturalist or materialist terms.

This leads to the third major shift brought about by Darwinism, and this is the end of the cooperative relationship between religion and science that had been the norm historically. Instead of cooperation, we have conflict. But the conflict is based on the false premise that science equals materialism and naturalism. What conflict exists is not between science and religion, but between two opposing belief systems, materialism and naturalism on one side, and theism on the other.

Thus, though Darwin didn't see evolution as conflicting with the existence of God, many of his philosophical adherents do. They consider his theory of evolution as putting science squarely in the atheist camp. In their view, evolution provides empirical proof that there is no God. The claim is groundless, says Francis S. Collins, head of the Human Genome Project and one of the world's leading scientists. A former atheist, Collins argues in *The Language of God* that there is a major and inescapable logical flaw in the Darwinist claim that science requires atheism, and this is that it goes beyond any possible evidence. If science is restricted to nature and matter as the Darwinists assert, and God transcends these, then science cannot prove or disprove his existence.[8]

Logic notwithstanding, Darwinists have used their conflict thesis to wage what amounts to an ideological war against religion. Battles have raged for over 150 years now, and have heated up again with the "New Atheism" ushered in with the 21st century. More than any other group, Darwinists have succeeded in creating a cultural climate where it is widely believed that faith and religion are incompatible with, if not the enemies of, reason and science.

AA was formed in this climate, and all of us alcoholics have been affected by the atheist enterprise. While much of our resistance to the spiritual and to God originates in a negative experience with organized religion, much can also be attributed to the spirit of contention that militant atheism and hostility to religion in general tend to foster.

By pretending that there is a conflict between faith and science, some of us can dismiss any evidence of a spiritual reality that might threaten our most cherished biases as not being "scientific." This can provide a convenient rationale that precludes the legitimate exercise of reason. It can reflect an attitude of close-mindedness that is pointedly described in the Big Book, in a quote attributed to Herbert Spencer, as "contempt prior to investigation" (p. 568).

But there is another way. If we are willing to consider the evidence, we will discover that faith and science have enjoyed a long and fruitful partnership. Historians of science generally agree that modern experimental science arose in the West, and a good case has been made that this was due in great part to the Jewish and Christian belief in a rational God who is the Creator of an orderly universe governed by an identifiable system of laws. Made in the image of God (*Imago Dei*), man was endowed with reason so he could discover these laws and act as God's steward over the natural world, thereby serving to advance God's purpose for his creation. This is, as we shall eventually have occasion to discuss, the original call for "love and service" that is expressed in Step 12 (12&12, p. 124).

Historians also widely acknowledge now that the "Scientific Revolution" originated in the religious monasteries of the Middle Ages, and that its major figures were men of faith. Historian Rodney Stark[9] shows that of its 52 leading scientists, only two were skeptics. The rest, 96.2% of the total, were Christians, of whom two-thirds were devout lay persons and the others ecclesiastics.

Among the believers, we find such well-known names as Tycho Brahe, Nicolaus Copernicus, René Descartes, Galileo Galilei, Johannes Kepler, Gottfried Leibniz, Robert Boyle, Blaise Pascal, and the acknowledged greatest of them all, Sir Isaac Newton, who in fact wrote more about theology than science. The Royal Society of London, the earliest institution for the advancement of science, counted seven believers among its ten founders, many of them clergy.[10]

Statistics also show religious belief to be well represented in the modern scientific community. A Carnegie Commission survey of more than one-fourth of all college professors in 1969 showed that a substantial majority in most science fields self-identified as religious. Of these, 60% were in mathematics/statistics, 55% in the physical sciences, and an equal percentage in the life sciences. Only in the social sciences did the religious constitute a minority (45%), and among these only in psychology and anthropology were nonbelievers a substantial majority.[11] Meanwhile, a 2005 survey of medical doctors showed that 59% believed in God and the afterlife.[12]

That religious belief is strongest in the "hard" sciences and weakest in the "softer" social sciences sheds light on the source of the science-faith debate. As Stark notes, practically all that was written on the subject during the twentieth century was written by nonscientists or *social* scientists (who are more inclined to philosophical assumptions).

Few in the hard sciences seem interested in stoking the conflict with religion. Einstein expressed a sentiment share by many of his colleagues when he said that "[s]cience without religion is lame, and religion without science is blind."[13] Arthur Schawlow, co-inventor of the laser and winner of the 1981 Nobel Prize in Physics, went even further. Quoting Psalm 19, he argued that religion provides "a great background for doing science," and that for him "scientific research is a worshipful act, in that it reveals more of the wonders of God's creation." The deeper the research the greater the revelations. This was given voice by Louis Pasteur, founder of microbiology and immunology. "A little science distances you from God," he wrote, "but a lot of science brings you nearer to Him." Along similar lines, physicist Lord Kelvin wrote that "If you study science deep enough and long enough, it will force you to believe in God." And theoretical physicist Werner Heisenberg observed that "The first gulp from the glass of natural science will make you an atheist, but at the bottom of the glass God is waiting for you."

A 2016 study of 9, 422 biologists and physicists in eight countries shows that participants who saw a conflict between science and religion were decidedly in the minority. The average for the eight was 22.5%, with the highest percentage in the United Kingdom (35%) and the lowest in Taiwan (9%). The U.S. average was 29%.[14]

Atheists expected the supposed gap between science and faith to widen as further scientific discoveries made a theistic explanation of the universe unnecessary and untenable. The opposite has happened. Science has not given us proof positive of God's existence, because as Collins noted, that does not lie within its province. But it has given us sufficient evidence on which to rationally ground our belief.

It has given us more than enough to meet AA's standard for faith in Step 2: whether "our present faith is reasonable" and whether it is "more sane and logical to believe than not to believe" (Big Book, p.53). This is a modest but completely adequate standard. In the final analysis, if we humbly accept the limits to human knowledge—and that is the big if—we can aspire to no more than that: what is reasonable and logical. Complete and absolute knowledge will always elude us. We shall see that, as regards God, science can point at best to probabilities, and that the available scientific evidence makes it more probable than not that God is.

The Big Book and the 12&12 make a case for the compatibility of faith and reason using mostly common sense and plain, ordinary logic. Everyday experience shows that faith is as necessary for life as reason. The same applies to science. It too accepts evidence for which there is no absolute certainty: "[D]oes not science demonstrate that visual proof is the weakest proof? It is being constantly revealed, as mankind studies the material world, that outward appearances are not inward reality at all" (Big Book, p. 48). The Big Book uses the example of the "prosaic steel girder" and its "mass of electrons" to illustrate the point that what we perceive through the senses is not necessarily what is there.

Indeed, the revolution in science ushered in by Einstein's theory of relativity and the laws of quantum mechanics has radically altered modern physics' understanding of matter, space, and time. This has thrown into question a fundamental premise of atheism: that our senses can fully apprehend reality. Since all we perceive is material, goes the argument, the material world is all there is.

This was never a good argument on purely logical grounds, for it could always be argued that we can only perceive the material because that is all we are physically equipped to perceive. That logic is now supported by quantum mechanics' description of wave/particle duality. Our senses, says physicist Gerald Schroeder, are all particle detectors. The other half of quantum reality is not accessible to them.[15]

Contemporary science's view of reality is radically different from that of the atheist and much closer to that of the theist. This can be illustrated with three examples. We can start with an update on that steel girder. As solid as it looks, physics says that chunk of steel is mostly empty space. Why? Because its constituent parts, atoms, are mostly that, empty space. The mass of an atom lies almost entirely within its nucleus. The nucleus, however, is but a tiny fraction of the atom's size. Between it and the distant cloud of electrons, there is a total vacuum. Thus, the steel beam and our perception of it are not the same.

Moreover, what we do perceive is but a fraction of what actually is. The atom's nucleus is made up of quarks and gluons that, like its orbiting electrons, cannot be seen. Physicist and theologian John Polkinghorne says of quarks that not only can they not be seen, they "are also invisible in principle," being "confined within the protons and neutrons they constitute."[16] Photons, which are elementary particles that carry the forces holding nucleus and electrons together and give solids the appearance of solidity, are equally invisible. We can perceive the effects of these entities, but not the entities themselves. We infer their existence from what they do. All of this tells us is that, contrary to the atheist, our senses are not a reliable guide to knowledge even of what we do see, much less of what we do not and cannot.

This conclusion is confirmed when we move from the micro-cosmos of the single atom to consider the cosmos in its entirety. The majority of physicists have come to accept the theory that most of the matter and energy in the universe is made of "dark matter" and "dark energy."[17] Dark matter is posited to account for the galaxies being able to cluster together; dark energy for the accelerating rate of the universe's expansion. They are called dark because they cannot be observed, measured, or detected with any available instrument. Yet they are said to account for as much as 95% of all the matter and energy in the universe.

But if only 5% of the matter and energy in the universe is accessible to scientific exploration, then the atheist can hardly appeal to reason as the ground for his absolute claims about the universe. The claim that the material universe is all that exists sounds more like dogma than fact. It has no basis in science.

The third consideration regarding the nature of reality as science sees it today has to do with space and time. We experience life in four dimensions, three of space and one of time. In an attempt to unify Einsteinian relativity with quantum mechanics, many scientists postulate the existence of a larger, multidimensional world. A widely accepted approach called string theory posits the existence of eleven dimensions to reality, ten of space and one of time. The additional seven dimensions are invisible and inaccessible to us.[18] Physics infers their existence because, like quarks, gluons, photons, dark matter, and dark energy, they help to account for what we *can* observe.

The same principle applies to God. We can infer his existence from his effect upon the universe, or what Christians and Jews call natural revelation. In the poetic language of Psalm 19, "the heavens declare the glory of God." We make a similar inference in Step 2. We come to believe because, though we can't see God, we see the effects of his grace, first in other alcoholics, then in us. Our faith is based, as Hebrews says in a paradoxical yet prescient turn of phrase, on the evidence of things not seen.[19] In a world of quarks and gluons, the seeming contradiction is progressively revealing its essential truth.

The atheist who believes with Carl Sagan that "nature is all there is, was, or will be" is not drawing a conclusion from the scientific evidence. What the Big Book calls "the perfectly logical assumption" that "underneath the material world and life as we see it, there is an All Powerful, Guiding, Creative Intelligence" (p. 49) is increasingly corroborated by an array of scientific discoveries. These are the "effects" in the visible universe of invisible causes, of a reality that lies beyond the reach of materialism and naturalism.

The biggest such effect is the Big Bang, the cosmic explosion of light and energy in which the universe was born some 15 billion years ago. For most of history, people thought the cosmos was eternal. This belief was held by the great philosophers of Greece and Rome and by the pagan religions of antiquity, and is still held today by eastern religions like Buddhism and Hinduism. Until the last century, even some scientists subscribed to it. The book of Genesis stood alone in declaring that God had created the universe *ex nihilo*, out of nothing.

With the Big Bang, biblical revelation appears vindicated by science. Einstein's theory of relativity, the second law of thermodynamics, and three other major lines of scientific evidence all support the conclusion that the universe had a beginning. Matter, space, and time all came into being together as a singular event. There was no preexistent anything.

The faith implications of this discovery are inescapable. The law of causality, which is the fundamental principle of science, states that everything that has a beginning has a cause. Hence, as theistic thinkers had argued all along in support of Genesis, the universe had a cause. And this cause, the Big Bang further confirms, had to come from outside the universe itself. That is, since there was no natural world of matter, space, and time, no natural laws and no natural anything until the Big Bang, its cause had to come from beyond nature. Put differently, the cause was supernatural. We could also say that it was metaphysical, as opposed to physical, or spiritual, rather than material. What we call God.

Though initially resisted, these implications were eventually acknowledged by leading scientists, including those involved in the work that established the Big Bang. Astrophysicist Sir Arthur Eddington conceded that the beginning had to be looked at as "frankly supernatural." Physicist Arno Penzias wrote of the best available data as being exactly what he would have predicted if all he had to go on was "the five books of Moses, the Psalms, and the Bible as a whole." And after his initial resistance to the theory, Einstein recognized the necessity of a "beginning."[20] He is later quoted as saying that he wanted to know how God had "created the world," that he wanted to "know His thoughts."[21]

Astronomer Robert Jastrow echoed similar views when he concluded that the evidence "leads to a biblical view"[22] of how the world came to be and makes it "a scientifically proven fact" that there are forces at work that can only be called "supernatural."[23] Astronomer Allan Sandage spoke of a "supernatural" and "creation" event that could not be explained "within the realm of physics."[24] Physicist Paul Davies also referred to the Big Bang as representing a "creation" event.[25] Theoretical physicist Stephen Hawking and physicist George Ellis wrote the universe began in a "space-time" singularity that was outside the known "laws of physics."[26]

"In the beginning God . . ." is the founding event of faith, the first miracle. Paul reclaims it when he declares: "By faith we understand that the universe was formed at God's command, so that what is seen was not made out of what is visible."[27] The Jewish and Christian claim has always been that faith is founded on fact, on objective truth. That is now corroborated by science, but thousands of years ago, before the advent of modern science and independently of human reason, the Big Bang was directly revealed to man.

A second major cosmological discovery that supports faith holds that the universe has not only a beginning but a purpose. That purpose is life. Physics calls this finding the anthropic principle. It tells us that the universe is fine-tuned for life, specifically human (*anthros* is Greek for "man") life. The universe operates according to laws that do not have a physical origin and which appear intentionally designed to make human habitation on earth possible.

Like the Big Bang, the anthropic principle is widely accepted by the scientific community. The principle designates a series of physical quantities or numeric values that must be exactly as they are for us to exist in the universe. The slightest variation would make life impossible. There are approximately 122 of these "anthropic constants" or "anthropic coincidences." Among the better known are such things as the rate of expansion of the universe, the speed of light, the gravitational pull, the 23-degree axial tilt of the earth, and the levels of oxygen and carbon dioxide in its atmosphere.

The implications of the anthropic principle are recognized by many scientists. Astronomer Robert Jastrow calls it "the most theistic result ever to come out of science." Astronomer Owen Gingerich says it shows that "the laws of nature are rigged not only . . . in favor of life, but also in favor of mind," and that "mind is written" into those laws "in a fundamental way."[28] Physicist Freeman Dyson adds that the way the universe is constructed "is consistent with the hypothesis that mind plays an essential role in its functioning."[29] Astronomer Fred Hoyle writes that a commonsense interpretation of the facts "suggests that a super-intellect has monkeyed with the laws of physics as well as chemistry and biology."[30] Physicist Paul Davis observes that "The impression of design is overwhelming," while astrophysicist Luke Barnes observes that "The whole system seems well thought out, something that someone planned and created."[31] Similar remarks have been made by many other scientists, including physicists Henry Margenau, George Greenstein, and John Polkinghorne.

The old argument from design that theistic thinkers had offered in support of biblical revelation now finds strong support in science. If the universe appears to be designed, that is probably because it is. Hence calling the designer God is entirely within the bounds of reason.

The anthropic principle strengthens the Big Bang's case for God. It says the universe is not the accidental product of some abstract First Cause or Prime Mover (or its modern variations), but the intentional design of a Creator, the guiding and creative intelligence referenced in the Big Book.

Furthermore, the anthropic principle refutes another basic tenet of atheism, borrowed from Darwinist materialism: that life on earth arose purely by chance. As a corollary, Darwinists have also held that life arose spontaneously out of what they consider inert matter: the infamous primordial ooze. Instead, says physics, life was written into the very design of matter and the universe from the very start. Referring to the fundamental forces of physics, Stephen Hawking notes that "The remarkable fact is that the values of these numbers seem to have been adjusted to make possible the development of life."[32] Astrophysicists now estimate that the value of the four fundamental forces (gravity, the electromagnetic force, and the strong and weak nuclear forces) were fixed "less than one millionth of a second after the Big bang."[33]

In biology too, a series of revolutionary findings is adding weight to the evidence that life is the product of intelligent design. Prominent among these is the discovery of DNA. The cell, the basic unit of life, is not just a bundle of chemical compounds but itself a complex micro-universe that operates according to a precise series of encoded messages. It is estimated that even the simplest, single-cell amoeba contains in its DNA a message so complex that its letters would fill 1,000 complete sets of the Encyclopedia Britannica.[34] A message of course presupposes a message giver. With Francis Collins, many scientists call this code of life the language of God.

This finding of an encoded message at the cellular level ties in with a similar concept in the subatomic world of quantum mechanics and again challenges the materialist understanding of existence. Werner Heisenberg, Nobel laureate in physics and one of the pioneers of quantum mechanics, suggests that rather than being the only thing there is, the physical may actually be a product of the metaphysical, for when we reduce matter to its smallest units, we find that they are not physical objects as commonly understood: "they are—in Plato's sense—Ideas."[35]

Heisenberg is not alone in this view. George Wald, another Nobel laureate, biologist, and organic chemist, declares that what we call physical reality is "mind stuff. It is mind that has composed a physical universe."[36] Mathematician and physicist Sir James Jeans writes that the universe is beginning to look more like "a great thought than a great machine," and that mind should be seen as "the creator and governor of the realm of matter."[37] And John A. Wheeler, Princeton physicist and winner of the Einstein Award, abandoned his view of reality as constituted of particles and came to see it as an expression of information.[38]

Citing these various views, Gerald Schroeder concludes that what these and other scientists now call idea, mind, thought, or information is what the Bible all along has called the wisdom of God,[39] or the Logos or Word,[40] what gave rise to and forms the "substrate" of existence. Or as we referenced earlier in the Big Book, the "Creative Intelligence" that is "underneath the material world and life as we see it" (p. 46).

Matter, space, time, and reality are just not what the atheist says they are. Neither is science. The idea that science can provide absolute, exact, and objective knowledge of things is just not supported by quantum and related theories. This new understanding has been given a name, the Heisenberg

Uncertainty Principle, and it holds that even with material reality, science can only deal in probabilities.

The way science works, according to what is known as "confirmation theory," is that it begins with a theory that has an initial plausibility. The accumulation of evidence does not result in certainty, but only increases or decreases the probability that the theory is true. The existence of God has an initial plausibility, according to one exponent of confirmation theory, because of its simplicity (as AA suggests), and because it offers a coherent explanation of the world in terms of a purposeful agent (as AA also suggests). The order evident in the universe "increases the probability of the theistic hypothesis." So do a growing number of scientific discoveries, some of which we have touched upon. It is therefore reasonable to conclude that, taking all the evidence into account, "theism is more probable than not."[41] This supports the Big Book's line of reasoning cited earlier.

Quantum theory, the Big Bang, the anthropic principle, and other findings of contemporary science have made believers out of many an atheist in the sciences, including the aforementioned astronomers Fred Hoyle and Allan Sandage. The same has occurred in other disciplines, including philosophy. These former atheists have been willing to follow the evidence where it leads, and it has led them to God. That's how Antony Flew describes his own journey.[42] The leading atheist philosopher of the second half of the 20th century, and the man who is said to have set the agenda for modern atheism, he came to believe because the evidence demanded it. Existentialists Jean-Paul Sartre and Albert Camus and Marxist Alasdair MacIntyre followed a similar path.[43]

Other atheists, scientists included, refuse to go where the evidence would take them. They seem unwilling to give up their philosophical bias against the supernatural. By their own admission, they have a prior commitment to materialism. They automatically reject any evidence of design or purpose (however compelling) and seek to replace it with alternative theories (however implausible) that might explain the universe while excluding the possibility of the supernatural.

Robert Jastrow explains that many scientists subscribe to a religious faith of their own. This faith is in the power of reason to find a material explanation for any natural phenomenon, given enough time and enough resources. They may believe that there is order and harmony in the universe and that there must be a cause for every effect, but they still can't believe that there is a *first* cause. It is not hard to see why. If the universe began under conditions for which the known laws of physics are not valid, and as the result of forces that he cannot discover, then, says Jastrow, the scientist has lost control.[44]

That is why it has been said that the science-religion debate is not one between faith and reason but between reasonable and unreasonable faith.[45] The theist needs to reconcile faith and reason, for as the Bible insists, his faith is useless if not grounded in truth.

The atheist, on the other hand, seems ready to forsake reason if it interferes with his faith, for, all his protests to the contrary, his faith appears to be not so much in reason or science as in materialism and naturalism. It's not hard to see why. Only within the realm of the material and the natural is he able to maintain the illusion of personal power and control. Once he accepts the existence of the spiritual, he is no longer in charge.

This accords with AA's understanding of things. Ultimately, the question of God is a question of power. This accounts for the belligerent atheist, his motivation, his inordinate passion against the divine. Contrary to popular belief, notes a writer cited earlier, atheism is not primarily an intellectual but a moral revolt. "Atheists don't find God invisible so much as objectionable."[46]

The atheist wants atheism to be true because, as philosopher Thomas Nagel[47] acknowledged about himself, he doesn't want there to be a God. Why? Because if the God of Genesis created the world, has a purpose for it, and declared it to be "good," then we live in a moral universe governed by God's will. Man's will is not sovereign but subordinate. We are not morally autonomous. We can't determine good and evil for ourselves. Adam and Eve had first-hand empirical evidence of God's existence, for he's said to have walked in the Garden with them. Their problem was that God told them they could not eat of a certain tree.

"The fool says in his heart there is no God," we read in Psalm 14. The Hebrew original doesn't reference someone who is mentally or intellectually challenged, but someone who is morally so: in his "heart," not in his "mind." The "fool" wants to live as if there is no God, so he must convince himself there isn't. This, as we have noted, is the spiritual root of the psychology of denial, and the militant atheist's true motivation. For the intellectually inclined in particular, it leads to an elaborate web of rationalizations. It is wishful thinking masquerading as reason. The atheist who accuses the believer of this mode of self-deceit may very well be suffering from a serious case of projection.

All of this supports AA's view that the atheist's problem is not one of the head but of the heart and the will. For the great majority of us, the barrier to faith is not intellectual. If we are honest with ourselves, we have to admit that a dispassionate examination of the evidence for and against the existence of God is not what turned us away from him. We were not moved by reason, but by negative emotion and a morally compromised character.

We indignantly and self-righteously blamed religion and God for what we found wrong with the world. We wanted sole control over our lives and refused to recognize any ultimate authority over us. We wanted to define our own truth and be the final arbiter of right and wrong. God stood in our way. We turned against God first, and then we sought ways to rationalize our rebellion. We found them in the various "isms" we have discussed, from Marxism to Freudianism to Darwinism and their many offshoots in Existentialism and a host of other contemporary creeds—or we gradually absorbed them from the culture.

This is why in AA the way to faith is not primarily through the exercise of the intellect or the accumulation of knowledge, but through shared personal experience informed by the practice of spiritual principles. The alcoholic who doesn't want to believe won't believe. No amount of evidence can change that. The willingness isn't there.

This explains why AA has raised willingness to the level of a virtue. Without it, the heart remains hardened and the mind closed. Willingness is what sets the process of "Attitude Adjustment" under way. Involved in this process is a key principle of the spiritual life. Proposed by Thomas Aquinas, it states that things are received according to the mode of the receiver. The principles of Step 2 are there to wean the unbeliever away from an ingrained disposition to self-will so that he may become receptive to the evidence of spiritual healing found in the rooms as others share their experience in terms that are personal, intimate, and direct.

Willingness is the point of departure, what frees us to move toward the other principles, however haltingly it may be. If the willingness is there, a spiritual awakening is possible, and with it a new "mode" or disposition, a different way of viewing and valuing things.

"We Agnostics" (pp. 55–56) and the personal stories section of the Big Book (p. 215) tell the story of a typical atheist, a rebel against religion who, nearing self-destruction, is confined to the alcoholic ward of a hospital. He is in utter desperation. All hell seems to be closing in on him. Suddenly, an overwhelming question thunders in his mind: "Who are you to say there is no God?" The man falls out of bed and onto his knees and his resistance melts away. A sense of peace and hope washes over him and with it, a new faith. That very night God began to restore him to sanity. He never drank again.

A spiritual experience healed the man from his alcoholism and his atheism. What made this "miracle of healing" possible is simple, we are told: his circumstances made him willing to believe. He humbly surrendered to his Creator, and then he knew. God is there and he will reveal himself to us if we are willing and humble enough. Sometimes he will do it suddenly and dramatically and sometimes he will do it slowly and imperceptibly. Invariably, his revelation will come in the wake of crisis, pain, and collapse. We may have to lose everything before we can find him. Or we may willingly surrender. But if we seek, we shall find.

That is the message and the promise that Dr. Bob carried to the very first meeting of the new AA fellowship in Akron as he read from the Sermon on the Mount.[48] It is echoed in the Big Book when we are assured that he will come to all who honestly seek him (p. 57).

Like the early AA's, many of us who entered the rooms as atheists eventually came to believe. We drew near to God and he disclosed himself to us. Those of us who haven't come to God, even after many 24 hours, will find that the road to faith still begins with the principles laid out in Step 2. The evidence for God is in the rooms, sitting next to us and across the table. To see it and accept it we need only surrender the pride that blinds us and be willing to listen honestly and with an open mind.

We also need to be honest with ourselves when we look at "what we used to be like" (Big Book, p. 58). Those of us who refuse to acknowledge the spiritual nature of our disease or who tweak "spiritual" to exclude God, will not admit to any connection between our unbelief and our failure in life. But we all have a need for ultimate meaning, a need which is at the very heart of what makes us human. AA suggests that only God can fulfill it, for as our creator he implanted it in us. In his absence, we tried to fill this need with our own little gods, and they failed us. Undeterred, we tried harder, and we proved Dostoevsky right.

With God out of the way, we could do as we pleased—and we did. We sometimes say that when we drank, we crossed lines we thought we would never cross. This is true, but it can become our version of "the Devil made me do it." Alcohol can become an alibi. The truth is that we were so spiritually and morally bankrupt that we could not even see some of those lines. We stepped over them blindly. Other times we saw the lines alright, but we *wanted* to cross them. Alcohol gave us the false courage to do it and numbed our conscience as we did. Alcohol was the great enabler and the great anesthetic. It wasn't God who was dead. We were.

We need to be honest about the connection between what we believed and how we lived. We also need to be honest about why we remain atheists. It will do no good to appeal to science and reason, for the advance of science has effectively closed that option. Science is re-emerging as one of the main pillars of faith, and there is a plethora of intellectually accessible and reader-friendly books written by respected scientists, thinkers, and scholars that can help us clear the road if false reasoning and discredited ideas are still blocking the way.

Are we willing to put in the effort? Do we honestly want to pursue the facts and follow the evidence wherever it leads? Or do we too have a prior commitment to unbelief? The reality is that we may admit we are powerless over alcohol and still want to retain ultimate power over how we live. God precludes that possibility. Therein lies the rub.

If we are to find the truth, about God and about ourselves, we need to be properly disposed. Practicing the principles in Step 2 helps us to do that and brings about a new attitude in us. It helps us to experience a change of heart and become receptive to the gift of faith. Without that, there is no amount of evidence, whether gathered in books or around the table, which will convince us. There is no number of miraculous stories told in the rooms that will touch us. We will turn a blind eye and a deaf ear.

The Agnostic

The chapter to the agnostic in the Big Book is the chapter to the atheist as well, for no clear distinction is made between the two. The 12&12, on the other hand, hardly addresses the agnostic, concentrating instead on the militant atheist, the believer, and assorted types of ex-believers. As a barrier to faith, agnosticism presents nevertheless its own peculiarities, and examining some of these may be of help to all of us.

Agnosticism properly speaking is a fairly recent phenomenon, having arisen as a response to the conflict between reason and religion stirred up by radical atheists in the 19th century, which we referenced earlier. One of the parties to the conflict, Thomas Huxley, is said to have coined the term agnostic to refer to the person who took a neutral position in this war between belief and unbelief. Agnostic literally refers to one who doesn't know (the two words share the same Latin root *gno*, as in *i-gno-rant*), in this case whether or not God exists.

If we are agnostic, we generally take one of two stands. One is avowedly subjective. It admits that, personally, we don't know if God exists. He might or he might not. We just don't know. Another sports an aura of objectivity. It claims that such knowledge is unachievable in principle. Philosopher Bryan Magee[49] is one of the best exponents of this position. Some aspects of reality, he correctly argues, are permanently beyond the possibility of human apprehension. For him of course, this includes God. As with the subjectivist, however, for him knowledge is a strictly intellectual or rational proposition, for as agnostics we have accepted the atheist's false premise that reason is the only way to knowledge of what is true or real. Having accepted the premise, we agnostics find that we are stuck, unable to reason with any degree of conviction for or against God. Eventually, we relinquish reason altogether, shelve the issue, and make vague feelings and emotion our compass.

Regardless of how we defined our agnosticism when we drank, in practice we acted as if God didn't exist. In this we were indistinguishable from the atheist. We differed from the latter only in the level of sentiment. Where the theoretical atheist in particular tended to be aggressive in his denial of God, we agnostics tended to be passive. It is hard to be a passionate agnostic. Indeed, a lack of strong feelings about the question of God may be the peculiar mark of the agnostic. It's just not that important to us, not something we care that much about. The agnostic is not just ignorant on the matter, but emotionally predisposed to ignore it, to not pay it any mind or give it any attention.

Our bland denial therefore achieved the same objective as the atheist's hardened rejection. We could live our lives free from any constraints that might come with a belief in God. This worked pretty well for a while. There were certainly plenty of the usual concerns and counterfeit gods to engage our passion: work, money, success, power, romance. Till these failed us, as idols always will.

Eventually, self-will and the bottle caught up with us and we began to hurt badly. Then, "crushed by a self-imposed crisis we could not postpone or evade, we had to fearlessly face the proposition that either God is everything or else He is nothing. God either is, or He isn't. What was our choice to be?" (Big Book, p. 53). Pain forces the issue. At the jumping-off point, we cry out with Bill W. and so many other desperate alcoholics: "If there is a God . . ." We surrender and ask for help. Then, as with Bill and so many others after him, a feeling of peace and assurance comes over us, and we know there is.

In the spiritual experience that pain and suffering make possible, the barriers to faith crumble and we come to a direct knowledge of God. Agnosticism and the rest of the fancy "isms" lose their hold on us. Step 2 becomes a reality. Some of us are blessed with such an experience early on in our recovery. Others not till much later, usually on the heels of another crisis and the even greater suffering that accompanies it. Still others come to believe slowly, pain prodding us along when we falter.

Somehow, the alcoholic who remains in the agnostic frame of mind well into sobriety has experienced a bottom that has not motivated her sufficiently into a search for God. This brings into relief a curious feature of agnosticism. In practice, functionally, agnosticism can often be the most comfortable stance toward God. It is almost a default position. When we want to behave shabbily, it helps to pretend that God is not there.

Moreover, taking a middle ground between belief and unbelief means that we don't have to commit one way or another. And lack of commitment always connotes a lack of effort. Why bother with Step 2 and the other God Steps when we have already stopped drinking? It is so easy to settle into a "soft and mushy" agnosticism (ibid.), particularly when cushioned with a generalized and rarefied spirituality that makes no demands either on our intellectual or our moral faculties.

The agnostic who is honestly confused about the question of God's existence, even after countless alcoholics have testified to his miraculous work in their lives, can certainly undertake a serious study of the matter. The rational, scientific evidence pointing to God is abundant, as suggested earlier, and unlike the early days of AA, today's technology makes it easily accessible to the average person. But if agnosticism can be so comfortable, why practice any intellectual virtue and make the effort to investigate the matter? Again, the motivation is lacking, and without a change in motivation, there is no change in outlook, and without these, no change in our emotional predispositions.

This brings us back to what we said may be characteristic of the agnostic, her lack of passion. The agnostic's problem may not be a case of "contempt prior to investigation" so much as a lack of interest. She may suffer from a sort of apathy or sloth. This may be of the ordinary or of the spiritual variety. The latter condition is known in the virtue tradition as acedia (Greek: not caring or indifferent), a defect that manifests itself in a disinterest in things spiritual. The agnostic may simply lack a hunger for God. Just as we will not get sober unless we have at least a desire to stop drinking, so we may not come to believe unless we have some desire for God.

Yet the Big Book maintains that the "fundamental idea of God" is implanted in all of us (p. 55), however obscured it may be by circumstance and worship of other things. That is the seed of faith that Step 2 helps us to cultivate. Our hunger for God will grow when we stop trying to satisfy it elsewhere and start to practice the principles in that Step and those that follow.

Spiritual apathy can be a problem for the believer as well as the unbeliever. If we honestly recognize our lack of faith, we can humbly ask for help. In the Bible, the example is set by the father who pleads with Jesus to heal his epileptic son "if he could," and recognizing in his choice of words the insufficiency of his faith, then cries out to him "I do believe; help me overcome my unbelief."[50] We are told that the man was helped and the boy was healed.

In one of its most reassuring passages, the Big Book says: "We found that God does not make too hard terms with those who seek Him" (p. 46). Simplicity and spirituality go hand in hand. As soon as we are even willing to believe that there is a Power greater than ourselves, we are assured that we are on our way. "It has been repeatedly proven among us that upon this simple cornerstone a wonderfully effective spiritual structure can be built" (p. 47).

THE EX-BELIEVER

To the agnostic and the atheist discussed in the Big Book, the 12&12 adds two other categories of alcoholics who face particular problems with Step 2 and the questions of God, religion, and faith. These are ex-believers, and not surprisingly, believers.

Of course, the agnostics and atheists in early AA were themselves at one time ex-believers, mostly Christians (if nominal) of diverse denominations who had ended up abandoning their faith altogether. There were few cradle unbelievers then. The usual route was, and to a lesser extent remains, from believer to ex-believer to agnostic to atheist.

The 12&12 focuses on the ex-believer who has yet to make a conscious passage into the two later stages of his progression away from belief, although for all intents and purposes he will operate as if he already had. It distinguishes four types among these alcoholics: the drifter, the intellectually self-sufficient, the prejudiced against religion, and the outright defiant. The lines of demarcation between these are not hard and fast, and a progression is possible here too, from drifter to defiant.

The alcoholic who has wandered from his faith and drifted into indifference is perhaps the most common among these types, a cousin of the agnostic. The 12&12 calls him "the bewildered one" (S2, p. 28). Those of us who fit this description lacked any conviction one way or another about God. We just didn't see him as being relevant to our life. We didn't rebel against our faith so much as we were diverted from it. We simply set out to make our mark in life, and the more successful we became the less did we feel a need for God.

We had the will to win, and that was enough for us. We pulled ourselves up by our bootstraps and claimed our abilities and achievements as our own, proud of being self-made men and women. Then alcohol caught up with us and reduced us to impotence, making short shrift of our cherished accomplishments. When God brought us to AA, we found others who like us had also lost their faith, and we rediscovered it among a group of drunks.

The intellectually self-sufficient is a stone's throw from where the atheist stands. If we belong to this group, we may have attended college and maybe even earned graduate and post-graduate degrees. We might have sported a string of initials after our name, proof positive of our academic achievement. Though we would be the last ones to admit it, we used our credentials to puff ourselves up into "prideful balloons" (ibid., p. 29). For us, knowledge was the measure of all things. "It's what you know that counts," we liked to say, and we judged people accordingly. Since we generally thought we were smarter than most, we looked down our nose at them.

We subscribed to the view propounded by Francis Bacon that "knowledge is power," rather than a means to the pursuit of God-given truth. Brainpower was our ticket to victory in our survival-of-the-fittest attitude toward life. The god of intellect replaced the God of our fathers, says the 12&12, and intellectual pride became our besetting sin. Eventually, we got into a power struggle with a power greater than ourselves, and we lost. Alcohol short-circuited our brain, inducing blackouts and reducing us to helplessness. Our vaunted knowledge had no power to save us.

When we came to AA, we found many who had scaled the same heights and fallen off the same cliff. "They helped us to get down to our right size. By their example they showed that humility and intellect could be compatible, provided we placed humility first. When we began to do that, we received the gift of faith, a faith which works" (ibid., p. 30).

For other unbelievers, the roadblock to Step 2 is their attitude toward religion. For the early alcoholics, that meant Christianity. It still does today, for many of us. It is our religious background, the faith of our parents and much of our culture, at least nominally, and thus the object of our rebellion. It is also the religion that most influenced early AA, and though we may strenuously deny it, the religion whose spiritual principles suffuse the Steps and the Traditions. All the more reason to resist.

Still, as the 12&12 tells us, it was often not the theology or the morality of the Bible that turned us against religion. What set us most against Christianity was its self-professed adherents, as we saw them. "We gloated over the hypocrisy, bigotry, and crushing self-righteousness that clung to so many 'believers' even in their Sunday best" (ibid.).

As the Big Book observes, this only shows we were substituting "negative for positive thinking," i.e., we became prejudiced. We looked at the all-too-human defects of these people and felt totally justified in judging and condemning the whole lot. "We talked of intolerance, while we were intolerant ourselves. We missed the reality and the beauty of the forest because we were diverted by the ugliness of some of its trees. We never gave the spiritual side of life a fair hearing" ("We Agnostics," p. 50).

In condemning the blatant defects of religious people, we made a tacit assumption. This is that those who believe in God should *ipso facto* be better people than those who don't. But as Tim Keller writes in *The Reason for God*, that is not what Christianity teaches. According to him, God gives what Christians call common grace to all, believer and unbeliever alike. Any act of virtue or other good, regardless of who performs it, is made possible by the power of God, who alone is the source of what is good.

Moreover, we don't know the substance of anyone's beliefs. We don't know who is a committed believer and who a nominal one, and to what extent their beliefs have anything to do with how they live. The nominal believer can hardly be expected to best represent the faith she professes. Even the committed believer, as Paul recognized about himself and as we shall see further below, may believe one thing and live another.

We also assume that all persons are equally endowed by nature, and that believer and unbeliever have the same starting point. But that is hardly the case. Virtue comes more easily to some than to others, regardless of their religious views. In addition, we fail to take into account the role that nurture plays in our moral development. Our character is necessarily influenced by the family and social environment in which we are raised.

As C. S. Lewis observes,[51] we might conclude a Christian's character defects are a product of her religion or at least proof of its falsity or inefficacy, not knowing what baggage nature and nurture may have saddled that person with and how much worse her shortcomings might be were it not for the mitigating effects of her faith. What follows if Christianity is true is not that a Christian should be a better person than a non-Christian, but that a Christian should be a better person than that same person would be had she not become a Christian.

The Christian may actually start with more than her share of shortcomings, for as Keller suggests, those who see their need for God and turn to Christ are often not the well and the virtuous but the seriously flawed, those whose character defects have exacted a heavy toll and forced them to their knees. For them, there is nowhere else to go. That is why according to the Bible Christ said that he came not for the righteous, but for sinners.[52] And sinners don't become paragons of virtue overnight.

When asked how he could behave so cruelly towards others and still call himself a Christian, Evelyn Waugh is said to have replied: "You have no idea how much nastier I would be if I was not a Catholic. Without supernatural aid I would barely be human."[53]

As we alcoholics soon find out, character growth is a drawn-out and gradual process, and emotional healing an even longer one. It is no different for the Christian. What this means, according to Keller, is that the church will typically be filled with the broken and the immature, people who spiritually, morally, and emotionally will still have a very long way to go. Quoting Abigail Van Buren, he notes that "The church is a hospital for sinners, not a museum for saints."[54]

The same can be said of the rooms. They are filled with defective people, us included. When we admit that, we become less intolerant, less self-righteous about other people and their religion, whatever that may happen to be. We see that condemning the shortcomings of religious people allowed us to feel superior to them and to avoid looking at our own defects. We realize that "Self-righteousness, the very thing we had contemptuously condemned in others, was our own besetting evil" (12&12, S2, p. 30). When we began to take our own inventory, we discovered that we were as flawed as the next person.

Defiance is said to be a distinguishing characteristic of many alcoholics. We don't take well to authority and obedience doesn't come naturally to us. It is inherent in our rebellious nature to resist any attempt to exert power over us. We start by resisting the authority of our parents and then of our teachers and eventually graduate to resist a Higher Authority. Whatever God's other attributes, we resent his omnipotence most. An all-powerful God doesn't sit well with us. Thus admitting powerlessness doesn't easily translate into accepting the idea of a Power greater than ourselves, particularly if that Power has a will for us. The whole concept rubs us the wrong way.

Sometimes when we were hurting very badly we appealed to this Power, but always on our own terms. We made demands and God failed to deliver. When we became drunks, we asked God to stop that, and nothing came of it. We had given faith a try, and we had "found it wanting" (ibid., p. 28).

Coming to AA, we saw that we had it all wrong. We were trying to get God to do our will rather than seeking to do his. We could not believe and defy God at the same time. "Belief meant reliance, not defiance." The fruits of a humble dependence on God could be seen in men and women who had been delivered from the ravages of alcoholism and restored to a reasonably useful and happy life. "This was not only faith; it was faith that worked under all conditions. We soon concluded that whatever price in humility we must pay, we would pay" (ibid., p. 31).

The Believer

The believer who can't get sober until she comes to AA represents a real puzzle, to herself and others. This is especially the case with the committed, as distinct from the believer in name only. The committed believer attends church regularly, observes the rituals, and adheres to the tenets of her faith. She may even be active in her congregation and serve in one capacity or another. Yet no matter how hard she tries, she can't stop drinking. Now here is AA telling her that God can free her from alcohol when she already believes in God, is a devout follower of her religion, has asked God for help, and it hasn't worked. It just doesn't make any sense.

We soon found out that the problem wasn't God. We discovered that we suffered from a false religiosity and that our problem was "the quality of faith, rather than its quantity." This was "our blind spot. We supposed we had humility when really we hadn't. We supposed we had been serious about religious practices when, upon honest appraisal, we found we had been only superficial." Other times we mistook zeal and fervor for true faith. Our beliefs had little to do with how we lived, and so our faith remained barren. "The fact was we really hadn't cleaned house so that the grace of God could enter us and expel the obsession" (ibid., p. 32).

We believed there was such a thing as sin and that we ourselves were sinners, but that was largely a theological abstraction. We never undertook a serious examination of how such sin expressed itself in our lives, of what was wrong with us, and of the wrongs we did to others. Nor were we in the habit of confessing to such wrongs. Either we didn't think our particular religious denomination required it, or where it did, we just went through the motions. It became a shallow ritual for us, not a serious spiritual discipline designed to change us and set us right with God and neighbor.

Making amends to those we had harmed past and present, if it occurred to us at all, was well beyond the scope of what we considered our religious obligation. Our prayers were often like the reading of a wish list, or dutiful but mindless repetitions of set formulas, rather than a way to place ourselves in God's presence and seek his moral will for our lives. We could recite creeds or scriptures from memory, but "The love of God and man we understood not at all. Therefore we remained self-deceived and so incapable of receiving enough grace to restore us to sanity" (ibid.).

However sincere and well-meaning, and however orthodox or theologically correct our beliefs, we were not practicing the spiritual principles that would allow God to work in our lives and bring healing to us and those around us. Religion became an end, rather than a means, a substitute for God. Until alcoholism intervened and forced the issue: God, or religion?

RELIGION, SPIRITUALITY, AND FAITH

For the believer then, no less than for the ex-believer, the agnostic, and the atheist, religion can become a stumbling block to Step 2. Some will find in it a reason to disbelieve, others a faith that doesn't work.

Consequently, in working this Step, the Big Book and the 12&12 guide us through an honest self-examination of our attitudes in this area. Such a survey most often reveals that if religion has become a barrier to God, we have built the wall with the brick and mortar of our negative attitudes and character defects. Pride, prejudice, self-righteousness, and intolerance have been our chief building blocks.

Other times we will find that religion was not a barrier but a detour that diverted us from a right relationship with God and neighbor. Yet the same character defects obtained, whether directed at our co-religionists, at those of other denominations or faiths, or at unbelievers. Religion and lack of religion both could be used to diminish others and avoid looking at ourselves. In this dishonesty and pride worked hand in hand.

AA is quick to reassure the newcomer who has a problem with religion that we are a spiritual and not a religious program. In part, this is a tactical response. Our own negative experiences and prejudices aside, the reality is that religion has become problematic in our culture. This is the result of its shortcomings as well as the relentless drive by secularist forces to marginalize religious faith. We want to get around this problem and help people get down to the business of AA. This business is to work the Steps and practice the principles of the program. It is a spiritual business, and it involves God directly, one on One.

That we practice a spiritual rather than a religious program is no evasion. It is one of the basic tenets of AA. For those who are hostile to religion, this is a distinction without a difference. They see spirituality as a thinly disguised attempt to bring religion in through the back door. Their problem is not with religion but with God, or to put it differently, with theistic faith. The shortcomings of religion make it easier for them to deny faith and reject God.

Many of the traditionally religious object to spirituality on diametrically opposite grounds. They see spirituality as a vague and elastic term that can be stretched to mean everything and nothing. It allows people to waffle on the question of God, to wallow in a comfortable agnosticism or dabble in Gnosticism and syncretism, even the occult. They point out that spiritual powers can be good or evil. Satan, after all, is a spirit.

All this says, however, is that spirituality as originally understood in AA can be distorted, just as religion can. Indeed, the tendency to distortion is inherent in the very fact that, in its modern context, spirituality arises in reaction to a negative perception of religion. Taken to an extreme, as we alcoholics tend to take things, religion is summarily condemned and we willfully deny the good that it has accomplished throughout the centuries, even in its organized form. We want a spirituality that is free of all of its traces. In practice, this leads some of us to a spirituality that is also free of God.

A convenient rationale for this view of spirituality is found in the fact of contemporary religious pluralism. During the early days of AA, religious pluralism meant primarily Christian denominational diversity, as it had meant from the time of America's founding. Today, the religious freedom made possible by its Judeo-Christian heritage has made America the most religiously diverse country in history. But living amidst a diversity of religions can be a challenge to one's faith, particularly if that faith is wobbly to begin with. Given so many religions and so many different and conflicting ideas about God, how are we to know the true from the false? Even just raising such a question might be deemed offensive. Better to dispense with religion altogether.

Religious pluralism provides a false incentive to resolve the tension between reason and faith that is inherent in theism. Agnosticism does this by abandoning both faith and reason. Spirituality can do the same, escaping the tension by opting instead for feeling, good vibes, a well-intentioned idealism, and a vague mysticism, with nature (the cosmos, the universe, whatever) filling in for God. This affords relief from the barrenness of rationalism and materialism while avoiding the exigencies of faith.

Such spirituality abandons the search for truth and becomes subjective and personal, self-defined and self-designed. It does not respond to a spiritual reality that could be said to exist objectively, much less transcendentally. There is no need for faith or God. Not incidentally, it reaches the same conclusion as atheism. The modernist apotheosis of reason and its postmodernist escape arrive at the same place.

Spirituality is necessary but God and faith are optional, in this view, which reflects the ethos of a characteristically New Age blend of Western and Eastern religious philosophy. Yet, Step 2 and AA spirituality is about nothing if it isn't about faith in God. Many good reasons exist why AA makes a distinction between religion and spirituality, but a denial of God is not one of them.

AA spirituality seeks a right relationship between faith and reason. It recognizes that we humans are rational and spiritual creatures and that our wellbeing lies in the proper use of both faculties. This is why the practice of the virtues is central to 12-Step spirituality, for their aim is precisely the right use of our faculties in pursuit of a sober life.

In its classical understanding, virtue governs the use of the abilities by which we function in life. Our tendency as humans is to misuse those abilities, and this is the source of our character defects or shortcomings. Virtue seeks to temper or moderate this tendency, helping us to attain a proper mean between two extremes: one of excess, the other of deficiency. Cowardice and recklessness, for instance, both reflect a poor use of our ability to handle difficult or threatening situations, in one case by lack and in the other by excess. In practicing the virtue of courage, we avoid both extremes.

In maintaining a right relationship and balance between faith and reason, AA spirituality steers a clear course between two forms of religion that misuse the rational faculty. We may consider these two forms of irrationalism, two misuses of our ability to think. Both lead to a misuse of the spiritual faculty, a distortion of faith, and a denial of God.

One proceeds, as we have seen, from a rationalist outlook or worldview. This considers the material the only reality, denies the spiritual realm and with it a part of our humanity, and makes reason a religion in its own right.

The other comes from the opposite pole. It proceeds from an anti-rational worldview that conflates the material and the spiritual and posits an abstracted spiritualized nature as the sole reality. It too denies a part of our humanity, seeing our ability to think and reason as a fatal liability. This is our original sin, in this view. It causes us to make distinctions and draw differences between things when all is really an indistinct and undistinguishable mass, a seamless continuum, an eternal now with no beginning and no end, no purpose and no meaning. Here spirituality is seen as becoming one with the One, merging with a divinized, non-rational Reality. Reason stands in the way, generating the illusion of a distinct and separate self, an illusion that is the source of all our problems in life.

AA spirituality speaks to our full humanity and denies none of its parts. It reflects what we may characterize as a recurring human attempt to recapture the meaning that religion perhaps once held universally but which is now lost to many. Stripped of its accretions over the centuries and restored to its original intent, re-ligion signifies to "re-bind" (its root still present in "liga-ment"). The original idea the word conveyed was that of restoring the binding connection between God and man.

Today we would use the word relationship to convey the same idea. When AA talks about a right relationship with God, it is hearkening to the original religious impulse. This is the goal of a spiritual awakening and the ultimate goal of the program. It is the essence of AA spirituality. One may repudiate organized or institutional religion, but one cannot dispense with religion altogether. God put in us the desire to seek him and to reconnect with him, and what we do when we respond to that desire, *that* is religion.

However, God also put in us the desire to seek and connect with our fellows. That communal instinct is the seed of corporate religion. As it developed over the millennia and is now traditionally understood, three aspects of organized religion may account for its negative perception among many. First, as an institution, religion claims the power of mediation and interjects itself between God and man. In so doing it displaces the centrality of a direct relationship with the divine, spirit to Spirit, and erects walls of its own. Second, reflecting men's passions, religious institutions throughout history have repeatedly assumed unwarranted secular powers and become more concerned with worldly than with godly affairs, with the tragic results all too familiar to us.

Third, organized forms of religion have tended to lose sight of the right relationship between their constituent parts. Central to most religions is a set of beliefs that is often formalized in creeds, a code of moral conduct usually expressed in injunctions and exhortations, and a pattern of worship often manifested in diverse liturgical traditions or practices. When creeds supersede deeds, when beliefs and rituals have no bearing on the way we live our lives, religion is reduced to that caricature of itself which elicits charges of hypocrisy and rightly earns the scorn of many—and which produces the man or woman who is filled with faith, yet "still reeking of alcohol" (12&12, S2, p. 31).

All of this brings to mind the story of the Pharisees, whose name has become synonymous with hypocrisy (from Greek for "actor," one who pretends) and who are emblematic of what can go wrong with religion.

The Pharisees constituted the religious establishment in first-century Palestine. They were so zealous about observing the letter of the Mosaic Law that they turned largely blind to its spirit. Righteousness became a matter of complying with a complicated code of do's and don'ts and observing an impossible series of external rituals. Meanwhile, their hearts festered with contempt for the common folk they looked down upon as "unrighteous" and "unclean." They famously persecuted a carpenter for associating with sinners and outcasts and for feeding the hungry and healing the sick on the Sabbath. In the end, they handed him to the Romans to be hung on a cross, all in the name of religion.

In effect, religion has often given God a bad name. Hence the movement away from religion so perceived and toward spirituality.

AA is part of this movement. Its early members were men and women who had failed to find sobriety and sanity through traditional religion. They first found help in a religious group that avoided meeting in church buildings and using traditional Christian language. The focus of the Oxford Group was on practicing certain principles that would lead to a spiritual experience and a direct relationship with God.

Yet the Oxford Group was itself saddled with many of the problems of organizations everywhere, and power, prestige, and ambition headed the list. Externally, on the national and international plane, it entertained ambitious missionary plans, and its ragged band of drunks, a downtrodden minority within the larger organization, didn't figure prominently in them. Internally, at the group level, there were issues of leadership, control, and religious dogmatism. The ensuing tension led to the Cleveland contingent of alcoholics in Akron breaking with the Oxfordites and meeting separately as a group which came to be known as Alcoholics Anonymous, after the title of their then recently published book. Akron itself soon followed suit.

Thus an entirely new entity was born, a bona fides spiritual Fellowship. Its 12 Steps are directed to a spiritual awakening and a right relationship with God as the basis for right living. Its 12 Traditions are designed to ground the Fellowship on spiritual principles under the sole authority of God. We come together as equals before him and before each other, without any intervening authorities, to help each other work a living faith.

In a misguided attempt to distinguish the religious from the spiritual, it is sometimes said in the rooms that "Religion is for those who are afraid of going to hell; spirituality is for those who have been there." This obviously plays on a stereotype of the religious person as one who is moved by fear of a punishing God. Some believers will no doubt see it as gratuitous put down of their faith. One may also detect a trace of smugness and self-satisfaction in the saying, implying as it does that we (alcoholics) are superior to them (the religious). There is as well the implication of a necessary conflict between religion and spirituality, that one cannot be both religious and spiritual.

The implication is false. Any acquaintance with the spiritual role that such religious figures as the Reverend Shoemaker, Sister Ignatia, and Father Dowling played in AA history will easily bear that out. So will any acquaintance with the larger spiritual traditions to which these figures belong. Religion and spirituality both proceed from the intuition that there is more to reality than what can be perceived by the senses. *The Spirituality of Imperfection*,[55] which uses storytelling to explore the relationship between spirituality and recovery, demonstrates that spirituality and religion historically have been tied to each other.

There is no such thing as a spirituality separate and apart from a religious tradition, whether Christian, Jewish, or that of any other faith. From the Desert Fathers in Egypt to Francis of Assisi, and from Julian of Norwich to the great Spanish mystics and Mother Teresa, the greatest exemplars of spirituality have also been deeply religious people.

Nevertheless, we in AA are in the spiritually healthy habit of looking for the good even in the flawed and the defective, and so we will find that there is some truth in the maxim under scrutiny. And the truth is that, when we drank, we alcoholics lived life so poorly and so recklessly so much of the time that we created our own hell right here on earth. We need to be rescued from that hell before we can be saved from any other. That is what AA promises to do when we come to the rooms and are shown a new way of living.

To the extent that its message doesn't address the reality of our daily lives in this world, to that extent religion doesn't speak to us and can't help us. Many of us alcoholics believe that God brought us to AA because we couldn't find him in such religion. Whether we came as rebels against our religious traditions or as believers still, AA gave us something we couldn't find in church, synagogue, or temple, no matter how often they might have preached about it in some of those precincts. This something was hope for today, the hope of release from the self-inflicted torment of our own everyday lives.

This is the message of Step 2. What makes us sober and restores us to sanity is not religion. It is God. We are restored to sanity by "a living Creator with whom we may form a relationship upon simple and understandable terms as soon as we are willing and honest enough to try" (Big Book, "There Is a Solution," p. 28). Those terms are laid out in the Steps. Through their spiritual principles we are led to a faith that works because it allows God's power to enter us, expel the drinking obsession, and make us whole.

AA sees religion as a friend and an aid to recovery. It encourages us to see where religious people are right and not close ourselves off to traditional religion, for AA cannot fulfill all of our spiritual needs. Many of us who do go back to church find that we are in fact able to "bring new purpose and devotion" (12&12, S12, p. 112) to our religious practices. We become contributing members, givers and not just takers, able to be of service to others.

But we also find another thing. We come to understand why, like the medical profession, the religious profession also failed the alcoholic. Religious leaders, not being themselves alcoholics by and large, have no practical understanding of alcoholism. They seem incapable of translating the principles of their faith into a spiritual program of specific and concrete steps through which God can work to bring the alcoholic to sobriety and a new life. The very concept may appear theologically suspect to them.

Nor do these leaders seem able to provide the fellowship environment necessary to grow in our relationship with God and neighbor in the everyday, practical way that AA does. Even when an attempt is made to create programs based on the 12 Steps, the organized and institutional aspects of religion exclude the practice of the 12 Traditions, without which the Steps cannot work in their fullness.

Hence many of us find ourselves going to church to worship and perhaps learn something about the Bible and the tenets of our particular religious group or tradition, but going to AA to work with others on how to stay sane and sober and put faith into practice on a daily basis. Church and religion seem to speak of a salvation that starts at some date in the hereafter; AA and spirituality speak of a salvation that starts today, in the here and now.

As regards religion, AA asks us to give up our prejudices and self-righteousness and not to dwell on its failures. But it doesn't ask us to make excuses for them. Neither attitude will help us to come to believe and grow in faith, for if one is lacking in humility, the other is lacking in honesty.

As regards the spiritual, AA asks us to focus on practicing those principles that can lead us to a right relationship with God, which if authentic will always lead us to a right relationship with neighbor, whatever his or her religion or lack thereof. Right relationship is the beginning and the end, our point of departure and our destination, and the very essence of our spirituality.

5

CROSSING THE THRESHOLD

Whatever our former views about God, religion, spirituality, or faith, they didn't work for us, or we wouldn't be in AA. We are here because those perceptions and understandings failed us. Our first task is to lay them aside. This is how we enter the process of surrendering unbelief in its manifold expressions. As we surrender unbelief, we will also surrender the character defects that enable it, replacing them with the virtues that make faith possible.

CAME TO BELIEVE: THE GRADUAL APPROACH

This is admittedly a slow process, and because of this, Step 2 takes a deliberately gradual approach. Key to this is the virtue of simplicity. We say that AA is a simple program for complicated people. When we drank, we had a tendency to complicate everything. This resulted in part from our need for control. We did not trust God and so could only feel secure if we held tightly to the reins. Unable to let go, we obsessed over things and tried to figure everything out. Rather than relieve our anxiety, this cluttered our minds with conflict and worry. Often we created a problem where there was none. Other times we compounded an existing problem and made things worse.

Complications also arose from a lack of humility, which is closely connected with a lack of simplicity. Incapable of recognizing our limitations, we would sometimes overreach and take on more than we could handle. Then, too, some of us thought of complexity as the mark of a superior intellect. We looked down on simpler folk as inferior, confusing simplicity—a virtue of heart and will—with simplemindedness—a defect of intellect. We affected an air of sophistication and liked to make "nuanced" arguments, which was nothing more than a way of avoiding straight answers to straight questions. The more we complicated things, the harder it became to live and the greater our failures and the emotional liabilities that followed in their wake.

We arrive in the rooms tangled up in a web of complexity and confusion. Our lives are unmanageable because our minds are unmanageable. We look at the Steps on the shades with those italicized words and the whole thing looks terribly complicated and impractical. Keeping it simple is essential if we are to act, and the gradual approach to Step 2 helps us to do that.

A POWER GREATER THAN OURSELVES

This is why Step 2 reads the way it does today. The original version stated: "Came to believe that God could restore us to sanity."[1] While rhetorically that sounds simpler, in practice it wasn't. Substituting "a Power greater than ourselves" was a way of breaking the Step into smaller, more manageable parts. "God" made a demand on our capacity for humility that many of us could not meet at this early stage. If we are powerless in the face of our alcoholic problem, then our hope lies in a Power greater than ourselves. We may in due time come to call that Power God, but we don't need to jump through that narrower hoop to get started.

AN OPEN MIND

In the same spirit of simplicity, we are told that AA doesn't demand we believe anything, that the Steps are just suggestions, and that Step 2 can be taken piecemeal. All we need is an open mind.

That can be an icebreaker because few will argue with the desirability of having an open mind. Modern society places a premium on progress and sees the acquisition of new information and greater knowledge as a means to achieve it. Open-mindedness is a necessity. Thus seen, open-mindedness is a secular virtue, one we took for granted we possessed when we drank.

A secular view of open-mindedness, however, carries a built-in exception where the virtue doesn't apply. That exception is God and the spiritual realm. For many of us being open-minded and believing in God were mutually exclusive.

This supposed open-mindedness was often no more than a self-serving ruse. It helped to camouflage our spiritual revolt. In the name of being open-minded, we could live as we wished and reinterpret the world to suit our selfish desires and ambitions. We didn't want what we dismissed as "traditional" and "old-fashioned" ideas to get in the way. By this, we meant of course religion, which obviously was for the closed-minded, the ignorant, and the superstitious. Eager to break "old taboos" and debunk "religious myths," we opened our minds to fashionable ideas and trendy rationalizations we found personally "liberating"—and we closed our minds to God. Slowly but surely, our heads filled with bits and pieces of philosophies and ideologies that poisoned our way of thinking, and we began to wither spiritually.

Step 2 seeks to reverse that process and restore us to spiritual health. It asks us to open our minds to the one thing against which they were tightly shut. Step 1 sets the stage for this next step in surrender: "Faced with alcoholic destruction, we soon became as open-minded on spiritual matters as we had tried to be on other questions. In this respect alcohol was a great persuader. It finally beat us into a state of reasonableness" (Big Book, "We Agnostics," p. 48).

Manifestly then, the practice of open-mindedness in AA is directed first and foremost to the spiritual life. Traditionally classified as an intellectual virtue, in AA open-mindedness is ordered first of all to the search for spiritual truth, which is seen ultimately as the foundation of all truth. Step 2 highlights its association with the virtue of humility, which also plays a role as an intellectual virtue in that it governs how we go about acquiring and imparting knowledge. If we think we know more than we do, we are not likely to succeed in either. Thus, in asking us to open our minds to the spiritual experience of other alcoholics, Step 2 is asking us to admit to the possibility that we know less than we suppose, and that perhaps, our ideas about God don't necessarily correspond to reality.

The gradual approach of Step 2 helps us to set aside the contentious attitude and adversarial pose that is typical of so many of us and which shuts our minds down. We alcoholics often tend to be overconfident and overrate ourselves. We are quick to speak and slow to listen. We are prone to raise objections, bring up issues, find fault, and complain. We like to argue, rebut, correct, and prove others wrong. We think we are better and know more, and we don't hesitate to show it. We want to have the last word. We want to fight.

These are all expressions of a spirit afflicted by competitive pride. If we are always ready to counter, then we are not really listening. If we are always right, then we can't keep an open mind. As we stop fighting, surrender, and "resign from the debating society" (12&12, S2, p. 26), our rebellious attitude loses its edge.

AA meetings are structured to help us do just that. If when we come to the rooms we listen and keep an open mind, we will lay ourselves open to Step 2 and the gift of faith will grow naturally within us. We will experience, gradually, the beginnings of a spiritual awakening and a new way of seeing things. Keeping things simple helps us to lend ourselves to this process.

Hence, we are often encouraged to look at the first phrase of the Step as working in three stages: came, came to, came to believe. First, we came to meetings and listened to the actual, real-life experience of men and women in recovery. Slowly, we broke out of the alcoholic fog and came to: "I woke up. I had to admit that A.A. showed prodigious results. I saw that my attitude regarding these had been anything but scientific. It wasn't A.A. that had the closed mind, it was me. The minute I stopped arguing, I could begin to see and feel." Then we came to believe: "Right there, Step Two gently and very gradually began to infiltrate my mind. I can't say upon what occasion or upon what day I came to believe in a Power greater than myself, but I certainly have that belief now. To acquire it, I had only to stop fighting and practice the rest of A.A.'s program as enthusiastically as I could" (ibid., p. 27).

TEMPORARY SUBSTITUTION

For the more defiant and close-minded among us, the temporary substitution of "a Power greater than ourselves" for God remains far too suggestive. That upper-case P raises multiple red flags, stirring up all manner of resentment about a deity we have rejected. The Big Book tries to deal with this by suggesting to these alcoholics that they use their own conception of God, an idea given full expression in the Step 3 notion of "God as we understood Him."

This is based on the assumption that the problem for the unbeliever has to do with his resistance to somebody else's conception of God. This is often the case with the ex-believer, but not always with the agnostic and the atheist. For the militant atheist in particular, the problem lies precisely in his own personal conception, which seals his mind tight against even the possibility of God's existence. The 12&12, written later, suggests a way out for this type of alcoholic. It is derived from the experience of those who have taken the method of substitution one step further and have made AA itself their "higher power," the initial letter of each word lower-cased to remove any hint of the divine.

The alcoholic is assured that "Even this minimum of faith will be enough. You will find many members who have crossed the threshold just this way. All of them will tell you that, once across, their faith broadened and deepened. Relieved of the alcohol obsession, their lives unaccountably transformed, they came to believe in a Higher Power, and most of them began to talk of God" (ibid., pp. 27–28).

Making AA itself the higher power works initially because as regards alcohol, those recovering in AA are by that very fact a greater power than the newcomer, who has yet to find a way out. The newcomer can surely place some faith in those who have found a solution. They will point her to its source and, seeing that it works for her too, she will come to believe.

This seems to work for most alcoholics. Yet "a Power greater than ourselves" had the potential to open up Pandora's box, or switching metaphors, to become a slippery slope. And it did. Before long we had "light bulbs and Third Avenue buses"[2] as stand-ins for God. Today it has become fashionable in some rooms to tell newcomers who bristle even at the mere mention of the G-word that they can make appliances, assorted inanimate objects, and anything else they fancy their higher power.

Granted, the intent is to defuse the issue. Yet this risks trivializing the concept of substitution and taking it out of its original context as a temporary, transitional measure. It is hard to see what it has to do with carrying the message, if the message is indeed spiritual. We may think that we are helping the newcomer keep it simple, but ours might come across as a message of duplicity rather than simplicity. Unwittingly, we may be acting as the purveyors of dishonesty, for we are not being straight with the newcomer, who is likely to see through the charade.

In AA a greater or higher power are not empty words or arbitrary linguistic constructs. They go to the heart of the program. "Lack of power, that was our dilemma. We had to find a power by which we could live, and it had to be *a Power greater than ourselves* (italics in the original)." The Big Book was written "to enable you to find a Power greater than yourself which will solve your problem" ("We Agnostics," p. 45). As an alcoholic notes in one of its stories ("Window of Opportunity," p. 421), no one is fooled by those words. Everybody knows what they stand for, and we cannot practice the principles by pretending otherwise.

We surrender to God because he is the "One who has all the power" (Big Book, p. 59), and in a limited and temporary way we can surrender to AA as a *channel* for that power. But we cannot surrender to a piece of furniture, which needless to say is neither the source nor the conduit of the power we lack and seek. We can honestly admit our powerlessness and our problem with the concept of God, but we cannot honestly pretend that an ashtray can help us. We can humbly acknowledge the possibility that our ideas about God are wrong and try to keep an open mind, but there is no humility in making a god out of our refrigerator. Frivolous substitutes will not help us practice the principles.

Coming to believe that a Power greater than ourselves can restore us to sanity is the first ray of hope in the Steps, the dawn of a new faith. But there is neither sanity nor hope in placing our faith in idols, animate or inanimate.

If honesty is of the essence for recovery as the Big Book insists, obfuscating on the issue of a Higher Power is doing the newcomer a disservice and setting a poor example. We AAs are said to talk from the heart and tell the truth. Why would we make an exception here? If we identify with his problem and yet came to believe anyway, any number of us can level with the newcomer and share our own experience.

Many of us have done just that, sharing our story along the following lines: "When I came to AA I didn't believe in God, but when I was drinking,

I sometimes acted as if *I* was God. That got me into a lot of trouble. I learned that the first step in AA is not so much to believe in God—it is to admit that *I* am not God. I have no power over alcohol and I need a Power greater than myself to get sober. That Power, whatever it is, was obviously working in AA, so it made sense to let AA be my higher power. When I did, I was able to work the Steps. Eventually, I came to believe in a Power higher than AA. I now call it God. All I had to do was to be willing and keep an open mind. Nobody knows how it will turn out for you. But you can start by leaning on AA. It works."

Being straightforward and transparent makes sense if we appreciate the spiritual nature of the principles underlying the Steps. To work Step 2 is to practice a set of principles. Key among these are the discipline of surrender and the virtues of humility, simplicity, willingness, open-mindedness, and honesty.

The goal of practicing these principles is that we may come to believe. We cannot achieve this goal by avoiding the issue of the spiritual and God, sacrificing principle for expedience. If we practice these principles, we will receive the gift of faith, and with faith, the gift of hope. Faith and hope not in a temporary substitute that sooner or later will wear thin and fall short, but in the God of the Promises, the one who can do for us what we cannot do for ourselves in the long journey of recovery.

BELIEF ON THE EVIDENCE: THE EXPERIMENTAL APPROACH

The atheist and the skeptic in general will find no conflict between faith and reason in AA. Ours is a rational program. We come to believe on the evidence, first of others' recovery, then of our own transformation. All we have to do is open our eyes to that evidence, and thereby open ourselves to receive the Power that will change us.

EXPERIENCE AND EXPERIMENT

As we saw earlier, Step 2 doesn't propose that we start our journey of faith by adopting a new philosophy or code of morals. Nor are we asked to adopt a set of religious doctrines. Instead, we are to conduct what in some ways is similar to a scientific experiment. In his address at the 20th Anniversary Convention of AA in St. Louis, Dr. Samuel M. Shoemaker spoke of how this works. An Episcopal clergyman, Shoemaker was the leader of the Oxford Group in NYC where Rowland H. and Ebby T. got sober and where Bill W. was initiated in the experience that eventually led to AA's formation. Says Shoemaker:

"The basis of that belief [in Step 2] was not theoretical; it was evidential. Right before us were people in whose lives were the beginnings of a spiritual transformation. You could question the interpretation of the experience, but you couldn't question the experience itself."[3]

This is a challenge to the atheist or skeptic who places a great deal of stock on empirical proof. He will find in the rooms of AA all the hard evidence he needs. The issue before him is not whether he will believe, but whether he will act. That is why we tell the newcomer "Utilize, don't analyze." The slogan is a call to simplicity. Still prone to complicate everything, the newcomer can get stuck in interpretation, succumb to "analysis paralysis," and fail to pick up the "simple kit of tools" (Big Book, p. 25) laid out before him.

The AA experience is that we could not think ourselves into right action when we drank, but that we can act ourselves into right thinking once we are in the rooms. Shoemaker explains that, when we have tried reason and reason has left us wanting, the time comes to make a decision and take action. The decision can be simple, such as entering into an experiment.

He sees the process as being more like science than like philosophy. Rather than reasoning things out using abstract logic, we choose a hypothesis. We then act as if the hypothesis is true and see whether or not it works. If it doesn't work, we dispose of it. If it is true, we will see the concrete results in our lives. That, he says, is how the experimental approach works. We first lean on other recovering alcoholics who have found a solution, and then we lean on the Power that stands behind them.[4]

To *experiment* with Step 2 is to give ourselves to the *experience* of Step 2. (The two words share a common root, meaning to try, proof, or test, and in Spanish and Portuguese, for instance, the same word is used for both ideas.) We let go of any resistance and practice the principles set out before us, following the example of those who give evidence of success.

Of course, the object of our experiment here is a subject, our own person, our innermost being, in fact. As such, there is a particular virtue related to honesty and simplicity that we need to highlight, for the experiment won't work without it. This is the virtue of sincerity.

To practice this virtue here means to give ourselves to the experiment with singleness of purpose and purity of intention. Contrary to the well-meaning but misguided slogan sometimes heard in the rooms ("Fake It Till You Make It") we cannot fake it or kid ourselves. If we participate in the process in all sincerity, the experiment will work, we will experience the results in our lives, and we will come to believe.

LOOKING AT AND LOOKING ALONG

We will no longer be looking at the experience of spiritual release in other alcoholics; we will be looking alongside that experience, for we will then be a part of it. C. S. Lewis makes a distinction between looking "at" and looking "along" which sheds light on the experiential nature of AA.5 We have been conditioned by a false scientism to believe that the external account of something is objective and "scientific" and trumps the account given from the inside, which is considered personal and subjective and therefore inferior.

The skeptic in AA looks from the outside at the spiritual liberation of those about him and scoffs: "They said God made these things possible, and we only smiled. We had seen spiritual release, but liked to tell ourselves it wasn't true" (Big Book, p. 55). He sees the results, but won't acknowledge the cause. He can't. He is on the outside, in the realm of conjecture and speculation. If he is intellectually resourceful and sufficiently jaded or cynical, he will come up with all kinds of clever explanations for what he sees, interpretations that try to debunk what those who have had the interior experience are telling him. Until he has the same experience himself. Then he will be looking along with his fellow alcoholics, living in a common solution by the grace of a common Power.

Having experienced a Power greater than ourselves from the inside, we can now "look at" with different eyes. For we need to do both, look at and look along. Being human, we live of necessity in an interpreted world, as Rilke says in one of the *Duino Elegies*. We need to interpret and analyze and try to understand if we are to continue to grow and make spiritual progress. But that comes later, and it is always grounded in experience. This is why looking along, from the inside, from personal experience, is the basis of sharing in AA meetings. We speak from experience, and when we don't, we are looking "at" and expressing opinions. We may be right or wrong, and others may agree or disagree, but they can't identify. To identify is to see in somebody else something that we realize is also in us, though up to the point of identification we may have had no consciousness of the fact.

Some of us go to meetings and read the Big Book and the 12&12 and come across the same concepts and ideas over and over again. But they are just words for us, characters on a page. Then somebody talks from the heart and shares her experience and all of a sudden some of those characters come alive and penetrate to our innermost selves. We identify and are deeply touched. The words reveal a significance we had never seen before. They become an experiential part of us and we are changed and perceive things in a new light.

Psychic Change and Spiritual Transformation

At the St. Louis Convention, Dr. Harry M. Tiebout, the psychiatrist who worked closely with AA, gives us a psychological take as he looks "at" the experiential/experimental process that Dr. Shoemaker describes.

Dr. Tiebout describes the typical alcoholic as having a "narcissistic ego-centric core" marked by an illusion of omnipotence which he must safeguard at all cost. He will defy God and man and fight for total control over his own life. The alcoholic must be, says Dr. Tiebout in language that evokes Ernest Henley's *Invictus*, the master of his fate.

The person who possesses these characteristics, he goes on to explain, finds it hard to accept God or religion. By demanding that the individual acknowledge God, religion challenges the alcoholic's very nature. But if the alcoholic is able to "*truly accept* the presence of a Power greater than himself, he, by that very step, modifies temporarily and possibly permanently his deepest inner structure and when he does so without resentment or struggle, then he is no longer typically alcoholic." And, concludes the doctor, if the alcoholic is able to "sustain that inner feeling of acceptance, he can and will remain sober for the rest of his life" (italics in the original).[6]

Here psychology and religion, or if you will spirituality, work harmoniously as well they should. Dr. Tiebout, having worked closely with numerous alcoholics, honestly and sincerely takes their explanation of their own experience at face value and tries to apply the tools of his trade to its understanding. His explanation of a "psychic" change is in harmony with AA's spiritual explanation. In this latter view, surrender and humility break down the intellectual and emotional barriers that keep us from accepting the presence of God in our lives and which block his grace from entering and transforming us. We open our minds and hearts to God, and he grants us the gift of faith.

Spiritual Awakening and Spiritual Experience

The gradual and the experimental approaches in Step 2 are not designed only for those who have a resistance to God. They address the reality that the average alcoholic in AA will come to a spiritual awakening in a slow and often painstaking process of recovery. This wasn't reflected in the original wording of Step 12, which read: "Having had a spiritual experience as a result of these Steps . . ."

Having had a sudden and dramatic spiritual experience that revealed God to him and instantly instilled him with faith, Bill W. proceeded to preach such an epiphany as the path to recovery. Others could not identify. He would soon discover that it was given to most alcoholics to have a spiritual experience only of "the educational variety," as William James had called it, meaning gradual and progressive as they interacted with others. That discovery led to changing "experience" to "awakening" in the second edition of the Big Book.

Even those who, like Bill, have been blessed with a sudden and dramatic spiritual revelation, will still find that more shall be revealed, as we are told in "A Vision for You." Even if our faith has come to us in a flash of light, it will grow only gradually as we grow in recovery. We are restored to sanity in the same manner.

Could Restore Us to Sanity

This brings us to the third part of Step 2. We have so far discussed the first two clauses: "came to believe" and "a Power greater than ourselves." The third, "could restore us to sanity," is less problematic than the others, but it can still raise issues, especially again as it regards the real spiritual nature of the Step.

In Mind, Body, and Spirit

Sometimes people in the rooms say something like "Well, I don't know about being restored to sanity, because I don't think I was ever sane to begin with." Some of us might identify with the sentiment. However, such a statement suggests an understanding of "sanity" and "restored" which falls short of its full import in the Step.

Sanity is sometimes seen primarily if not exclusively in terms of its mental, psychological, or clinical connotations. But sanity in AA is best understood in the larger context of recovery. Sanity is our progressive healing from our three-dimensional illness. The program provides no basis for interpreting sanity reductively in terms of mental pathology, clinical or otherwise.

This is clear in "How It Works" in the Big Book: "There are those, too, who suffer from grave emotional and mental disorders, but many of them do recover if they have the capacity to be honest" (p. 58). These alcoholics may not recover in the clinical sense, but their obsession can be removed and they can recover in a larger sense that includes but transcends the emotional and the mental.

The practical definition of insanity popular in the rooms and attributed to Einstein says that insanity is doing the same thing and expecting a different result. We are ill both in the doing and the expecting. We keep doing the same thing because our defects are ingrained in us and have the force of habit. We are powerless to do otherwise. We expect different results because we deny our powerlessness and thus deceive ourselves. We think that the repeated application of willpower will get us what we want.

In this we are irrational, i.e., we act contrary to reason. Irrationality is a mark of the active alcoholic, we are told in the 12&12, and we generally have no clue of the fact. Ironically, the more irrational we are rendered by alcohol, the more rational we claim to be, particularly in our denial of faith. This is especially so of the radical atheist, as we have observed. Taken to an extreme, G. K. Chesterton suggests, such rationalism can result in mental insanity: "The madman is not the man who has lost his reason. The madman is the man who has lost everything except his reason."[7] Such a person is un-balanced, literally. Nietzsche, who reasoned his way to lunacy, is a famous case in point.

Irrationality and rationalism are cut from the same cloth. They have the same self-deceiving motivation and effect. Because of this, as active alcohol-ics we couldn't see the full extent of our illness. The 12&12 cites "soundness of mind" as a definition of sanity: "Yet no alcoholic, soberly analyzing his de-structive behavior, whether the destruction fell on the dining-room furniture or his own moral fiber, can claim 'soundness of mind for himself'" (S2, p. 33).

Once sober in the program, we begin to make concessions to the reality of our disease. We admit to our physical and mental condition, our obsession with alcohol, our addiction to it. Fully admitting to our moral and spiritual bankruptcy is another story.

Our insanity lies deep in our ego, in the self-centered core of our being. From that vantage point, we appear to be in control. Reality is what we want it to be. We live in a fantasy world where the law of cause and effect doesn't apply to us. Ultimately, our insanity is the end product of our attempt to live as if there is no God. The disease extends to the emotions, the intellect, the will, the imagination, our conscience, the moral and the aesthetic sense, and all the God-given faculties that make us specifically spiritual, distinctly human.

AA retains the broad meaning of sanity which in the original word (Lat-in *sanus*) encompasses health, healing, wellness, and wholeness and covers the three dimensions of our existence: physical, mental, and spiritual. The idea is captured in an ancient motto: *mens sana in corpore sano*, a sound mind in a sound body.

Most of us alcoholics come to AA in a sorry state of physical health. Our obsession took so much of our time and energy that we cared little about eating well, getting enough sleep, or exercising regularly. Nor did we care for regular medical or dental check-ups. And then, we poured all that beer, wine, and liquor down our throat. What was that, if not a slow poisoning of our ourselves?

We were physically and mentally addicted and suffered the consequences in mind and body. We admit to that, and we wish to be restored in those areas. But the third part of Step 2 raises again the issue we would like to avoid. Sanity, narrowly interpreted to refer to the mental only in a medical sense, opens the door to reducing this part of the Step to a materialist viewpoint, enabling some of us to sidestep the spiritual dimension of our disease.

This medicalizing reductionism can be extended and is by some to include the whole program. In this view, recovery is only about mental health. We stop drinking and go to meetings for group therapy. Some may admit to the physical as well. We can easily make a religion out of diet and exercise. Health thus conceived can even become a new obsession.

But when we focus on mind and body to the exclusion of spirit, we are practicing another program, not AA. Bring your body and your mind will follow, some like to say in the rooms. No it won't. Not if it is closed to God. We are at first restored to sanity in the sense that the obsession to drink is removed. We are then at the dry point. We have recovered in that partial and limited sense. But the full sanity that Step 2 promises goes beyond that and encompasses a growing spiritual and emotional sobriety. And that growth comes with the practice of spiritual principles—disciplines *and* virtues. That is why a contemporary manual of psychology we referenced earlier calls itself a "manual of the sanities." Spiritual health is the foundation for both emotional and physiological soundness.

What are we to make of "restore"? No doubt many of us had lost our sanity narrowly defined long before drinking became a serious problem. But if we are alcoholic, the obsession developed and the "allergy" kicked in at a certain point in time, when we "crossed the invisible line." Whatever our mental, emotional, and spiritual condition before, it certainly worsened once we stepped through that threshold. Our health deteriorated in all areas. Our ability to think, feel, make decisions, tell right from wrong and connect with any spiritual reality, all became impaired.

To restore is to make possible the normal use of our mental and rational faculties, to recover our moral sense, our sense of beauty and wonder and the numinous, and to fully feel again, freed from the grip of obsession. To restore also means to revive, to revivify, to resuscitate. It means to bring back to life. For if we were physically and mentally impaired, we were also spiritually dead. As God restores us to sanity, our spiritual awakening begins. We are made whole in all three areas: mind, body, and spirit.

OF POWER AND GOODNESS: COULD AND WOULD

We now come to the "could" in the phrase. This little word implies a condition. God can and will restore us to sanity *if* we do something. That something is to seek him. This is the third of the ABCs we referenced earlier (Big Book, p. 60). In AA we seek God by taking "certain Steps" through which we are initiated and grow in faith in a direct, personal relationship with him. Step 2 is the start of our faith journey. It is a beginner's faith. It is faith as belief. It involves a largely cognitive process that results in "being convinced." The more fundamental and more distinctly spiritual element of faith as trust is not yet present.

In Step 2 we are focused primarily on one attribute of God, and that is his power. We see God's power at work in AA and this makes prospective believers out of us who are powerless and hopeless. But the trust issue is not yet resolved. Power can't be the object of trust; only goodness can. Power often inspires fear, suspicion, and resentment. Only when it serves goodness can it gain our confidence. And God's goodness, says AA, is expressed through the grace by which he restores us. Indeed, in grace, God's goodness and God's power are one. As we experience his freely given favor and transforming power, we start to trust God. We go from surrendering unbelief to surrendering our will and our lives to him. This is a greater step in faith and the next Step in the process of recovery.

As we proceed to Step 3 and go on to the ones that follow, we will find ourselves coming back to the fundamental questions raised by Step 2. How do we come to believe? What is the Power that is greater than ourselves? How does that Power heal us? And what is the sanity to which we are restored? Though some of us may not reflect much on these questions, in practice we cannot work the Steps without addressing them, for whether we are conscious of it or not, the answers we give inform the actions we take.

Step 2 rests on a set of specific principles, and these principles are practiced with reference to God. They have no other object. The discipline of surrender and the virtues of humility, simplicity, willingness, open-mindedness, and honesty are all geared to bring us to faith and hope in a Power that can make us whole. Their practice gradually whittles away and progressively displaces the attitudes and character defects that block our path to him: rebellion and defiance, intellectual pride and religious intolerance, willful self-deception and denial. They are the principles upon which we begin to build our relationship with God. We practice them in all our affairs because a right relationship with God is the necessary foundation of all we do as we grow in our journey of recovery.

Ultimately, in the larger spiritual sense, being restored to sanity means being brought to a relationship with God that we have never experienced but for which we were originally intended. It means becoming, one day at a time, the persons God created us to be. This is, ultimately, what we come to believe, our faith and our hope.

The 12&12 declares that Step 2 is "the rallying point for all of us," that whether we are believers, agnostics, atheists, or ex-believers, "we can stand together on this Step" (p. 33). Why is that? Isn't that counterintuitive, given the disparate nature of such a group? The reason is simple. What is needed to get started is not faith. What is needed is "humility and an open mind." Humility disposes us rightly toward God; an open mind disposes us rightly toward the AA message. Given these, "every AA meeting is an assurance that God will restore us to sanity."

STEP 3

"Made a decision to turn our will and our lives over to the care of God <u>as we understood Him</u>."

"There is only one key, and it is called willingness. Once unlocked by willingness, the door opens almost of itself, and looking through it, we shall see a pathway beside which is an inscription. It reads: 'This is the way to a faith that works.'"

—12&12. p. 34

STEP THREE

6

The Turning Point

With Step 3 we come to a turning point in our recovery. Our ability to work the rest of the Steps and to practice the principles of the program in all our affairs rests upon the choice that we make here.

In Step 2 we come to believe. In Step 3 we act upon that belief and enter into a relationship with God. Our decision to turn our will and our lives over to the care of God as we understand him opens the way to this relationship. This decision brings us to a faith that works and allows a Power greater than ourselves to restore us to sanity.

Steps 1 and 2 are preparatory Steps. Their objective is to bring us to the decision we make in Step 3. Sometimes called the "surrender Steps" as we previously noted, these three Steps take us through a process of spiritual and emotional change summed up in a simple AA formula: "I can't. He can. I'll let Him." We move from admitting we can't fix ourselves, to accepting there is a Power who can heal us, to allowing that Power to work in our lives. We come to acknowledge that Power to be God, as we understand him. We become willing to surrender our self-will and our self-directed lives, not only as regards the problem of alcohol, but in all that we do.

We work Step 3 through seven primary principles. These are the disciplines of surrender and prayer, and the virtues of humility, willingness, acceptance, serenity, and faith. The practice of these principles is directed toward one aim: entrusting our will and our lives to the care of God. By this we seek a spiritual transformation whereby, from a natural inclination to self, we become habitually inclined toward God. We move from self-seeking to seeking God and his will for us. We aspire to a spiritual condition best described by the Big Book as one of "complete abandon" (p. 59). Finding our rest in God, we find that we are free at last.

The Spiritual Malady, or the Nature of the "Ism"

We are not likely to understand much if any of this when we first come to this Step. In fact, the words of Step 3 may have no practical significance for us. For some, this may remain the case for a very long time. What does it mean to turn my will and my life over to the care of God? What exactly do I do? We find it hard to wrap our minds around what seems an elusive and improbable proposition.

The words don't register and we gloss over them. Sometimes we write them off as no more than a well-meaning ideal. In either case, we are not particularly inclined to work the Step. Still, we are told that the entire program hinges on this Step. We can hardly afford to ignore it, give it lip service, or put it on the shelf till a later date.

For some of us the difficulty with Step 3 arises from a continuing resistance to the spiritual nature of the AA program, much as we saw with Step 2. For others, it arises from a lack of clarity about the spiritual nature of the alcoholic disease.

When we say that alcoholism is a threefold disease, we can readily name the physical and the mental aspects of the illness. We say we suffer from an allergy of the body and an obsession of the mind. Using different language, we may say that we have a physical and a mental susceptibility to alcohol that makes us addicted to it. Yet when it comes to the spiritual root of our disease, we lack a single, transparent word like allergy, obsession, or addiction to refer to it.

Unable to name the spiritual malady, we are left with a vague and general notion of how it is that we are spiritually afflicted. At times we may even wonder whether there is such a thing as a spiritual disease, whether the concept amounts to no more than a religious interpretation of a problem that is just an emotional extension of the mental obsession, and which is best explained by secular psychology or one of the newer sciences that study the brain. The situation is analogous to that which we face concerning "these principles." They are essential to understanding and practicing the program, yet we can't quite get a handle on them.

Even if we concede that we might have some sort of a spiritual problem, and even if we are open to taking the steps the program proposes, a lack of clarity cannot but affect our practice. Many of us spend years with the uneasy feeling that we have not made that much progress with Step 3, that maybe we have not really "taken" it. When our recovery falters, we suspect it has something to do with that Step, but we can't put our finger on it. Some of us may figure that it has something to do with faith, but we are at a loss to see how and to translate that understanding into action.

So what *is* our spiritual malady? Ironically, the Big Book and the 12&12 never tell us, at least not in the sense of making a direct propositional statement that explicitly defines it. This is ironic because the entire program is expressly about the underlying spiritual disease and its solution. In AA's view, there is no cure for the physical allergy, and the mental obsession is lifted only as the result of a spiritual process. Emotional sobriety too is said to be dependent upon our spiritual progress. The spiritual is the part of the disease we can actually treat directly, through the program of action, and hence where we are called to concentrate our efforts.

Notwithstanding the absence of an explicit definition, the spiritual disease is amply described throughout the basic AA literature. Perhaps the fullest description is to be found in Step 3 in the Big Book. There we are pointed first of all to the source of the disease. That source is the self. "The first requirement" to start working Step 3, we are told, "is that we be convinced that any life run on self-will can hardly be a success." Why? Because "On that basis we are almost always in collision with something or somebody" (p. 60), even when our motives are good.

"How It Works" points specifically to selfishness and self-centeredness as "the root of our troubles." We are "driven by a hundred forms of [self-based] fear, self-delusion, self-seeking, and self-pity" (p. 62) which are the primary cause of all our difficulties. A quick check of the dictionary will yield an expanded list of these hyphenated liabilities: self-absorption, self-involvement, self-interest, self-importance, self-aggrandizement, self-promotion, self-indulgence, self-gratification, self-sufficiency, self-satisfaction, self-deception, self-justification, self-righteousness.

The "hundred forms" are all character and emotional handicaps based on self and willpower. Like most people, we "try to live by self-propulsion" and want "to run the whole show." Consequently, we are often at odds with others. The harder we try to have it our way, the more discord and conflict we create. In this the alcoholic is no different from most people, and so by implication the spiritual malady is not unique to him. But the alcoholic represents a special case, for he is "an extreme example of self-will run riot." No other expression in the Big Book better captures the magnitude of our problem. In a rare use of hortatory language, we are admonished that more than anything we "must be rid of this selfishness. We must, or it kills us!" (ibid.).

Until we came to the rooms and heard AA's description of our condition, many of us didn't regard ourselves as being particularly selfish or self-centered. Once sober, we didn't have too much difficulty admitting to the fact that, when we drank, we were mostly concerned with ourselves, our problems, our needs, our plans, our goals. But that is as far as we went.

We fail to appreciate the full dimension of the disease that afflicts the self because we tend to construe selfishness or self-centeredness narrowly and thus to minimize it. So deeply ingrained in us is what more broadly may be called selfness (an admittedly unfamiliar term), that most of the time we are not even aware of how it manifests in us, inwardly or outwardly. We who are exquisitely sensitive to the shortcomings of others—to *their* selfness—

are numb to our own disease. That is why it can rightly be said that we are spiritually dead, and why a spiritual awakening and rebirth is our only hope.

And why only God can bring that about, for "there often seems no way of entirely getting rid of self without His aid"(ibid.). Our own efforts, be they based on moral convictions, philosophical precepts, psychological analyses, therapeutic strategies, or—we may now add—knowledge of the latest crop of scientific theories about brain functioning, can by themselves do little to reduce our self-centeredness. We are as powerless to get rid of self on our own as we are to get rid of our alcoholic obsession. We need God's help.

We are powerless because self, selfishness, and self-centeredness are natural to us. They constitute a condition that is innate to us, as observing any two-year-old in action will make patently clear. These are not just things that we learn from our parents or society and that we simply outgrow as we develop and mature, as some schools of psychology hold. Nor are they the product of oppressive systems that we can be liberated from through revolution or social engineering, as the ideological heirs of Rousseau will never cease to claim. These things are inherent in the human condition. They are part and parcel of the self, a disease of spiritual and not social origin.

The self is by definition that part of the person that is conscious of its own individual being and identity as distinct from the world and other selves. Its very existence therefore holds the potential for its claiming a place of preference at the center of things. Self-centeredness is built into us.

Some philosophies and their psychological and sociological offshoots try to deny that self-centeredness is natural to us by denying the existence of human nature and locating the cause of the problem in family and society. Some religions try to do the same by denying the existence of the self and locating the problem in the illusion that there is any such thing to begin with. This of course flies in the face of common sense and ordinary experience. We don't speak of two-year-olds having illusions. Yet, they leave no doubt that they have a self and that the universe revolves around it. Rather than outgrow it, our inherent ego-centrism only deepens with age.

The evidence is undeniable. We are naturally inclined to self-centeredness. But to want to be at the center of things is to claim a place that doesn't belong to us as created beings. Spiritually understood, it is ultimately to want to usurp the place of the Creator. AA comes closest to naming our spiritual malady when, explaining the how and why of Step 3, it tells us that, "First of all, we had to quit playing God. It didn't work" (Big Book, p. 60). Playing God: therein lies our disease. That is the natural impulse to which we are all subject and often enslaved.

AA calls this the bondage of self (ibid., p. 63) and sees it as the end result of self-will. This understanding is consonant with the Judeo-Christian view of the problem. It explains why the first commandment says "Thou shalt have no other gods before me." The self is the first god we put before God. That is the cause of our downfall.

In C. S. Lewis's take on Genesis, this turning from God to self is man's original sin. Lewis sees it as the only sin possible for a being that God called "good" upon creating him. It is possible because "the mere existence of a self—the mere fact that we call it 'me'— includes, from the first, the danger of self-idolatry. Since I am I, I must make an act of self-surrender, however small or however easy, in living to God rather than to myself."[1] This is precisely the act that Step 3 calls us to make.

What St. Augustine termed original sin is the original act of self-will, a rejection of the creature's true position vis à vis its Creator. Our remote ancestors wanted, in the words of Lewis, "some corner in the universe of which they could say to God, 'This is our business, not yours.'" They wanted "to be like gods," to "set up on their own as if they had created themselves—be their own masters— invent some sort of happiness for themselves outside God, apart from God. And out of that hopeless attempt has come nearly all that we call human history—money, poverty, ambition, war, prostitution, classes, empires, slavery—the long terrible story of man trying to find something other than God which will make him happy."[2]

The result of this spiritual rebellion was that man was left on his own, as indeed he wanted to be. Cut off from God, says Lewis, his human spirit was also cut off from the source of its power and became subject to the laws of the natural order governing his material existence. Thus did man become powerless, his fallen will losing control over his body, his mind, and his psyche.

AA of course has no opinion on how the problem of self-will originated or how it led to our condition of powerlessness. But it does tell us that, in creating us, God gave us instincts, desires, abilities, and faculties that are good and necessary for our existence, and that it is when we are driven to exceed their God-given purpose that they cause us "great trouble, practically all the trouble there is" (12&12, S4, p. 42).

This, in different words, is the message of the Genesis account Lewis conveys. It explains why surrender is the essential discipline among the principles of the program, and the necessary remedy for our malady. Our natural tendency—our fallen nature—is to put self front and center, before God, before others, before everything. We reenact the fall time and time again. The consequences are the same. Without a willing surrender of self, we cannot connect with God, and severed from God, we cannot live in harmony with ourselves or with his creation. Everything, says AA, gets "out of joint." Or as Yeats puts it, "things fall apart," for "the center cannot hold" when we strive to usurp it.

It remains for us to connect the dots and see how, if surrender is the discipline essential to our cure, humility is the requisite virtue. To be humble is to have a proper view of myself, one that corresponds to the truth, to the reality of things. It is, as Bill W. keeps reminding us, to have the right perspective. This is first of all to recognize that, in the created order, I am the creature and God the creator. Second, it is to acknowledge and accept that I am a flawed human being, or a fallen creature, in theological terms. Before these two facts, a proper view of who I am is of necessity a low view. Only by adopting such a humble attitude can I find the willingness to surrender my natural propensity to succumb to "delusions of grandeur" (12&12, S5, p. 58), displace God, and take center stage.

The opposite of humility is pride, and so it is not surprising to find that AA places pride on the same level as self, referring to both equally as the source of all our troubles. We may recall that in its survey of the Seven Deadly Sins in Step 4, the 12&12 refers to pride as "the basic breeder" of most of our difficulties and the "chief block" to real progress. It is pride that leads us into "perverting or misusing" (pp. 48–49) our instincts and every gift God has given us, starting with the very self which constitutes our essential being.

Thus pride and self are of a piece and are often used interchangeably, self being understood as the sorry condition into which the self has fallen. Robert C. Roberts sheds light on the connection between the two when he writes that "[T]he systematic obstacle to every virtue is human selfishness . . . Ambition, scorn, envy, greed, injustice, cruelty: the disease in every case is traceable to the same source—the self's non-negotiable claim to be Number One in the universe."[3] Pride is the mark of self, the wellspring of self-centeredness. We are expressing the same idea when we say in AA that ego stands for "easing God out." When we do, we also ease the good out and let the darkness in.

We may say then that spiritual self-centeredness, arising from pride of self, is the spiritual malady from which we suffer. It is the self turning from God and becoming its own center, playing God with its own life and the life of others in countless ways both big and small of which most of us don't even have the slightest clue. This is, finally, what in the absence of a better term we sometimes like to call our "ism," the disease that is left after alcohol is gone and the source of every sin, of every character defect and emotional deficiency.

Self-improvement, or Self-surrender?

If self is the problem and God the solution, then the choice that Step 3 presents to us is as stark as it is simple: me, or God? Do we hold on to self-will and power our lives by it or do we surrender our will and our lives to God, conform our will to his, and live by his power?

The path that Step 3 beckons us to walk is a spiritual path, and the issue is whether we are willing to walk it. Our decision confronts us with two questions, questions that will arise again at every juncture as we work our way through each subsequent Step. Are we willing to grow along spiritual lines, or will we devolve to our natural selves? Are we willing to go to any lengths to realize AA's vision of a life that is happy, joyous, and free, or will we settle for half measures?

How we answer these two questions determines the kind of program we are going to work: a self-help program or a spiritual one. The self-help movement is generally a positive development, in its origins and inspiration a uniquely American phenomenon. The problem-solving impulse and the individual drive to raise oneself by one's own bootstraps are deeply ingrained in our culture.

Self-help is an expression of this. It is also reflective of dissatisfaction with medicine and religion, a response to the limitations and failures of the church and of secular psychology, psychiatry, and therapy as professional enterprises driven from the top by leaders and experts who are "looking at" our problem only from the outside, and not "looking along" with us, from the inside, from personal experience. AA is in part a product of this movement, has done much to inspire it, and continues to influence and be influenced by it.

But AA transcends self-help. It has to, because transcending self is precisely our objective. The concept of self-help is problematic for the alcoholic. It presents a temptation. That temptation is to fall back upon self-reliance. For us alcoholics, whose problem is deeply rooted in the self, a self-help program risks devolving into a self-determined and self-serving enterprise, directed and controlled by the self for its own inevitably selfish ends. The best of intentions cannot keep such an undertaking from giving way to the self-centeredness that characterizes our spiritual illness.

The AA solution goes beyond self-help to God-help, beyond self-improvement to self-surrender and a spiritual transformation of our being. In *Alcoholics Anonymous Comes of Age*, Bill W. describes it as a "regeneration . . . the loss of one's old life as a condition for finding a new one."[4] We are to become, not just a better version of who we were, but a new spiritual self in God. We suffer from a disease that cannot be treated with self-prescribed remedies or secular group therapy, but which requires divine intervention.

AA is a spiritual program and Step 3 is a quintessentially spiritual Step. It is the ultimate anti-self Step. Thus, in a very real sense, we cannot practice the 12 Steps of AA merely as self-help. They are not intended to be.

Step 3 is a watershed. We can reduce Step 1 to admitting that we are powerless only over alcohol. We can reduce Step 2 to believing in AA or in any number of human agencies or even whimsical material objects as the small-p power that can restore us to sanity, and we can further deconstruct it and reduce sanity to not drinking. But Step 3 resists deconstruction and reduction, however much we may tinker with those famous last words: "as we understood Him." For we still have to contend with the sixteen unequivocal words that precede those four. Any entity to whose care we can meaningfully turn over our will and our lives has to be, by that very fact, nothing less than God. The words are nonsense otherwise, and so is the Step.

Its spiritual implications make Step 3 an even bigger stumbling block than the preceding two for many alcoholics, and not only of the agnostic or atheist persuasion. This is where many of us get sidetracked and go off on a path that diverts us from the goal of working all of the Steps and practicing their principles in all our affairs.

Some of us retreat to Step 1 and eventually settle into two-stepping, self-help by another name. Others skip to the Steps associated with inventory-taking and making amends, viewing these as "realistic" action Steps where we can do something "really" practical and concrete. The problem with this attitude is its tacit divorce of the real from the spiritual. Presumably, Step 3 is not realistic, and by implication, the so-called realistic Steps are not spiritual. By not working Step 3 we rob these other Steps of their spiritual foundation. By trying to work these other Steps bereft of their distinct spiritual dimension, we deny ourselves the possibility of reaching the fundamentally spiritual objectives of each. The self-help impulse still drives our actions.

How searching, we may ask, how fearless, how moral can an inventory be which is self-motivated and self-directed? If I have not turned my will over to God, who is in the driver's seat? And how do I admit the exact nature of my wrongs to a God to whom I have not surrendered? Indeed, how can I even know their exact nature without God's guidance?

If I am bent on circumventing the spiritual, it is a foregone conclusion that I will bypass Steps 6 and 7, which for that very reason are rightly called the "forgotten Steps." Yet those Steps are precisely where my inventory and admission in 4 and 5 are meant to take me, for they constitute the next turning point in my journey: it is there that I abandon "a self-determined objective" and strive "for the perfect objective which is of God" (12&12, S6, p. 68). Shortchanging myself, I will not become entirely ready to have God remove the defects that separate me from him and my fellows. Nor will I humbly ask him to do so, for I have not laid the groundwork and built the necessary relationship with him in Steps 3 through 5.

Predictably, I come to the amends Steps spiritually handicapped, hanging on to my old natural self. My survey of the past, of my character, and of my relations with others is not based on the spiritual principles of the program and guided by God. Nor is the understanding I bring to Step 8 of the harm I have done to my fellows. I cannot approach them in a spirit of surrender in Step 9. Nor do I take God with me when I go to them. All of these deficiencies will undermine my work in Step 10.

Stumbling on to Step 11, I will find that I have failed to lay the groundwork for improving my conscious contact with God, and that praying for knowledge of his will for me and the power to carry that out amounts to no more than mouthing words, if I utter them at all.

If I have not been willing to work Step 3 and have remained reluctant to working the other Steps on a spiritual basis, I will come to Step 12 only to find that I have not had "a spiritual awakening as the result of these Steps," for such an awakening is their ultimate goal, and I have been resisting it all along.

Self-help will not bring us to a spiritual awakening. To work Step 3 is to move beyond self-reliance and even beyond dependence on AA, our home group, our sponsor, or any human power. We are not being asked for a limited acquiescence to finite human agencies that can dig us out of a temporary hole, but for a total and complete surrender to an infinite and eternal Power, so that as we move forward in our recovery we can "grow in the image and likeness of [our] own Creator" (12&12, S6, p. 63, *As Bill Sees It*, p. 159).

In the end, recovery can have no higher goal than this: to recover that resemblance and thus to be restored to our true, our real, our original self. It is how we can live in harmony with God and with all of his creation. It is how we can attain our full humanity.

HUMILITY CAN LEAD US TO FAITH

The surrender of Step 3 entails growing into a kind of faith that is largely foreign to us. Yet the Big Book tells us there is a principle that can lead us to such faith. This is the virtue of humility.

WILLINGNESS: THE MUSTARD SEED

We can start very small, with a quality we were called to draw upon in the first two Steps. This quality is willingness. We can look at it as the mustard seed of humility. AA considers it the key that unlocks the door to Step 3 and indeed to all of the Steps. We may do well therefore to probe a little deeper into this quintessentially AA virtue.

As a form of humility, willingness manifests itself initially as a preliminary internal shift away from self, a slight bowing of the will. We bend a little and leave ourselves open to at least exploring the spiritual course of action proposed by AA, before we are entirely convinced, before all our questions are answered and all our doubts resolved. It is a lowering of resistance, a letting down of one's defenses.

Perhaps we can understand willingness best if we consider the opposite quality in the alcoholic, the character defect to which it is a corrective. That quality is willfulness. A typical dictionary defines being willful as "to be obstinately bent on having one's way, to persist stubbornly in a self-determined course of action."

That describes just about most of us when we were active. Having come to AA and seen where our own way had gotten us, we became receptive to a different way of looking at things.

This receptivity is central to the virtue of willingness, as it is also to the closely related virtue of open-mindedness. In Step 1, pain and despair deflate our ego and break down our defenses. Out of sheer necessity, we become willing to listen to AA's message that we have a disease before which we are defenseless, that we are alcoholic. Still reeling from the pain, we become open-minded enough to listen to the spiritual solution AA presents in Step 2.

We may say that in these two Steps our receptivity has to do generally speaking with the processing of information and the acceptance of facts. This is primarily a function of the intellect. In Step 3, however, our receptivity goes deeper and engages the heart and therefore the emotions. To become willing in this Step is to make ourselves open to receive and accept, not so much information or facts, as direction and guidance.

Guidance and direction are not things we alcoholics take to very well. We are a defiant lot. Yet we displayed this modicum of willingness when, for all practical purposes, we made AA our Higher Power and began to follow the program's "suggestions," a term expressly intended to circumvent our resistance and ease us into a receptive mode. Thus we made a beginning on Step 3 and started to turn our will and our lives over to the care of a power greater than ourselves, at least as concerned our drinking problem.

This was a step away from sell-will, and potentially, a step towards God's will for us. "The willingness to grow," we read in *As Bill Sees It*, "is the essence of all spiritual development" (p. 171). Without willingness, no spiritual progress is possible. The reason for this is stated with utter simplicity in one of the Step 3 sayings: "Without God, I can't. Without me, He won't."

This slogan is based on an understanding of which we may not be necessarily conscious but which justifies AA's unusual stress on willingness as a key virtue. Implicit in the Genesis story cited earlier is the idea that God created the self with a free will, giving us the freedom to choose and thereby setting a limit on his omnipotence or power. He can't help us if we won't let him. For his grace to come into our being, we have to make ourselves ready to receive it and voluntarily let it in. Willingness gives God the necessary opening.

By practicing willingness, we become teachable, malleable, and open to change. We release our will and allow it to be drawn in a spiritual direction that we would otherwise not be inclined to follow; we acquiesce in acts of surrender which we would otherwise tend to resist.

Though it may initially be occasional, tentative, and lukewarm, when fully established as a virtue, willingness grows into a new attitude, one that is marked by a complete readiness to accept and act upon spiritual principles and to seek God's direction for our lives. We become spiritually and emotionally disposed toward God.

Willingness is the requisite point of departure to get started on our searching and fearless moral inventory in Step 4. It is equally instrumental to admitting our wrongs in Step 5, to God, to ourselves, and to another human. In Step 6 this willingness finds its highest expression when we become entirely ready to have God remove our defects of character. When we humbly ask him to remove our shortcomings in Step 7, we have laid the necessary groundwork for the next two Steps. We become willing to make amends to all those we have harmed.

Surrendering our will and our lives to God and practicing the principles of the program in all our affairs is the undertaking of a lifetime. We will never do it with perfection. If we could attain it, writes Bill W., he would define perfect humility as a complete willingness at all times and in all places to seek and do God's will (*As Bill Sees It*, p. 106). Yet we are gently reminded in "How It Works" that "We are not saints. The point is that we are willing to grow along spiritual lines" (Big Book, p. 160). To be willing is to say "Yes" to spiritual growth. It is to say "Yes" to God, even if we cannot always measure up and our efforts will inevitably fall short.

A New Pair of Glasses is an old book popular with some AAs. Its thesis is contained in its title. What AA gives us is a new way of looking at reality: God, the world, ourselves. It is a spiritual way, the way of faith. The book's message is grounded on the metaphysical principle cited earlier in Step 2: that things are received according to the mode of the receiver. The principles of the program change our mode of perception and valuation, our "concerns" and "construals," and with that our response to life. Willingness is the virtue that gets the process under way.

Willingness is the smallest shift in attitude that allows us to open the door to Step 3 and catch a glimpse of that sign which reads, "Here lies the path to a faith that works." Step 3 invites us to walk through that door and start upon that path.

RIGHT DEPENDENCE, TRUE FREEDOM

If we become willing to make the decision that Step 3 puts before us, we have taken the necessary step to grow in the kind of humility that is characteristic of this Step. This is "the place of entire dependence upon God." When God created the universe, writes Andrew Murray, he made us for a relationship of "unceasing, absolute dependence"[5] on him. Therefore, turning our will and our lives over to the care of God is an act of humility that responds to the real nature of things, to the order that he set in place. We are contingent creatures, dependent upon our Creator. We have no life apart from him, for, even if he remains unknown to us, "In Him we move and live and have our being."[6]

In the account of Genesis referenced earlier, C. S. Lewis explained his view that by rebelling and declaring his independence from God, man fell into a state of dependence upon natural forces within his material being and external environment that his spirit was then powerless to control. Thus separated from its source in God, man lost his freedom. Step 3 aims to reverse that process. With it, we begin to reestablish our dependence on God through the surrender of our will and our lives. In this surrender we recover our freedom.

Acknowledging and accepting our dependence on God is to Step 3 what admitting and accepting powerlessness is to Step 1. The two are closely linked. We are powerless because we are dependent. The power we need to live originates in a source beyond ourselves. If our humble admission of powerlessness is forced on us by circumstance in Step 1, in Step 3 humility is a deliberate choice and thus a true virtue. Our admission of dependence and our decision to surrender are freely made.

As with personal powerlessness, our instincts are innately resistant to the idea of dependence. This is not surprising. It is a symptom of our spiritual illness. We can't very well take center stage and take charge if we admit to any dependence. Blinded by pride, we claim a status of autonomy for the self that it cannot have. Indeed, personal autonomy has become for many of us the highest good, the *summum bonum,* in the language of philosophy. It is enshrined today in an unabashedly self-serving conception of choice. We claim a false intellectual and, above all, moral independence, with self the sole arbiter of right and wrong.

And so we are willing to depend on AA when it comes to our problem with alcohol, but that is as far as we will go. As concerns the rest of our lives, we will decide for ourselves. Independence is of course another word for power. Our admission of powerlessness over alcohol in Step 1 remains that, an admission of powerlessness over alcohol. In Step 2 we still cling to intellectual self-sufficiency, coming to believe in a power that is greater than ourselves, but certainly no greater than a "group of drunks," or whatever power we can "plug" into at will, on our own terms and for our own ends. Any "god" will do, so long as we pull the strings.

Before we came to AA, we had plenty of experience practicing such moral and intellectual independence. And if we are honest with ourselves, where did that lead us if not to the bottle? Did we not then lose any ability to choose? Were we not then left at the mercy of our addictions? At the end of the road the fiction of personal independence led to the reality of our dependence on alcohol. As booze rendered our lives more and more unmanageable, our dependence spread to other areas. We became increasingly, sometimes even pathologically, dependent on others. How many times did we not have to rely on others to bail us out and rescue us from ourselves?

We experienced many such forms of wrong or faulty dependence, says the 12&12 as it acknowledges why "the word 'dependence' is as distasteful to many psychiatrists and psychologists as it is to alcoholics" (S3, p. 38). But what AA claims is that wrong dependence, by which is meant essentially *emotional* dependence, is the result of a lack of right dependence, by which is meant essentially *spiritual* dependence, right reliance on God.

Leave out the spiritual and "dependence" has no other reference point but, at best, weakness, at worst, neurosis and pathology. But AA sees it differently. In the spiritual life, it says, a predisposition to self-reliance and self-sufficiency leads inexorably to pride and pride to ordering my affairs, not in accordance with an objective moral order, but in accordance with the imperative to serve myself.

In our striving for a false because self-seeking autonomy, we end up becoming dependent on the very things we hope will make us independent. We think independence will make us free. What happens in reality is that we become subject to our instincts, feelings, disordered emotions and desires, our obsessions, compulsions, and impulses. Being thus at the mercy of our drives and passions, we become dependent on those things which the world tells us, and we readily believe, will satisfy them. But as many of us discover, these forces in us can never be satisfied. We always want more, and so dependence becomes dependency becomes addiction.

The truth is that there are very few areas, if any, in which we can achieve any sort of independence, and even then not for very long. A wave will sooner or later roll in and sweep away any castle we build upon the sand.

We came into this world as dependent beings and we will leave the same. In between the first cry and the last sigh, we get to choose between two forms of dependence. If we don't choose God, we choose self. And if we choose self, our choices will always be determined by people, places, and things, even when ostensibly we are doing the choosing. This remains the case even when, in a final and futile assertion of pride, we indulge in the ultimate act of selfishness and opt to end our alcoholic lives by our own hand.

The spiritual life is full of paradox. We saw in Step 1 that strength comes out of our admission of weakness, and that by accepting powerlessness over alcohol we became the recipients of a power that removed our obsession to drink. So it is with Step 3. The 12&12 says of the AAs who were first tested in WWII that "their dependence upon a Higher Power worked. And far from being a weakness, this dependence was their chief source of strength" (p. 39).

Out of right dependence on God comes true independence from the forces in ourselves and in the world that would otherwise hold us in bondage. In freely choosing to turn our will and our lives over to the care of God, we begin to regain the freedom we had long lost.

The Question of Trust

The essence of humility in Step 3 is acknowledging and accepting our dependence on God. The essence of faith is trusting God.

Reason and our personal experience as active alcoholics show us the rightness of dependence on God rather than self. But knowledge, whether intellectual or experiential, does not automatically translate into practice. We still need to act to humble ourselves and let go of our natural desire to rely primarily on ourselves, keeping God out of our lives or calling on him only when our backs are against the wall.

Reason and experience can also bring us to believe in a God who can restore us to sanity. But he can only do so if we turn our will and our lives over to his care, and we won't do that unless we have the faith to trust him. The decision we need to make in Step 3 is not a decision of the head, but the heart. It is a decision that from now on we are going to trust God and rely on him completely.

The agnostic or the atheist who has assented to the proposition that God exists and who has now become a believer in this preliminary and rudimentary sense is still confronted, like all believers, with the central question of faith: the question of trust. The issue is no longer the reality of God, but his reliability.

We saw in Step 2 that faith is a fact of ordinary life and not just the province of religion or the spiritual. We unconsciously make numerous acts of faith every day. So does the scientist in his research and experiments. We need faith to function. Dependence is equally a fact of life and inherent in the human condition. The connection between the two is obvious: we are necessarily dependent on others; hence we need to rely on and trust them.

Yet our faith in others, our trusting them, cannot be based on need or dependence alone. We have to have reasonable grounds to justify our trust. Faith properly understood is trust that is warranted, whether by reason, authority, or experience. On these grounds, we trust that something is probably true even though absolute proof or certainty may be lacking and indeed may be impossible to achieve. Without such warrant, trust is arbitrary and devolves into wishful thinking or naiveté. Rather than reflecting the virtue of faith, such trust is more likely to reflect the vice of gullibility, a lack of discernment and prudence.

Trust is essential to any relationship. It is one of the first casualties of our alcoholic drinking, and often the hardest to remedy. We frequently violated the trust placed in us by those close to us. In some cases, we may never be able to restore that trust, no matter how much we may have changed and how sincere and thoroughgoing our amends may have been.

That hard reality notwithstanding, one of the results of practicing the principles of the program in all our affairs is that in due season we do grow into trustworthy individuals. There comes a time when people recognize that and find reason again to trust us: relatives, spouses, children, friends, employers.

We also become trusting individuals ourselves. As we take personal inventory in Step 4, some of us may discover that an inability to trust constitutes one of our shortcomings. Even when there are reasonable grounds for doing so, we may find it difficult to trust others.

This may be the result of that threefold emotional handicap of fear, anger, and resentment. We may have been on the receiving end of betrayal, and having had our own trust violated, we find it hard to trust again. Or it may result in part from pride. We don't trust because we don't want to appear dependent and indebted to others, lest we be perceived as weak and looked down upon or taken advantage of. Lacking humility, we lack a proper, which is to say a spiritual, appraisal of our worth. Ironically, the result is that we make it dependent on other people's opinions and actions.

But a lack of trust may also reflect another character trait, one that stands directly against the virtue of faith. This is the vice of suspiciousness. Those of us who are afflicted with this defect tend to suffer from an ingrained, chronic questioning of other people's motives and intentions. We are prone to suspect and judge their character and integrity. We find it hard to give them the benefit of the doubt. They always have to prove themselves to us. We may be so blinded by distrust that we cannot see them for who they are. This leads us to adopt a self-protective shell and maintain a certain emotional distance from them, so that our relationships remain shallow and tentative. In a love relationship in particular, this precludes any real intimacy.

Having a suspicious attitude may also affect our relationship with God. We may have trouble trusting God because an inability to trust is part of our character and emotional makeup. Such appears to have been the case with a figure that has gone down in history as doubting Thomas. As one of his disciples, Thomas had had a long and intimate relationship with a man who had given him ample reason to trust his word. This man had often predicted that he would die and rise again from the dead. When this prediction was fulfilled, Thomas's closest friends testified to the fact. Thomas even saw this man standing in front of him and heard him speak. Yet he demanded still more proof.[7]

Thomas was suspicious beyond a reasonable doubt. Doubt is a necessary part of faith, which believes what reason dictates to be true based on the available facts. Yet, suspiciousness can lead even the believer to interpret facts in a manner that excludes or undermines faith. Habitually prone to question and doubt, the suspicious person will always find a reason not to trust the evidence.

The problem with this person is not primarily intellectual, as it is with the skeptic, but deeply emotional. It is more than just doubt. Even if we are not suspicious by nature, doubt will always arise. Accepting this truth led C. S. Lewis to an understanding of faith as a necessary virtue. Faith, he tells us, is in this sense, "the art of holding on" to those things once accepted by your reason "in spite of your changing moods."[8]

Mood changes are a fact of our emotional life, for it is intrinsic to the emotions that feelings are in flux (hence "e-motion"). As our moods change, we will be assailed by doubt sometimes, no matter how firm the rational grounds for our faith. Hence the need to develop faith as a virtue to give us anchor. As a virtue, faith requires training. Only by practice can it become a habit, a stable disposition capable of weathering the instability of our moods as well as of changing circumstances. Like other virtues, faith can give shape to our emotions. Hence, one of the signs of our spiritual progress as we gain in faith is the freedom we achieve from frequent and wild mood swings and an increased emotional stability.

If trust is fundamental to any relationship, it is all the more so when it comes to our relationship with God. For in our relationship with God we are called to practice a trust that is total and unconditional. Yet this call is problematic. If we don't know God—and most of us don't have a sense that we do—how can we trust him? Moreover, how can we trust a Power that is infinitely greater than ourselves, a God that ultimately has absolute power over us? We saw this problem with Step 2. We noted there that, by and of itself, power inspires not trust but distrust, and beyond that fear, resentment, and rebellion. Power can be trusted only when it is in the service of goodness.

This is the issue that we now face in Step 3. It is an issue that goes back to one of the most dramatic and problematic examples of faith found in the Bible or anywhere in literature. Asked to sacrifice his beloved son Isaac, Abraham makes a decision that in terms of recovery we could rightly characterize as a 3rd Step: he turns his will and his life over to the care of God and proceeds to carry out his instructions.

We have here a twofold dilemma. God had made a promise to Abraham that could be kept only if Isaac lived. At the same time, the promise could only be kept if Abraham trusted God fully, for God could not work through a man who insisted on doing things his way, as Abraham had repeatedly shown in his relationship with God. Now on Mount Moriah, Abraham was being asked to let go absolutely. And he did, surrendering all at last.

The story of Isaac's sacrifice has made more atheists out of us than probably any other in the Bible. How could God be so cruel? But seen from a Step 3 perspective, things take on a different light, for it then becomes evident that the story is telling us of two very different conceptions of God, and linking the decision in the first part of the Step to the understanding in the second.

At first, we hear the voice of a God who had haunted mankind throughout the ages and who was worshipped still throughout that part of the world, a far and distant and omnipotent deity who was greatly feared and who needed to be appeased by human sacrifice. This God, the God of the Universe (*Elohim*) is the one who calls on Abraham to kill Isaac. But then, through an angel, we hear the words of a God who is caring and loving and intimate, and this God, the Lord (Yahweh), is the one who stays Abraham's hand and spares the boy.

The moral of the story is that God is a moral God. With Abraham and the Hebrews man's sense of the spiritual and his sense of the moral come together for the first time in a new understanding of God. He is a God of power and might and also a God of goodness. We are not "as flies to wanton boys," where the gods "kill us for their sport," as a despairing Gloucester and many of us would come to see it on our journey away from faith.

Thus while we usually focus on Abraham's trust in God, there is another side to it. Because Abraham trusted God, God was able to show Abraham, and through Abraham all his descendants, that God was trustworthy. The story is about God's trustworthiness as much as it is about Abraham's trust. The latter has its warrant in the former.

Through this and many other stories, Scripture carries a message that undergirds and gives Step 3 its justification: if we place our faith in God, if we trust him, he will be faithful to his promises. "They will always materialize" (Big Book, p. 84).

In Step 3 we are asked to trust a God who has proven to be trustworthy. At the outset we are offered no evidence but the experience of other AAs whose call for help God has faithfully answered. In due time, if we work the Steps, this evidence will be confirmed by our own experience. Our own recovery will stand as proof.

One of the reasons some of us may have trouble with Step 3 is simply that we fall short of fully trusting God. We may have had experiences in our own lives, tragic ones perhaps, that have resulted in our questioning God's goodness. Or we have looked at pain and suffering in the world, whether originating in nature or the acts of men, and concluded God could not possibly be good if he allows such evil to take place. Or we may be psychological heirs of Thomas.

The inability to trust God accounts for the failure of many of us to practice these principles in all our affairs. We may not consider ourselves agnostic or atheist, and may even believe in God and attend church regularly. But not trusting God wholeheartedly, we cannot surrender to him completely. We practice the spiritual principles of the program without conviction and slip into the default modes of self-help and two-stepping.

We become practicing deists. God is up there and I am down here, on my own As we saw in Step 2, the God of the deist may be a God of power, but he is not a God of goodness: he created the world and then left it to its own devices. He is indifferent to my plight, and hence irrelevant to my life. He is a Power greater than myself all right, but he cannot restore me to sanity.

As We Understood Him

This brings us to the question of "God as we understood Him." If we are going to go beyond believing in God's existence to personally trusting him with our will and life, we have to have an understanding of God that would allow us to do that. Step 3 points us toward this needful understanding. It says that we surrender our will and our lives to the *care* of this God.

Certainly "to the care of" suggests that we are to understand God as a God who cares. In specifically practical terms, a God we can trust to do what we came to believe he could do: to restore us to sanity. We are being asked to take a step toward greater faith, from passive belief that he *could*, to active trust that he *would*.

God as we come to believe in him in Step 2 is a God of power and might. With Step 3 we begin to gain a view of him that ultimately finds its highest expression in AA's understanding of a "loving God" who restores and guides the individual alcoholic, protects and preserves the Fellowship, and informs the conscience of the group. A God thus understood we can trust completely. We can ask "His protection and care with complete abandon."

Growing in this understanding is a process, and it works if we willingly give ourselves to it. Again, willingness is the key. Hence AA makes every conceivable effort to help us become willing, to open every possible door and close none. This accounts for the expression "as we understood Him."

If we take a close look at the phrase "to the care of God as we understood Him," we may discern a tension, a semantic dissonance even, between the set of four words to each side of "God." One set seems to suggest a specific understanding of God; the other appears to pull back from such specificity.

The tension reflects AA history. We know that Step 3 did not originally include "as we understood Him" to qualify God. The phrase was appended later, and if it appears conceptually out of harmony with "to the care of," that's because it is.

If, as has already been noted, my understanding of God is that he is an indifferent and distant power, then I cannot possibly turn my will and my life over to his "care," for I don't believe that he does. The same applies if my understanding of God is that, let us say, he is only a figment of people's imagination and he doesn't really exist; or that he only wants to punish me and send me straight to hell; or that he is an It, an impersonal force, energy, or some other entity in which the attribute of caring cannot possibly inhere. My understanding of God has to be compatible with, or at least amenable to, the idea that somehow he cares about me for me to surrender to him. Otherwise I can't and I won't.

That is why the program insists on my letting go of the old ideas I had when I drank. If they didn't work then, they won't work now. I can't hold on to my old understanding of God and practice Step 3 when that understanding precludes my surrender. Giving up that old understanding is precisely what the Step is first asking me to do. The dissonance introduced by "as we understood Him" is therefore very real.

As with "a Power greater than ourselves," the addition of "as we understood Him" was a compromise between most AAs (half of whom, we might recall, started as atheists and agnostics) and a handful who had not yet come to believe and objected to the use of the word God. The modifying clause made it possible for these AAs to hold on to their individual understanding of whatever power they thought had enabled them to gain sobriety. The modification also threw the door wide open to any alcoholic who had a desire to stop drinking, regardless of religious belief.

Ironically, the compromise was a throwback to the more religious Oxford Group. Sam Shoemaker had used a similar expression to signal the group's openness to all and encourage those who had a problem with religion to start with whatever faith they could summon. The idea was to surrender as much of ourselves as we could to "as much of God" (sometimes he would say "Christ") as we understood.[9] This earlier formulation harbored no ambiguity. It presupposed a benign disposition. The understanding lent itself to the surrender, which was in turn proportionate to the understanding. The will posing no obstacle, continued growth was a matter of putting one foot in front of the other along an accepted if not always clear path.

Similarly, for the believing AAs at least, "as we understood Him" was a way to encourage the newcomer to get started on the spiritual journey and a relationship with God. No need to delay action because there are some things about God we don't understand (there will always be such things), or because we have objections to certain religious tenets, or because we have had a bad experience with religion, or because we don't like some religious people. We keep it simple and start where we are. All we need is a little bit of humility and the willingness to lay aside our old ideas and prejudices and give the Steps an honest try.

This was a grand compromise, crucial to the spread and growth of AA. It seemed totally warranted. Given a willing attitude, experience had shown that, at the outset, "our own conception of God," however "limited" (Big Book, pp. 46-47), was sufficient to get started on the spiritual road and make our first conscious contact with him. As we were assured, God doesn't play hard to get.

This was a temporary measure, and in time, we would find ourselves "accepting many things which then seemed entirely out of reach" (ibid., p. 47). Many of us would come to the requisite understanding of a loving God who would relieve us of our alcoholism and restore us to health, and in time we would "call Him by name" (12&12, S12, p. 109). We sometimes witness how this works when an AA shares in the rooms, and giving thanks to her Higher Power, she then proceeds to add: "whom I choose to call God." It is a choice she might never have made had the door not been left open.

This was after all what had happened to most of the AAs. Nearly all of the 100 or so alcoholics who participated in the work leading to the final version of the 12 Steps and the publishing of the Big Book had come to share a common understanding of God in just this fashion.

This was an understanding forged in the crucible of their common experience. Starting out as nominal believers, ex-believers, agnostics, and atheists (invariably of Christian backgrounds), they had gained a common view of the alcoholic problem, and had "discovered a common solution" (Big Book, p. 17). This solution was a spiritual experience leading to a direct relationship with a God who has discernible attributes and works in discernible ways. Their understanding of God in terms of these attributes and ways suffuses the Big Book and the 12&12 and gives the Steps and the Traditions their spiritual foundation.

Thus "as we understood Him" stands in its seeming ambivalence as a twofold invitation: Start with your own understanding of God, just as we did, but be open to growing in that understanding, just as we were, for therein lies our common solution. If it worked for us, it can also work for you.

Reaching out in this manner shows an attitude of goodwill and generosity typical of AA, virtues in their own right both of the program and of the Fellowship. In this same spirit, many reassurances can be found in the Big Book and the 12&12 that are designed to relieve any fear of dogmatism of whatever sort. There is simply no intention of imposing a particular understanding of God on anyone.

Yet it is necessary to stress that these reassurances reflect no ambiguity or ambivalence about how God is understood in the two basic texts of AA. Any notion to the contrary is dispelled from the very outset in the foreword to the First Edition of the Big Book, where in a statement already cited, we are told that the main purpose of the book is "to show other alcoholics *precisely how we have recovered*" (p. xiii, italics in the original).

The book proceeds to do just that. "Here are the Steps we took," it says (p. 59), listing a series of specific actions that carry implicit and explicit understandings of God and that are said to produce specific results attributed to this God's agency. Having explained the alcoholic problem and its spiritual solution on the basis of these understandings, the Big Book then goes on to relate how "we"—the early members of the Fellowship—acted on them.

This describes a process that unmistakably centers on establishing and growing in a relationship with this God and relinquishing those attitudes, beliefs, and understandings—the old ideas, the selfish concerns and self-centered views—which close us off from him. Through it we come to a spiritual awakening and receive the power to live a sober life.

That these understandings of God are seen as instrumental in AA recovery is evident throughout the Big Book narrative. They are later reaffirmed in the same straightforward manner in the exposition of the Steps and Traditions in the 12&12.

Telling characterizations of God abound in both texts. God is called by the name of "Providence," for he will remove our obsession to drink and supply what we need to live a sober life. The name links God to the story of Abraham cited earlier, for there God "provided" a ram as a substitute for Isaac, whose life he spared. Providence has since been synonymous with God's care, his loving guardianship of his children, and his divine direction. Hence "to the care of."

This God is understood as a supernatural and transcendental entity, above and beyond nature and the material world, a "Power greater than ourselves," a "Higher Power," an "Infinite Power," a "Supreme Being," a "Spirit of the Universe," a "living Creator," our "Maker," an "All Powerful, Guiding, Creative Intelligence" who brought all things into existence and who sustains them.

He is also an immanent being, the "Great Reality" that can be found "deep down within us," an intimate personal God of "Infinite Love" who can dwell in us and transform our lives. He is a purposeful God who has a "will" for how we are to live, a God of "grace" who offers himself to us freely and who, through such gifts as faith, hope, serenity, courage, wisdom, and the other virtues, can infuse us with the power to know and to do his will, for our good and in service to others. He is the "Father," and we his children. If we honestly seek him and relate to him rightly, in a spirit of humility, we will become conscious of his "Presence" in our lives, and he will restore us to health and do for us what we cannot do for ourselves.[10]

Whatever differences the early AAs had among themselves, most shared these various understandings of God. These are manifestly theistic. They are summed up in the one proposition on which they all strikingly agreed: they had gained access to and believed in a Power that had "in each case accomplished the miraculous, the humanly impossible" (Big Book, p. 50).

God thus understood is the God to whom we surrender in Step 3, initiating the relationship that will revolutionize "our whole attitude" and give us the new outlook on life and the new motivation that come with a spiritual awakening.

Thus, as C. S. Lewis writes, "we trust not because *a* God exists, but because *this* God exists,"[11] a God with a certain character and divine attributes which give us reasonable and rational grounds for placing our trust in him and believing that he will do what the program promises he will do. To this God we can entrust our will and our lives completely.

Taken in the spirit in which it is offered in the Big Book and the 12&12, "as we understood Him" can serve its intended purpose of widening the path to a relationship with a healing and restoring God. It has for countless alcoholics. Many of us would not have stayed in the rooms long enough to discover the loving God AA talks about and would have ended up in prison or dead.

Yet it is also true that, taken in a different spirit, "as we understood Him" can have the unintended effect of impeding our surrender in Step 3 and diverting us from the path to a relationship with God. We can, explicitly or tacitly and even unconsciously, interpret the expression to mean that one's understanding of God is irrelevant to recovery. Or we can take it to mean that the early AA's understanding of God as reflected in the Steps and the basic texts has little or no bearing on how the Steps are worked. Or we can use it as a rationale to flatly deny that AA offers any particular understanding of God. When we do any of these things, the first sixteen words of Step 3 become gibberish, and so does much of the rest of the program.

Yet there are times when some of us do all of them. An expression meant to forestall dogma becomes itself a dogma and a new form of denial. Thus it is argued that AA has nothing to say about God except "as we understood Him." Isolated phrases from the Big Book and the 12&12 (the reassurances referenced earlier) are cited to support this view. So are some later citations from Bill W., particularly a 1966 letter quoted in *As Bill Sees It*, in which Bill writes: "When we say that A.A. advocates no theological proposition except God as we understand Him, we greatly simplify A.A. life by avoiding conflict and exclusiveness" (p. 162).

Of course, Bill is absolutely right. As a program, AA certainly does not "advocate" any theological propositions: we are a program of attraction, not promotion; a spiritual program, not a religious one. And as part of the Fellowship, we AAs can believe as we please: the only requirement for membership is a desire to stop drinking (Tradition 3). Nor do we discuss religious doctrine or dogma: we share our experience, strength, and hope.

Clearly, Bill is stressing something we already know but which still bears stressing: that AA doesn't tell anybody what to believe regarding God. But he's not trying to deny the obvious: that as a program, AA is built on particular understandings of God. As we have stated, this is evident throughout the first 164 pages of the Big Book where that program is laid out, and throughout the 12&12 where it is unequivocally reaffirmed. And the program found on those pages *is* the AA program; there is no other.

So while AA advocates no theology, the program does rest on certain understandings of God, and these of necessity do have their theological connections and underpinnings. All of the characterizations of God cited above do.

That God can restore us to sanity; that he cares about us and can be trusted with our will and our lives; that he will listen to our admission of wrongs and forgive our derelictions; that he can remove our character defects along with our obsession to drink; that he is accessible to direct and conscious contact; that he has a will for us and can give us the knowledge and the power to carry that out; that he can effect a spiritual transformation in us and grace us with such gifts as peace, love, and joy—these and other understandings of God's attributes which are integrated into the Steps and the principles therein all have theological links and foundations.

Like "religion"—and for similar reasons—"theology" has become suspect among us. We use it emotively as a term of reproach, seeing it narrowly and prejudicially as synonymous with dogma and sectarianism. But theology (Greek *theo* for "god," *logo* for "study"), formally defined as the systematic application of reason to the understanding of God, is involved in any considered statement we make about God, even if the statement is that he doesn't exist. In this we are all theologians, just as we are all philosophers, espousing particular views of God and life.

Of course, being flawed and imperfect human beings, reason can always lead us astray, as we discussed in Step 2. But this is true of any discipline requiring the use of the rational faculty, not just theology. If through our recovery experience a "loving God" becomes part of our understanding, we are following in the footsteps of countless men and women who throughout the long march of history have arrived at that same understanding through the application of their God-given reason to similar experiences, in their own personal journey as well as in that of others who preceded them.

The early AAs are counted among this number. Bill saw faith and reason—joined in love—as the ground of spiritual practice and growth. "Theology helps me," he wrote, "in that many of its concepts cause me to believe that I live in a rational universe under a loving God, and that my own irrationality can be chipped away, little by little. This is, I suppose, the process of growth for which we are intended" (*As Bill Sees It*, p. 294).

At its most rudimentary level, theology is what we do when we try to think through and understand our experience of God. And our experience does need to be understood, if we are to integrate, consolidate, and grow further in it. Again, we need to look "at" as well as "along." It is inherently human to want to understand, things in general and God in particular. Philosophies and religions that deny or suppress our need and capacity to reason and understand also deny and suppress our humanity and the spirit within us.

Divorced from experience and seen as an end in itself, theology can undoubtedly become a stumbling block to faith and right action. It can lead to ossified, dead dogmas which can repel the believer no less than the atheist. No one knows that better than the alcoholic who attended church regularly and held all the theologically correct beliefs and still couldn't get sober. Sometimes that alcoholic was a priest, a pastor, or a rabbi, as we well know from the rooms.

In AA we don't come to God through theology but through experience, mostly of the humbling and humiliating variety, often reluctantly, and sometimes even kicking and screaming.

The understandings of God underpinning the Steps and the principles therein grow out of an accumulated wealth of such experience, and they help to guide us in our own individual walks so we can continue to grow along spiritual lines in our relationship with God. We work those Steps and practice those principles and our experience in doing that is what we share. If we speak from the heart and our experience is real, it will bring strength and hope and help someone.

Thomas Aquinas is widely acknowledged to be one of the great theologians of all times. He reasoned tirelessly in his attempt to make sense of God, and his literary output, culminating in his 5,000-page *Summa Theologiae* ("The Summa of Theology"), was nothing short of prodigious. One day late in life, while celebrating Mass in a small chapel in Naples, he fell into a trance. He later remarked that compared to the vision then given him, all his writings seemed like straw. He never set pen to paper again, and his *magnum opus* remained unfinished. We are greatly indebted to Aquinas and we can rightly thank God for his work. But it in no way diminishes his accomplishment to recognize that, by his own account, it was in a spiritual experience that the theologian found the real sum and summit of his life.

A spiritual awakening or experience is the AA goal, and it begins in earnest with Step 3 as we turn our will and our lives over to the care of God. "As we understood Him" can ease the way if we let go of our old preconceptions, or it can block it if we hold on to them. In the latter case what was intended as a temporary measure to help the newcomer get started can become a half-measure instead, and of the chronic sort—just like the earlier compromises we saw in Step 2. It can be seen as an invitation to wallow in the character defects that keep us from growing in faith: intellectual self-sufficiency, self-reliance, skepticism, and distrust. It can easily become an excuse for sloth and procrastination, and even an incentive to pride, dishonesty, and rationalization.

Many of us can spend years not going to Big Book or 12&12 meetings. Gradually, the twelve discrete sentences we call the Steps are abstracted from their context in those basic texts and from the collective experience that gave them birth and imparted them with meaning. They can then be made to mean anything we want them to mean. We reach a point where we no longer share "a common solution." AA is no longer one program, but many programs. You work yours and I work mine. Nor do we believe there is any objective spiritual truth to be found in the Steps. There is only my truth and your truth. "Rigorous honesty" is supplanted by a self-serving relativism.

There is a spiritual maxim that is echoed in the long form of Tradition 12. It says that our blessings are our curses and our curses our blessings. The curse of alcoholism brings us to defeat and despair and we hit bottom. Out of pain, we are led to AA and to the promise of healing through a relationship with God. We are then blessed with the gift of sobriety. As our lives get better, we regain a sense of confidence and independence, and we fall back upon relying on ourselves. This becomes our curse. We go off a fork and abandon "the Road of Happy Destiny," striking out on our own again. We may stay sober, but we are not going anywhere spiritually, not becoming all that God intends us to be.

Once complacency has reared its ugly head, I can become quite satisfied with the understanding of God I had when I entered the program, "however limited." With pain no longer a motivating factor, I lose what incentive I had to grow in that understanding. I tell myself the program is not about understanding, but about doing. It's a program of action: don't drink and go to meetings. Anyway, who can understand God? The rationalizing impulse reappears, and I ease God out.

Such attitudes keep me from making any serious effort to grow in my walk with God. I can coast along for a long time on a few catchphrases and a handful of slogans I echo as mindless mantras, never venturing beneath the surface of things, the principles reduced to a series of well-meaning and nice-sounding platitudes. Though I may zealously apply my God-given intellect to other pursuits, I don't apply it to the business of understanding him, so that I may know him better and love him more—his purpose in giving me the power to reason in the first place. I remain wrapped in my spiritual diapers.

Ultimately, "as we understood Him" can be approached from a disposition of pride or from one of humility. If I am still smarting from my negative experiences with religion; if I am still clinging to intellectual self-sufficiency and a false spirit of independence, and if I still get mileage and a sense of power from defiance—if I still suffer from any of these spiritual liabilities— these four words are an unintended boost to my ego. They tell me it is only about how *I* understand God. The "we" in the phrase loses its historical anchor in the real-life experience of a group of drunks who found a common spiritual solution and are carrying a message whose understanding of God is central to that solution.

Rather than an invitation to explore and share in that understanding, I see a license to continue to play God, confirming me in my disease. I take those four words to mean that I can create God in my own image. After all, it's *my* Higher Power.

But there is another way. "As we understood Him" can be read from a place of humility. It can be a reminder of an ego-puncturing fact: our understanding *is* limited. What we can apprehend of an infinite and all-loving God with our finite and divided minds and with our troubled and unsteady hearts is precious little. This is true of the believer no less than of those who have not yet come to believe.

Nevertheless, the program tells us that God wants us to understand him, through all the faculties that he has given us, our intellect not least. Our job is to humble ourselves and accept that God is God and that the initiative is on his side; that we can understand only what God reveals and only to the extent that we make ourselves ready to receive it, and even that "through a glass darkly."[12]

Admitting, as "A Vision for You" (p. 164) suggests, that "we know only a little," we express a desire to know as much as God wants us to know, trusting that he will "disclose more" and grant us the grace to know him better, so that that we may the better do his will. We work the Steps without reservation, holding back nothing, practicing all of their principles, and excluding none from any part of our lives.

If I choose the way of humility, the experience of alcoholics everywhere guarantees that I will grow in my relationship with God, and thus in my understanding of him. And I will do so in concert with others whose understanding too is growing, in and out of AA. If I choose pride, I am back in Genesis territory, reenacting the fall, going it alone, doing it my way. If I have not kept the memory green and forgotten where that once took me, I have probably also forgotten the definition of insanity.

Though "as we understood Him" is underlined, the emphasis in Step 3 is not on those four words, but on the decision that precedes them. Understanding in its cognitive or intellectual sense can help us knock down certain barriers to faith, namely erroneous ideas and attitudes. This was the case with some of the one-time agnostic and atheist thinkers and scientists we quoted earlier, men and women like Francis Collins, Fred Hoyle, Allan Sandage, Antony Flew, Nancy Pearcey, and C. S. Lewis himself. Understanding can also help us strengthen our faith once we have acquired it. But it is not likely to *lead* us to faith. Only humility and surrender can do that. More precisely, only God can, if we humble and surrender ourselves to him.

Our natural inclination is to believe that understanding is a prerequisite to faith. That is not what AA says. We are told instead that faith is a gift we receive when we put humility ahead of intellect (12&12, S2, p. 30). The intellect can then properly do its job. St. Anselm stipulated the right relationship between the two when he wrote that faith seeks understanding. Augustine elaborated further when he wrote: "I believe, in order to understand; and I understand, the better to believe."[13]

Putting faith first means putting God first, and letting him shape my understanding. That understanding in turn helps me to strengthen my faith. On the other hand, putting intellect or understanding first means putting self first, choosing what to believe on the basis of my limited reasoning power as directed by self-will. The result is that I make progress neither with faith nor with understanding.

Humility and surrender are the cornerstones of the faith on which Step 3 is built. James Spiegel points out that even when our understanding of God is such that we are convinced of both his power and his goodness, we can still fail to trust him. Why? Because we want to remain in charge. Trusting someone is ceding power and control, and our disordered desire for both is at the very heart of our disease. It is the vice or character defect most virulently opposed to the virtue of faith: "If to exhibit faith in God is to actively affirm his control over one's life, then to lack faith is to assert one's control over it."[14]

To trust God is therefore to humble ourselves and surrender all power and control to him. This is the decision we are called to make in Step 3, a decision that is implemented through concrete action as we work the Steps and practice the principles of the program in all aspects of our lives. Our faith grows from there, and with it our understanding.

7

Working the Steps, Practicing the Principles

It is not uncommon for many of us to look at faith as mostly a matter of feeling, or of adhering to certain religious precepts, performing certain duties and rituals, or observing various feasts and holidays. But while these elements may be present in faith, they do not constitute its core. Nor is faith merely a passive proposition. Properly understood, faith is a matter of specific acts of the will, all of which are underpinned by humility and surrender. As James Spiegel points out, "Faith is trust put into action," and it "is displayed through behavior."[1]

This echoes the 12&12's explanation that, like the rest of the Steps, Step 3 calls for positive or "affirmative" action. The reason it gives is crucial: only through action can we "cut away the self-will" which has "blocked" God entry's into our lives (p. 34). Here again we have a clear statement of the spiritual disease and its solution, and with it, an express understanding of God, of how he works. The understanding is not a prerequisite to the action. If we take the action, the understanding will follow, as the results manifest themselves in our lives. Nonetheless, if our understanding of God is such that it precludes our taking the action, reason would have it that we need to forfeit that understanding.

The 12&12 adds that "faith alone," understood as a passive sort of belief, will avail us nothing, for we can have such faith and still bar God from our lives. Our job is to find the specific ways in which we can "let Him in." This is what we begin to do with Step 3, which together with the rest of the Steps is designed to take us on a journey that will transform our spirit and reconstitute our character and emotional makeup.

A Faith That Works

Without positive action, faith is barren and bears no fruit. Hence the theme that is present throughout the seminal AA literature, starting with Bill's story in the Big Book: "Faith without works is dead." Taken from the book of James in the New Testament, these words drive home the point that the faith that restores us to sanity and a sober life is of a particular kind: vital and active, purposeful and productive: "a faith that works."

This understanding of faith is central to the program. It arose out of necessity and experience, as the early AAs sought to apply spiritual principles to the business of not drinking and living sober lives.

Being based on experience, such faith seeks to be rational. We have stressed the rationality of AA faith elsewhere and it needs to be underscored here as well. We observed in a previous chapter that AA experience can rightly be seen as a successful attempt, on a personal level, to follow a process of experimentation and verification which, in principle, is not unlike that at work in scientific inquiry.

Experience and experiment can be seen as sharing a common objective: the acquisition of knowledge by trial and error. The "veri-fication" (literally the truth-making) is the result, what confirms whether a theory or hypothesis we are testing is demonstrably valid. In our case, the proposition that faith of a certain kind, practiced in certain ways, produces certain results.

In the Steps then, faith is practical and practicable, experience-based and results-oriented. This becomes clear from a closer examination of the expression "a faith that works." In it, "works" bears a double meaning. On the more transparent level, it denotes a faith that as we have just suggested produces *results*. Less obviously, it denotes a faith that *exerts* itself. The relationship between exertion and result is one of cause and effect. We put in the effort, and certain things ensue.

When holding hands in a circle we conclude our meetings with the confident assertion that "it works if you work it," we are giving voice to this fundamental truth about faith. Granted, to the extent that we give it any thought, "it" stands for "program" in our minds. But what makes the program a spiritual program is that it exists as a channel for the power of God, and that power works through faith. Thus a deeper meaning behind our closing words is that *faith* works if you work it. If we trust God and we put our trust into action by working the Steps and practicing their principles, faith will not disappoint. We will become sober and live a reasonably happy and useful life.

As a virtue, faith needs to be practiced repeatedly and consistently until it becomes habitual, akin to a second nature that slowly displaces our natural bent toward unbelief, skepticism, distrust, self-reliance, and self-will. Working the Steps and practicing the principles is how we do that in AA, how we practice a faith that works.

In the business of recovery, faith cannot be divorced from works, nor works from faith. A faith that is not vigorously exercised withers and becomes sterile. Works that are not founded upon and directed by faith degenerate into self-reliance and self-will. In either case, there is no spiritual harvest.

Our faith rests upon a God of love and grace who has a will for us. To trust him is to order our lives in keeping with that understanding. Our exertion therefore, our efforts, are directed toward subordinating our will to his. Our job is to take the action and leave the results to his care. We do this by working the Steps and their principles. That work is directed to chipping away at self-will and opening our spirits to the grace of God. The results are the product of that grace, of God's work in us.

The relationship between human and divine agency, between faith and works, is summed up by Paul in a passage that echoes James's view of a faith that works. "Work out your own salvation with fear and trembling," Paul tells us, "for it is God which worketh in you both to will and to do" according to his good purpose.[2] As C. S. Lewis observes,[3] the first part of the sentence seems to say that everything depends on us, while the second part makes it look as if God does all and we do nothing.

The apparent contradiction dissolves in AA. From its perspective, practicing a faith that works is a cooperative effort involving the human and the divine, the alcoholic and God. Sidestepping long-standing religious controversies, AA reconciles faith, works, and grace. In recovery we need all three. We need to be "willing to go to any lengths" (Big Book, pp. 76, 79) and make "strenuous efforts" (ibid., p. 64) so that we may become receptive to the gift of grace by which we are delivered. In spiritual development and character formation, it is God's will for us to be men and women of faith, and therefore to grow in all the other virtues, for that is how our faith plays itself out in practice. Many if not most of us may doubt our ability to pursue this course. We need not, for as an AA saying assures us, what God wills for us, he will also give us the power to carry out. If we turn our will and our life over to God, he will direct and guide us in our recovery. But, again, we have to put in the effort, because the *effort* is what he will direct and guide. We row. He steers.

Exactly how all this works from God's side we don't know and cannot possibly know. To presume otherwise is to try to put ourselves in God's place once again. All we know is what we are called to do. If we do our part, God will do his. If we practice a faith that works, faith will work.

MADE A DECISION

We are brought to Step 3 and to a faith that works by practicing the principles of willingness, humility, and surrender. We are now offered three additional principles to practice as we make, and act upon, the decision to humble ourselves and surrender our will and our lives to the care of God. These are the principles of prayer, acceptance, and serenity.

Prayer is probably the practice we most associate with the spiritual life. As our disease progressed, prayer was reduced for most of us to its foxhole variation, a gesture of last resort we made when drinking got us in trouble. Not practicing a faith that works, our prayers didn't work either. We kept digging a bigger hole—until we hit rock bottom. In our anguish and despair, we cried out to whatever God there might be. Then something happened and we stopped drinking.

Coming now to Step 3, we are initiated in prayer as a distinctive spiritual *discipline*. We begin to practice it regularly, faithfully, and consistently day in and day out until it becomes part of the fabric of our lives. As part of this, we are introduced to two prayers, the 3rd Step Prayer and the Serenity Prayer.

THE 3ʳᵈ STEP PRAYER

The 3rd Step Prayer is a spiritual tool we use when making the decision to yield our will and our lives to God. Within the sequential order of the Steps, the prayer is our first attempt to establish conscious contact with God and enter into a relationship with him. Its text is found in the "How It Works" chapter of the Big Book (p. 63):

> "God, I offer myself to Thee—
> to build with me and to do with me as Thou wilt.
> Relieve me of the bondage of self,
> that I might better do Thy will.
> Take away my difficulties,
> that victory over them may bear witness
> to those I would help
> of Thy Power, Thy Love, and Thy Way of Life.
> May I do Thy will always."

We can see from these words that our decision is not just a mental note we make in our minds or an assent we give to a proposition. Nor is it a willful resolution we make to ourselves. Rather, our decision is a surrender of our entire being to God, an offering of ourselves to his providential care and to his service, a yielding to his will. It presupposes and reflects an internal conversion of the heart that we externalize and verbalize in prayer.

As the prayer shows, the decision is a radical one in that it goes to the root of our spiritual disease of selfishness and self-centeredness. It implies, if followed through, a deep realignment of our character and emotions and with that of our lives. Being foundational to the rest of the Steps and the entire program of recovery, it is far more than an expression of good intentions.

The word "decision" may obscure the fact that, like every Step, the 3rd Step involves a process. We start with as little as a wisp of willingness but grow toward greater willingness and a stronger desire to follow God's lead. We take an honest and fearless look at those attitudes in us, arising from self-centered pride, which keep us from initiating our relationship with God—self-reliance, distrust, suspiciousness, the need for power and control—and we become ready to let them go. We humble ourselves, acknowledging and accepting our dependence upon a Power who is infinitely greater than ourselves yet intimately cares for us. The decision is the culmination of this process and the prelude to a faith that works.

With Step 3 we stand at the turning point. Do we surrender and ask for "his protection and care with complete abandon" (Big Book, p. 59), or do we hold back?

If our decision should not be postponed, because our recovery is riding on it, neither should it be rushed and taken lightly, and for the same reason. In both cases, our working of the remaining Steps may suffer and our recovery stall. We are told in the 12&12 that we need continuous action upon the other Steps as a way of life, but that we can practice them successfully only when we have given Step 3 "a *determined and persistent* trial" (p. 40, our emphasis).

Thus we need to apply ourselves to Step 3 *in preparation for* and *in the course of* working, say, Step 4. If we are going to do his will in the process of inventory-taking, we need to turn our own will and our lives over to the care of God at every turn, especially where we might feel fearful, overwhelmed or discouraged, or where dishonesty might tempt us and undermine our work. It is the same with every other Step. Each is built on the foundation of our decision to surrender will and life and abandon all resistance so that God can guide our efforts and direct them toward accomplishing his purpose for us.

This explains why "the effectiveness of the whole AA program will rest upon how well and how earnestly we have tried to come to 'a decision to turn our will and our lives over to the care of God *as we understood Him*'" (ibid., pp. 34–35).

"How well" and "how earnestly" bear highlighting on our copies of the 12&12. We cannot be lackadaisical about spiritual matters. Nor can we make the decision without going through the process that culminates in the decision. We get out of the program what we put into it, as it is often said. A faith that works is a faith that works.

Our decision entails the start of a conversion experience and a marked spiritual and emotional shift as our outlook and motivation are gradually altered. As the Big Book explains, it presupposes and is preceded by two other decisions. First, the decision to "quit playing God." Second, the decision "that hereafter in this drama of life, God was going to be our Director. He is the Principal; we are His agents. He is the Father, and we are His children." These decisions form the foundation of "the new and triumphant arch through which we passed to freedom" (p. 62). We go from being self-centered to God-centered.

In what is sometimes referred to as the promises of Step 3, the Big Book describes how, *while still working Step 3*, we begin to change:

> "When we sincerely took such a position, all sorts of remarkable things followed. We had a new Employer. Being all powerful, He provided what we needed, if we kept close to Him and performed His work well. Established on such a footing we became less and less interested in ourselves, our little plans and designs. More and more we became interested in seeing what we could contribute to life. As we felt new power flow in, as we enjoyed peace of mind, as we discovered we could face life successfully, as we became conscious of His presence, we began to lose our fear of today, tomorrow or the hereafter. We were reborn" (p. 63).

What Step 3 promises then is nothing less than the beginning of a spiritual rebirth, an awakening that begins in earnest with our decision to surrender completely and unconditionally to God's care. This is where our hope for a restoration to sanity begins to find its fulfillment.

Given the nature of the decision that we are to make, we are counseled not to take the Step unless we can act with conviction. If we are not spiritually disposed to take the Step, any outward attempt to do so will remain a mere formality and effect little change. When we have worked the Step by working on our attitudes about God and the realm of the spirit (a task we began in Step 2), then we will come to the point of making a decision to start on our spiritual journey. The 3rd Step Prayer is our vehicle for doing this.

It takes many of us a long time to get going. And yet, it is nevertheless a fact of AA experience that for some, Step 3 comes sooner rather than later, and sometimes quite unexpectedly. We are in the middle of a difficult or painful situation and seemingly out of the blue we decide to act in a way that goes contrary to how we have acted in similar situations all our lives. In the midst of this experience, or perhaps later, we realize that we have moved away from self and turned our will and our lives over. The 3rd Step prayer subsequently becomes a tool for consciously and deliberately reaffirming and cementing that decision.

The Big Book says that the wording of the prayer is optional and that what counts is expressing the idea humbly, honestly, and without reservation. This is all true, but most of us find that we have trouble doing this effectively without a written prayer, and few of us can improve on the original. Hence we generally end up using the prayer as is. In this we follow another one of those maxims closely related to Step 3: "If it ain't broke, don't fix it." This is another call to the virtue of simplicity: if it works, work it. Don't reinvent the wheel. Let things be and don't try to change what doesn't need changing.

Using the 3rd Step Prayer as it is makes sense for another reason. As has been noted, taking Step 3 is not a one-time affair; we need to make its decision again every time we work each of the other Steps. Moreover, we also find that we need to turn our will and our lives over to the care of God in the ordinary course of our lives, practicing the principles of surrender, prayer, humility, and faith on a daily basis. A simple and by now well-tested prayer, the 3rd Step Prayer can help us in this disciplinary endeavor. It's a tool we can use to begin our day each morning as part of our 11th Step work of prayer and meditation. Indeed, it is not hard to see that Step 3 and its prayer foreshadow and culminate in Step 11's goal of seeking conscious contact with God, and through it knowledge of his will or us and the power to carry it out.

Regularity, consistency, and repetition are hallmarks of practicing a discipline and turning it into a habit. Sticking with the same prayer can facilitate our efforts. With time, we come to memorize it. This can make the prayer a more effective spiritual tool, inasmuch as in memorizing we internalize and make something an integral part of us. We come to know it "by heart," an expression that is very much apropos here. Nor is it of no significance to consider that, when we say the 3rd Step Prayer, we are joining in spiritual fellowship with countless other AAs praying the same prayer everywhere. It fosters humility to practice a "we" program, and the knowledge that we are in the company of others is reassuring. It comforts and inspires hope.

Turning It Over

If regular use of the 3rd Step Prayer can help us start the day by yielding our will and our lives to God, the Serenity Prayer can help us meet the challenges we face as the day unfolds in the same spirit of humility and surrender.

The Serenity Prayer

It is for this purpose that the prayer is introduced in the concluding paragraph of Step 3 in the 12&12, where we read that, when faced with indecision and emotional disturbance, "we can pause, ask for quiet, and in the stillness simply say . . ." (p. 41).

With this prayer we begin to practice on a regular basis the virtue of acceptance, to which we were first introduced in Step 1. Intimately connected with acceptance is the virtue of serenity (referred to variously as peace, peace of mind, and harmony). The two are interconnected, with acceptance fostering serenity and serenity facilitating acceptance.

As we know, the Serenity Prayer has become the signature corporate prayer of the Fellowship, serving to open most and close many AA meetings. We learn in the AA literature[4] that it was discovered in the obituary section of a New York paper by a member who brought it to the attention of Ruth Hock, the fledgling group's secretary.

A January 1950 Grapevine article attributes the prayer to Reinhold Niebuhr (1892–1971), a Christian theologian who taught at Union Theological Seminary in New York City. Though some have contested the attribution, there is little disagreement that the prayer reached AA through the work of Niebuhr. He reportedly had passed a similar prayer to the Federal Council of Churches, which in turn had given it wide distribution by printing millions of copies for U.S. soldiers during WWII.

Niebuhr's was a longer prayer, consisting of 14 lines. Though explicitly religious as we would naturally expect, it is nevertheless worth reflecting upon, as it might shed some spiritual light on the 4 lines we have kept. The version most in use today reads as follows:

> God, grant me the serenity
> to accept the things I cannot change,
> the courage to change the things I can,
> and the wisdom to know the difference.
> Living one day at a time;
> enjoying one moment at a time;
> accepting hardship as a pathway to peace;
> taking, as Jesus did,
> this sinful world as it is,
> not as I would have it;
> trusting that You will make all things right
> if I surrender to Your will,
> so that I may be reasonably happy in this life

and supremely happy with You forever in the next.

Seen in its fullness, it is fairly evident that the primary request of the prayer is for a spirit of peace, acceptance, and surrender. This is not always clear from the first four lines alone, which are the only ones familiar to us and which appear to focus equally on two other distinct petitions: the courage to change and the wisdom to know. Abstracted from the rest of the prayer, these four lines sometimes can be something of a puzzle. Particularly as newcomers, when simplicity is in short supply, we might be tempted into puzzle-solving instead of praying, trying to figure out in our heads which things we can change and which we cannot. Such mental gymnastics is of course far from the intention of the prayer, as it is conducive neither to serenity nor wisdom.

Structurally speaking, the prayer is an extended sentence, and a colon could properly substitute for the period following the word "difference." That is, the ten lines that follow (made up of five gerund or -ing phrases) are an elaboration of the first four. The things I cannot change are people, places, and things, or "this sinful world," which I am to accept "as it is" or "as Jesus did," rather than try to change it to conform to my will. Serenity comes through the acceptance of reality, peace by accepting the hardships inherent in a troubled or fallen world.

Acceptance allows me to live in the present and enjoy the gift of life as it comes to me one day and one moment at a time. Trusting that he will accomplish his good purpose in me, in others, and in all things, I surrender my will and my life to God. Through surrender I am given the serenity to accept. Through surrender also I am endowed with the courage to change, a courage born of faith. For the things I can change are mostly within me, in my attitudes and character, and I can only change them as I allow God to work his will in me. It is through this humble reliance on God that I can hope to find a "reasonably happy" life here, and a "supremely happy" life in the presence of God in the hereafter.

Without the last ten lines, the broader significance of the prayer, rich in AA principles, is lost. In what appears an attempt to compensate for this, the 12&12 inserts a new, fifth line to the four found in Step 3: "Thy will, not mine, be done" (p. 41). These words help to re-center the prayer in the spirit of surrender, humility, and acceptance which infuses the original. Indeed, they may be said to be the heart of the prayer, and the very essence of Step 3. Repeated throughout the Big Book and the 12&12 with minor variations, these six little words may even be said to represent the heart and soul of the entire program of AA.

For the biblically literate Christian, they evoke the ultimate act of acceptance and surrender as, praying in the Garden of Gethsemane, Jesus prepares to give his life on the cross. Regardless of our religious tradition or lack thereof, however, we can all profitably reflect on this act and its connection to Step 3. We have in this narrative a man said to be the Son of God. This man humbles himself before his Father, yielding his will and his life and accepting death on a cross so that all may be forgiven and reconciled to their Creator. By humility, acceptance, and surrender, he becomes a perfect instrument of God's will, and through him God is able to do for us what we cannot do for ourselves. The rebellion that originated in another Garden is over and peace is restored between man and God.

The six words the 12&12 adds are dropped when the Serenity Prayer is said in most meetings. But at some, collectively or individually, there are AAs who recite the prayer exactly as it appears in Step 3, echoing the words of the suffering man and identifying with him even as, we are told in the story, he identified with us.

The Serenity Prayer is a vehicle for taking what we may call a "God pause" where, faced with a stressful situation, we avoid an immediate and instinctive emotional reaction that is likely to produce more harm than good. Instead, we still the clamors of the self and reconnect with God. We re-center in him and pray that his peace may prevail within us, so that we may accept, surrender, and act as he would have us act, for our good and the good of all concerned.

Our first task when dealing with emotionally challenging situations then, is to stop and pray, making a decision right then and there to turn our will and our lives over to the care of God. With humility, acceptance, and surrender as a spiritual foundation, we are then in a position to use other tools the given circumstances may demand. That is, we can then work other Steps and practice other principles that may be fitting and constructive.

We can grow in acceptance through prayer if we practice both the virtue and the discipline regularly until they become habitual. Rather than reacting automatically in our usual fight-or-flight, attack-or-withdraw mode, the time will come when God will be our first thought, and "Thy will, not mine, be done" our prevailing frame of mind. Acceptance will displace anger and fear and we will experience peace and serenity. Our emotions will increasingly conform to the spirit of God working in us. Where there is discord, we will bring harmony.

Serenity and Acceptance, Courage and Wisdom

We have said that with Step 3 we are introduced to the discipline of prayer, and in the Serenity Prayer, to the virtues of serenity and acceptance. Before we discuss the practice of these two virtues further, we might consider why courage and wisdom, the other two virtues asked for in the prayer, are not included here as among the key virtues characteristic of this particular Step.

To do this we need to go back to the relationship between the three petitions (serenity, courage, wisdom) made in the prayer. Serenity and acceptance are at the heart of the prayer. They are the attitudinal stance and the spiritual and emotional dispositions that allow wisdom to tell us what, if anything, in the given circumstances can be changed. When faced with a difficulty, lack of acceptance adds to emotional stress, and this blurs our vision and reduces our ability to act wisely and hence courageously. Conversely, acceptance fosters the calm state of mind and emotional stability that allows wisdom to surface. If making a change is the counsel of wisdom, then we can rightfully pray for the courage to act.

Early in sobriety, when we are first working Step 3 and practicing surrender through the Serenity Prayer, we don't carry a lot of wisdom in our spiritual toolbox. We are not equipped to tell the difference between what we can and cannot change. The program offers us the wisdom of its long collective experience to help us make that distinction. The issue for us is whether, lacking in our own individual wisdom, we will accept the program's and put it to use.

This collective wisdom is expressed in a plain and empirically verifiable fact: most things in life are beyond our ability to change or do anything constructive about. We are powerless over them and therefore wisdom dictates we accept them. Otherwise, we are banging our heads against a wall and making ourselves (and others) pretty unhappy, and possibly inviting even further trouble.

For practical purposes, as regards the ordinary course of our lives, the bulk of those things we cannot change falls within two basic categories: people and the past. Our attitude toward the past is to learn from it, repair the damage done, put it behind us, and try to not repeat it. We do that through Steps 4 to 9. If we do our job, what is mendable will mend, and the guilt, regret, shame, resentment, depression, and other distressing feelings concerning the past will abate. We will then use its lessons to do better ourselves as well as to help others. As regards people, we accept them unconditionally. This doesn't mean we approve of their behavior, condone what they do, or necessarily maintain ties with them. It simply means we recognize we are powerless to change them and opt to change what we can instead.

In most cases that is simply ourselves, as the program clearly tells us. We go about doing that by practicing the spiritual principles in 4 through 10 and the rest of the Steps. In changing ourselves we change our outlook, our view of the past, people, and circumstances and of the things that matter to us. We begin to see difficulties as opportunities to grow and to pursue the good, whatever the situation.

That we are powerless over most things and therefore need to accept them, and that most of what we can change lies within us, that is about all the wisdom we need to put the Serenity Prayer to work daily as we begin to turn our will and our lives over to the care of God in Step 3. We could therefore say that, when we ask for the wisdom to know the difference between these things at this particular stage of our recovery, we are basically asking to be reminded of the program's inherited wisdom—and to be given the grace to accept and practice it.

Though it makes three distinct petitions, then, the emphasis in the Serenity Prayer is on acceptance and serenity. This is not to say that courage and wisdom are not integral to it, but that its cornerstone is those two other virtues. Courage and wisdom are built upon that foundation.

Moreover, though courage and wisdom are integral to the Serenity Prayer itself, they are not virtues that are integral to Step 3. Their practice is not the focus there. That is why they are not included among the virtues proper to that Step in the present discussion. The practice of courage as understood in the prayer begins with Step 4, where we need it to make a fearless and searching examination of ourselves so that we can find what needs to change in us and then take the action to change it. Wisdom begins to develop gradually from there as we work the other Steps and grow in our spiritual awakening. It becomes integral to Steps 11 and 12.

What this means is that as regards Step 3 and the Serenity Prayer, internal change comes to us through the practice of acceptance and serenity as distinct ways of surrendering and turning our will and our lives over to the care of God. As we practice these and the other principles of prayer, humility, willingness, and faith that are central to the Step, we begin to change inside. This change comes imperceptibly and almost as a natural by-product, rather than as the result of any overt acts of courage on our part. This is because all of the virtues—and not just courage—are agents of personal change, working to replace our character defects and foster our spiritual and emotional renewal.

When we are new to the program, it is suggested that we don't make any major changes the first year. The focus is on accepting things as they are. The only things we may have to change are those situations (e.g., an abusive relationship) that might bring harm to ourselves and others.

Prudence (another word for wisdom) is recommended because at this stage we are necessarily lacking in it. As newcomers, we can't see straight. We are in no spiritual or emotional condition to discern the wisdom of making any major changes. So it is suggested we don't. Again, we are asked to lean on AA experience and the program's collective wisdom.

Another reason for the suggestion to wait has to do with the relationship that usually obtained between change and acceptance when we drank. Serenity and acceptance were largely foreign to us. Change was more familiar, more our style, at least for many of us. When things didn't go our way, the impulse was to grab the bull by the horns and try to change them, rather than to adapt and adjust ourselves.

As many of our stories show, we were often addicted to change and to the anticipation, novelty, and excitement it brought, even as we were often filled with apprehension about how things might turn out. This all made for widespread instability, emotionally, financially, relationally, and otherwise. We just couldn't stay still for very long. True, many of us didn't fit that profile. We were not so prone to upset the apple cart. But that was mostly a function of our passivity and fear, not of a spiritually informed acquiescence. Such surface stability did not necessarily bring us peace, for we were often just white-knuckling it through life, the victims of circumstance, able neither to change nor to accept. In many cases, we just resigned ourselves to the way things were.

Whether we are of the active or the passive sort, our natural tendency is still to try to change the outside rather than the inside, and that temptation reasserts itself early in sobriety. As soon as our one-year waiting period is over, we are ready to go at it. We are eager to make changes and implement plans we had hatched while we were still drinking, or to resume a path we had started under the influence. We just don't give ourselves enough time to reevaluate things in light of our recovery.

If we consider the Serenity Prayer at all, we are likely to focus on the line that really appeals to us: changing the things we can. And here we come up against a quandary: though we can't change most things in the external world, there are obviously enough of them we can. I can leave my spouse or significant other, quit my job, start a new career, move to a new city. But should I? Certainly, the wisdom to know the difference when it comes to making external changes cannot refer simply to knowing what I can and cannot change. I may be able to change something, but that doesn't mean it is the wise thing to do.

What then are we asking for when we pray for the wisdom to know the difference as regards what external changes we can and cannot make? We are first of all asking for the wisdom to know what *has* to be accepted, if for no other reason than that it cannot be changed and therefore not accepting it can only cause emotional turmoil and probably occasion harm. But we are also asking for the wisdom to know whether what *can* be changed *should* be changed.

Plainly, knowing what can be changed doesn't tell us whether it should be. And plainly too, knowing what should be changed requires greater wisdom than knowing what can be, and again, such wisdom is practically non-existent when we first start working on Step 3. As we suggested, that greater wisdom is tied to the practice of seeking conscious contact and knowledge of God's will for us in Step 11, and it is the fruit of our spiritual awakening come to maturity in 12.

If we reflect a little on the second petition of the prayer, we might see that "should" is implicit in it and that it qualifies "can," as in *can and should*. But that is far from obvious, and many of us may be oblivious to it. We need to go back to an earlier version of the prayer, in this case of its first four lines, to appreciate the true nature of the request: it is not just about *ability*, but about *advisability*.

The source again is Niebuhr. In a sermon delivered during World War II, the same period he apparently composed the longer prayer, the theologian included the following prayer:

> "God, give us grace
> To accept with serenity the things that cannot be changed,
> Courage to change the things that should be changed,
> And wisdom to distinguish the one from the other."[5]

There are a few things made explicit here that are only implicit in the version AA inherited, which clearly has been fine-tuned into a better rhetorical tool. It is easy to see why it was that version of the prayer that became popular. It is more memorable, a lot catchier.

But perhaps what it has gained in pithiness it has lost in coherence. Obviously, there is no virtue, no courage, and no wisdom in changing what we can but shouldn't. Rather, we would consider that rashness and folly, character defects typical of our power-driven ways when we drank, precisely the things we seek to surrender with the help of the Serenity Prayer.

The stipulation "and should" needs to be understood at the end of the second petition of our version because it keeps the "can" anchored to its spiritual and moral foundations. It raises the question of "should" according to whom and in the service of what. The implicit answer, of course, is according to God's will, and to serve his purpose of restoration and renewal. Especially as regards major external changes, it is a question we cannot fail to ask if our change is not to be self-willed and self-serving.

Does this mean that our Serenity Prayer is less than an effective tool? No, it means that we need to use it as more than mere rote and reflect sometimes on its underlying richness. This is what we are called to do at the end of Step 12, where the Serenity Prayer resurfaces to conclude the study of the 12 Steps: "may every one of us sense more deeply the inner meaning of AA's simple prayer . . ." (12&12, p. 125). It is at this stage of our recovery, when we have worked all the Steps and have had a spiritual awakening, that serenity and acceptance can join with courage and wisdom. We are equipped to practice the four virtues of the prayer in all their fullness.

There is one more observation worth making. Niebuhr asks for the wisdom to "distinguish" rather than to "know." This is because wisdom involves more than just knowledge. What characterizes this virtue is the ability to make distinctions between things, to perceive or apprehend differences, to discern the true from the false, right from wrong, and proceed to take practical action based on an accurate grasp of reality and the consequences of such action.

Fortitude and Endurance

We now come to the last general consideration regarding the relationship between the four virtues in the Serenity Prayer. We recall that virtues are character traits that help us to deal well with a variety of distinctly human situations. The prayer embodies three virtues that apply to the business of how we can best conduct ourselves in the face of challenges, difficulties, hardships, or threats to our wellbeing. These are as we have seen the virtues of acceptance, serenity, and courage. A fourth virtue, wisdom, is essential in these situations because it helps us to discern when accepting things is the best course of action and when changing them is.

Generally, we tend to see acceptance and courage as juxtaposed to each other in the prayer, and serenity as associated with the former rather than the latter. But placing the prayer within the virtue tradition may help us to see the relationships among these virtues with greater clarity and hence practice them to better effect.

The virtue tradition sees the ability to face threats or difficulties well as essential to the good life. It therefore makes the virtue that makes this possible a "cardinal virtue," so-called because other virtues ordered to the same goal "hinge" or depend on it, as we saw in an earlier chapter. The traditional name for this overarching virtue is "fortitude." The 12&12 mentions it in connection with the serious financial difficulties faced by some AA, difficulties which are nevertheless faced with "fortitude and faith" (S12, p. 114).

Now, fortitude is often translated today as "courage," but its root meaning is "strength" (cf. "fort" and "fortress"), and it includes both the strength to let things be and the strength to change them. This means that what we call acceptance and courage in the Serenity Prayer are two parts or component virtues of the main virtue of fortitude, two related kinds of character strengths.[6]

Courage is the part that moves to deal with a threat or difficulty well by taking action to change or remove it. Acceptance is the part that is unmoved by it, seeking to face it well by standing fast, carrying on, "hanging in there" and making it through without letting the challenge derail us or break our spirit. The traditional name for this virtue is "endurance," which conveys the idea of hardening or making something strong and long-lasting (cf. "duration"). The 12&12 brings it up in connection with WWII, when the spiritual dependence alcoholics had learned in AA enabled them to "carry through" and "endure" the misery and monotony of war. They showed as much "endurance and valor" as other servicemen (S3, p. 38).

Rather than opposites then, courage and acceptance are related and complementary virtues. They work together under the master virtue of fortitude to help us deal with adversity. And serenity can accompany both.

It may sound odd to speak of the strength to let things be. But trying to change what can't or shouldn't be changed shows weakness, expressed in self-defeating and even self-destructive acts which are driven by character defects and render us even weaker.

Accepting what cannot be changed can involve its own characteristic kind of courage, especially when we are facing great adversity, such as suffering through a serious illness or loss. This is a quiet kind of courage, less dramatic, less episodic, more enduring. As for changing the things we can and should change, we are more likely to find the courage to do that after we have accepted a situation and desisted from futile attempts to change those things about it that are impossible or unwise to change. A serene and confident calm will underpin that kind of courage.

Whatever the trial we may confront, facing it well always begins with accepting with serenity the circumstances that prevail. Besides, in the end, whatever the situation, after all the striving for change is done, we will still have to accept the new set of circumstances and endure through its own likely challenges. These are facts of life. There is no escaping them. We start with acceptance and end with acceptance. That is why in the virtue tradition, in the Serenity Prayer, and in AA, acceptance or endurance is the greater part of valor, to paraphrase an old saying.

It is nevertheless worth adding that AA has taken the virtue of acceptance beyond the traditional understandings associated with endurance. In AA acceptance is more than endurance. We don't just make it through a difficulty. We seek to bring good out of it, for ourselves and others involved. Thus, though we may endure what people do, this doesn't mean that we just try to put up with them the best way we can. Rather, we accept them as they are, seeing past their defects and looking for ways to help them bring out their own strengths in the situation, if through no other way than by practicing ours. In AA's book, then, acceptance is a higher virtue, including but surpassing endurance.

We can now turn our focus back to the practice of acceptance and serenity in Step 3 itself, where the two virtues help us to surrender our will and our lives to the care of God.

ACCEPTANCE

Our release from the compulsion to drink began the moment we were willing to accept two facts: that we were powerless over alcohol, and that dependence upon a Higher Power could set us free. With Step 3 and the Serenity Prayer, we begin to extend the practice of acceptance to all our affairs.

At this juncture, we come to recognize and accept the reality that we are powerless over most things in life. It is through such total acceptance that we begin to find peace of mind, for we are no longer trying to control and change everything around us.

Letting fewer and fewer things bother us is a sign that we are making progress in this virtue. To borrow from a Grapevine story, we may find ourselves at the supermarket, waiting at the checkout counter for 10 items or less. We notice that somebody ahead of us seems to have more than that in his cart. Where that might have aggravated us in the past, now it has no effect on us: we remain unmoved, impassive. That speaks of acceptance, and our lack of reaction shows that it is becoming natural and effortless. This is confirmed when we don't try to count the items to prove to ourselves that we are right. And that speaks of serenity, the reward that accompanies such acceptance.

At the checkout counter and in many similar and ordinary situations where we frequently find ourselves, the practice of acceptance and serenity begins with not focusing on the problem, but on the solution. We don't indulge our eyes where to persist in looking is looking for trouble. Thomas à Kempis suggested as much when he wrote: "It is more profitable to turn away thine eyes from such things as displease thee than to be a slave to contention."[7] We turn our eyes elsewhere and our attention to more pleasant or edifying pursuits.

But we seek more than problem avoidance or distraction. We seek the good. The virtues form a unity, and we can practice acceptance by practicing gratitude, which is a way of focusing on the good in things. At the supermarket, we can always find something to be grateful for—an abundance and great variety of goods, for instance, with all the conveniences of modern shopping. To our ears, this may sound silly and perhaps even preposterous. But that is only because we take what we have for granted. When we take the good for granted, we tend to look for the bad, an attitude that precludes acceptance. Sometimes we have to lose what we have (think hurricane, tornado, earthquake) to realize how good we have it.

We can also practice forgiveness at that checkout counter, remembering how often we did things that were selfish and inconsiderate (or just plain clueless), recognizing ourselves in the shortcomings of others. Identifying with others in this way is always an aid to forgiveness and acceptance. A forgiving heart fosters the virtues of tolerance and patience (part of fortitude), which in turn further the ability to accept.

Acceptance may sound like a glum enterprise to some, something like white-knuckling it or gritting our teeth. Others may see it as assuming an attitude of indifferent stoicism or mystic detachment designed to avoid any feelings of discomfort or pain. To still others it may speak of passive resignation where we really long for things to be different but feel helpless to change them and so suffer in silence.

Sometimes it is suggested that acceptance simply means to have a laid-back attitude, to "go along to get along" and to "go with the flow." We are always looking for popular and catchy ways to convey ideas. This can be a good thing, as most of our AA slogans attest, and no doubt these suggestions are well-intentioned. But catchy doesn't mean true.

The same laid-back attitude that supposedly can help us to be more accepting can lead us by default into accepting the wrong things. It can also dampen any desire to change what can and should be changed, particularly in ourselves, leading us into inertia and complacency. As for going along or going with the flow, if the flow is taking us in the wrong direction (spiritually, morally) then we certainly don't want to go with it and accept it. We want to get out of the flow and swim to safety.

As a spiritual principle, acceptance has little to do with any of these popular notions. Virtue seeks to replace diseased emotions with healthy, spiritually fruitful emotions, not to ignore, suppress, or escape them. Our aim is not only to avoid anger, resentment, worry, anxiety, fear, depression, and all the other harmful emotions that often are the result of not accepting those things we cannot change, but to exercise the virtues which can foster countervailing and constructive emotions in the service of right action. We will know that we are practicing acceptance as a true virtue when we experience a sense of peace and serenity, of inner harmony and tranquility, even of freedom sometimes.

It is a spiritual axiom, we are told in Step 10 of the 12&12 (p. 90), that whenever we are disturbed, regardless of the cause, there is something wrong with *us*. Hence, however trivial or serious the situation we face, our first task is to accept things exactly as they presently are: our circumstances, ourselves, and those who are about us. *As Bill Sees It* (p. 44) characterizes this as adopting an attitude of "realistic humility." Without it, we cannot begin to make any real progress. That is always our starting point and the place to which we shall always return. It is an exercise in the practice of acceptance, he declares, from which we (and those around us) can profit each day.

This is what Bill W. calls *right* acceptance (ibid., p. 20). We humbly recognize the reality of things as they are, and the limitations we face in bringing about change. In the light of the Serenity Prayer, we can see that defeat does not have to mean disaster if it is rightly accepted. We realize that we don't have to run away from our problems or try to overcome our difficulties by another self-defeating display of willpower that can only deepen and multiply them.

We neither run nor fight. We accept. And then we are freed. For through acceptance we are released from the control that our character defects, the character defects of others, and the ills of "this sinful world" exercise over us.

EXPECTATIONS AND DISAPPOINTMENTS

Defeat, failure, and great adversity are inevitable but infrequent occurrences for most of us. Where acceptance is put to the test most often is not in these big, yet rare setbacks, but in the little challenges of ordinary life. On a daily basis, it is the small frustrations and disappointments that we have to contend with. These too are inevitable, for even our little, everyday goals, purposes, and desires will not always be satisfied. Acceptance, resting on a "realistic humility," applies here as well. It can help us to view or construe things from a spiritual perspective, reorient our concerns and align our motivations accordingly, and bring the most good out of our daily pursuits.

Perhaps the biggest cause of frustration and disappointment is the expectations we have of people, places, and things. The greater our expectations, the greater our emotional liabilities when we fail to meet them. Yet expectations are one of those things we can actually do something about, one of the things we can change. We cannot just rid ourselves of them, for they are part of our mental makeup, our built-in disposition toward the future. But we can alter, amend, adjust, or modify them. We can apply the principles of the Serenity Prayer to bring them in line with reality, mitigate the emotional impact of disappointments, and forestall harmful conduct.

There is wisdom in the idea that we cannot change people. This wisdom lies in the fact that people will do what comes naturally to them. And what comes naturally to people, as the long version of the Serenity Prayer suggests, is to err and do wrong. We all fall short. Hence we will disappoint. This is the larger picture that a spiritual perspective can open to us. Fully grasped and accepted, our disappointments can become occasions for growth and demonstrations of faith which can benefit all.

Expectations respond to the way we view and value things, to our outlook and concerns, how we see and what we care about. Sometimes our outlook is self-centered and our concerns selfish. In such cases, disappointment is guaranteed. If we adjust our vision and valuation spiritually and conform them to God's will for us, our disappointments will be fewer and our emotional reactions less damaging.

But even when we are not being patently selfish or self-centered in our expectations of others, self-centeredness may remain a problem. This is so because in expecting a certain conduct from others, we are also implicitly expecting them to see things the way *we* see them and to give things the importance *we* give them. We fail to take into account how *they* look at things and what's important to *them* in a given situation. Naturally, they will respond to their own views and concerns and act contrary to our expectations, leaving us disappointed.

Sometimes disappointment and frustration follow from what we believe to be a sincere attempt to help another. Yet we can be sincere but misguided. The disappointment comes from expecting certain results from our efforts when in fact we have no control over such results. We may mean well, but our intention is compromised by our expectations and robs our action of virtue, for as we have noted, right intention is essential to truly right or virtuous action.

In a popular booklet called *Acceptance: The Way to Serenity and Peace of Mind*, the author gives some cogent reasons why acceptance is a necessary disposition even when we are trying to help others. After many years of thinking that it was his "duty to try to solve other people's problems, arbitrate their disputes, and show them how to live their lives"—and getting hurt in the process—he finally learned that "you cannot help people unless they really need help, are willing to be helped, want you to help them, and ask you to help them. Even then, you can only help them to help themselves."[8] Remembering these five little facts of life can help us to assist others without the burden of expectations, whether of them or of ourselves.

As built-in dispositions, expectations arise more or less naturally and automatically. But we do not necessarily have to entertain or indulge them. When we do, we often set ourselves up for hurt feelings and emotional stress. We then compound the problem by indulging the negative emotions and trying to manipulate others. When a person or circumstance falls short of our expectations and we are visibly upset or angry, we deny the fact. We are just "disappointed," we say. This is often a way of putting the onus on the other person in order to induce guilt and elicit an apology or some response that will soothe our hurt. This type of approach will disappoint as well, if not backfire. In such cases, being honest with ourselves is the first corrective measure.

Repeated disappointment is very likely to make us feel discouraged. This is another sign that our expectations are out of line with reality. If we get discouraged by people's failure to meet them, we are not accepting people as they are. We are expecting from them what they cannot or will not give us. Lowering our expectations is the only rational response.

A principle of the spiritual life says that you can't give what you don't have. "A Vision for You" in the Big Book takes note of this principle as it applies to helping others. If we don't have a right relationship with God and our own house is not in order, we can't carry the message of a spiritual awakening and "transmit it" to others (p. 164).

The same principle applies when it comes to accepting others. Sometimes people won't give us what we would like and could reasonably expect from them, not because they don't want to, but because they don't have it in them to give. It is not who they are. This may or may not reflect a defect in them. But in any case, it is not there, and the sooner we recognize that and accept it, the better for them and for us.

The truth is that expectations is oftentimes a nice word for the unreasonable demands that we place upon others, as Bill W. recognizes about himself in his Grapevine article on emotional sobriety. We think the world owes us and that people are somehow obligated to us. But the question goes beyond what may or may not be reasonable. Even when reasonable, expectations are of necessity self-based, projections of desire onto the future, anticipations of results.

To expect something is to see it as likely to happen or believe it should happen. It involves making certain assumptions and often connotes an element of presumption as well. But if I do certain things with the expectation that I will wrest certain results from life—or from God—I am not turning my will and my life over and there is no humility in me. I am still trying to run the show. I will be disappointed and discouraged. To accept is to let go of results and hence I need to wear my expectations loosely and shed them fast when they are not fulfilled.

There is also an issue of right and wrong dependence here. Our expectations and demands may be a sign that we are relying on others when we should be relying on God. People are fallible and liable to disappoint us. They can't give us what they don't have, and if we insist they do, we will be left wanting. Nor can they give us what is not theirs to give if it belongs to God alone and only he can satisfy it. More often than not our expectations are misplaced and we set ourselves up for disappointment and frustration, thereby making our spiritual and emotional wellbeing dependent on people rather than God. We will find no emotional sobriety down that road.

This doesn't mean that we don't have standards of right and wrong or that in certain settings or situations (e.g., when we are in positions of authority or enter into binding or reciprocal agreements) people don't have certain obligations that they can be rightfully expected to meet. It means that we don't invest ourselves emotionally in their meeting them. We accept people as they are, and when they do the right thing, we are grateful, for ourselves as well as for them. When they don't, we remind ourselves of who they and we are—fallen, fallible, sinners—and we accept. Then, and only then, with the serenity that comes from acceptance, do we ask for the wisdom to discern what we can and should change and for the courage to go ahead and do it.

Being repeatedly reminded of what we have already learned is vital, as Samuel Johnson once observed, echoing a similar observation by Plato. It helps us to avoid having to learn it the hard way all over again. It is one of the reasons we go to meetings, and why we try to "keep the memory green" through sharing. Flawed, powerless, alcoholic, not God: these are some of the things, the true understandings or accurate construals, that we need to remind ourselves of if acceptance is to be ingrained in us as an abiding disposition, a virtue that we can naturally practice in all situations where it governs right action and emotion.

Sometimes we are disappointed with ourselves. We don't measure up to our own expectations of who we think we should be or what we think we should accomplish. Even in sobriety, we continue to make unreasonable demands upon ourselves. This is a sign that we need to check our humility gauge. If we don't measure up, it is probably because we are not sizing ourselves up accurately, not accepting who we are.

It should be clear that self-acceptance is not equivalent to self-complacency. As Flannery O'Connor observes, "Accepting oneself does not preclude an attempt to become better." To accept myself doesn't mean that I overlook, downplay, or resign myself to my shortcomings. On the contrary, those are the things I will do if I *don't* accept myself. Self-acceptance is a necessary condition for change. As in Step 1 regarding alcohol, we have to admit and accept before we can change. We have to accept who we are if we are to become who God wants us to be.

Non-acceptance reflects and reinforces denial. It generates character defects and emotional reactions that blur our vision of the truth about ourselves. Self-acceptance forestalls these and makes possible the sober and serene state of mind where we can see clearly who we are and what, with God's grace, we can change one day at a time. Self-acceptance is therefore part of self-surrender. With it we abandon all self-condemnation and self-serving expectations.

In place of expectations regarding myself, I begin to practice hope. When, despite my best efforts, I fail to attain even what I am convinced is the will of God for me, I can turn that failure over too. I can trust in God's mercy, continue to put one foot in front of the other, and place my hope in his redeeming grace, for as an old hymn echoed in the Big Book reminds us, "the Lord has promised good to me."

The same applies to my expectations of people, places, and things. Instead of anticipating behaviors or results, I can let them go, accept, and practice hope. Seen from a secular perspective, hope is just another word for expectation, even wishful thinking. But as a spiritual virtue hope indulges neither. It proceeds from a faith that works, that involves God-guided effort and produces God-given results. In AA, it is sustained by a set of promises that are being fulfilled in the lives of others and which therefore can be fulfilled in ours as well.

Our attitude toward those promises is not one of expectation but of trust. Newcomers are sometimes told to "expect a miracle." The expression is an oxymoron. A miracle by definition runs counter to all expectation. It is equally by definition an act that is totally within God's control, a product of his grace, not something that we have coming to us in response to anything we might do or anticipate.

If we expect a miracle, we will probably miss it when it comes. Our experience is that, more often than not, we become aware of God's miraculous work in our lives only in retrospect. At the time, the miracle may not feel like anything we might expect at all. It might even coincide with failure and defeat. This reality is reflected in another adage we use to encourage those who are still struggling, one that is more faithful to the AA message. "Don't quit before the miracle happens," we say to them. If we trust God and persevere in right action, our hope won't be in vain.

A hope that is grounded in God does not disappoint. The Big Book tells us that he is trustworthy and has the power. In the end, his will shall always prevail. He would not be God if it didn't. My acceptance of reality is based on the fact that God is God. He is in control, or as the religious or theologically inclined prefer to say, "sovereign," Lord of all.

When the Big Book tells us that with Step 3 God becomes our Employer, it is giving us a spiritual outlook, a construal of our situation that can help us let go of our expectations. This way of looking at things applies not only to the work that we do for a living, but to everything we do. We do a good job at work and do the right thing in every department of our lives because we see ourselves as working for God. In the words of Scripture (which inspired the way Bach signed his works) we do it for the glory of God. Nothing can be more liberating, for we are beholden to no person, organization, institution, or circumstance for approval or reward. We are invested in God and God alone.

In the "Personal Stories" section of the Big Book (p. 407), we read the story of an alcoholic who discovers in acceptance the solution to all his problems. His great insight is that serenity is inversely proportional to our expectations. The higher our expectations, the lower our serenity. A sister 12-Step fellowship offers another helpful insight when it tells us that "expectations are resentments waiting to happen." It is out of such practical insights, accumulated over time, that we grow in wisdom and give ourselves to God "with complete abandon." We live not in the future but the present. We live in a state, not of anxious or excited anticipation, but of blessed assurance, knowing that God is faithful and that his promises will always materialize.

UNDERSTANDING AND ACCEPTING

There is another attitude that works against acceptance, particularly in our relations with those closest to us, and it has to do with the role of the intellect. We assume, tacitly, that if we are to accept people, we have to understand them first: we have to "figure" them out, know what makes them "tick." This is similar to the problem of the relationship between faith and intellect that we discussed earlier. We saw that we tend to put intellect ahead of faith, thinking that reason will enable us to understand and hence to believe.

If we can understand our spouses better, we think to ourselves, then we will be able to manage our relationship better. Maybe it will be easier to accept the things about them that we don't like or find objectionable. This sounds reasonable but it is really putting second things first, or as the 12&12 has it, putting the cart before the horse (S12, p. 115).

If we don't accept our spouses as they are, our chances of gaining any useful understanding of them are very small. We will continue to look at them through the same defective lenses that have warped our view of them all along: our defects of character. The definition of insanity applies here. We can't keep looking through the same glasses and expect to see something different.

If we don't accept our spouse and turn our understanding of him or her over to God, where is "right understanding" going to come from? One of the revelations we get from a serious self- examination in Steps 4 and 10 is how little we understand about ourselves. This is a lesson in humility. If our understanding even of ourselves is so limited, how much more so is our understanding of others? We grow in self-knowledge as we practice the principles of the program, *including self-acceptance*. It works the same way with others: we accept them, practice the principles, and understanding ensues.

As a spiritual principle, acceptance of other people is a matter of the will and of the heart before it is a matter of the intellect. We are called upon not so much to engage our rational powers as to surrender our will and soften our hearts. I turn my will and my life over to the care of God and accept people as they are, letting God come between me and them. This acceptance immediately allows me to relate to them differently. I am no longer objecting, judging, criticizing, rejecting, psychoanalyzing, and otherwise taking their inventory, something that is always sensed by the other person, even if I'm doing it only in my own head.

Accepting others is a form of love, and when I accept, I am following God's will to love my neighbor. When I accept God's will and accept others, understanding will gradually follow. I will be experiencing others as they are rather than as a function of me, of the ways I have accustomed myself to seeing them or the reactions my attitudes tend to elicit in them.

Much of the interaction in our intimate relationships is reactive, and the more we accept when faced with the other person's perceived shortcomings, the less will we react. And the less we react, the less of a reaction will we provoke in the other person. We will then find that not only will we gain a clearer, less distorted view of that person, but that the person, allowed to be who he or she is, will also be free to see more clearly who that might really be. Understanding can then grow on both sides.

As we therefore wake up spiritually and begin to change and the character defects through which we always perceived people are progressively chipped away, we gain a different perspective on them. We are gradually given the only understanding that in the final analysis truly matters, and that is the understanding that will enable us to extend a helping hand and bring peace to our relationships, whether with our spouses, children, parents, or other family members, or with our co-workers, our friends, or our neighbors.

Understanding becomes a matter of the heart, expressed in tolerance, compassion, and acceptance. Such understanding is a virtue of the affections before it is a virtue of the intellect. It is concerned first with feelings and emotions before it is concerned with facts and information. It is a disposition to see and feel things through somebody else's eyes and heart. We move out of our self-centered perch and begin to identify with others.

The proper relationship between understanding and acceptance, then, is that acceptance comes first. That is the point of departure. We can paraphrase Augustine and say that we accept in order to understand, and we understand the better to accept. As with faith, putting acceptance first means putting God first and letting him shape our understanding.

We are blessed that in the rooms of AA we can find a sort of spiritual lab where we can experiment with acceptance, experiencing and practicing it. Many of us never felt accepted until we first entered those rooms. As people identified with our stories rather than judge or reject us, we began to feel the acceptance we so desperately sought and never found when we drank. As we identified with *their* stories, we found we could accept them in turn. Eventually, we came to see the love and acceptance we found in the rooms as evidence of God's presence among us. We could now accept ourselves and the world around us because, as Bill W. writes, we could now accept that God is all and loves all (*As Bill Sees It*, p. 293). "As we understood Him" was fleshing out and becoming for us a concrete, experiential reality.

Every meeting is an exercise in acceptance. We accept our weaknesses, even as we strive to learn from each other how we can be freed from them. We accept our past and let go of regret, seeing how its lessons can be of help to our fellows. We accept our present circumstances as they are, even as we seek to learn from the experience of others how best to handle them and what in them we can and cannot change. It is through such practical experience, in and out of the rooms, that guided by the grace of God we are granted the wisdom to know the difference, and the courage, born of faith, to change the things we can according to his purpose.

SERENITY AND PEACE

So are we granted the serenity we seek through the practice of acceptance in its many forms, of which we have considered but a few. A faith that works is a faith that through God-directed effort bears spiritual and emotional fruit. As we work Step 3 and practice the various principles that are instrumental in turning our will and our lives over to the care of God, we begin to acquire the peace of mind that eluded us when we drank.

Letting God be God and moving off center stage, abdicating our self-appointed role as arbiters of other people's beliefs and behaviors, relinquishing the reins of power and control over others, accepting our creaturely dependence upon our Creator, acknowledging our common condition as fallen human beings in need of redemption and deliverance, trusting God's providential care of our lives and of the universe—these are the things that will bring us mental tranquility and stability. They are grounded in a spiritual, God-centered view of ourselves and of the world that makes possible the peace of mind we long for.

We have observed that serenity is associated with like terms such as peace, peace of mind, and harmony, all of which may be considered different aspects of the same virtue. It is one of those human qualities we have called emotion-virtues, qualities that describe both character traits and emotional states and have a direct bearing on emotional sobriety.

We might note that in early sobriety our practice of serenity has a distinctly defensive and protective orientation. That is, at this stage serenity is directed primarily to limiting the damage to ourselves that may result from the habitual mental turbulence with which we are often afflicted, particularly when confronted with serious difficulties. It is inner-directed, aimed at producing a calm state of mind in *us*. While externally beneficial in our interaction with our fellows, it is so mostly by omission, a by-product of our effort not to cause harm to ourselves, and only by extension to others. Simply put, we practice serenity mainly to stay out of trouble.

However, with the continued practice of surrender, acceptance, and the other disciplines and virtues that foster peace of mind, serenity begins to take root in our character. It then becomes a virtue that we deliberately externalize to bring peace and reconciliation directly to the lives of others, even when we are not a party to a particular trial. Having interiorized and become wholly disposed to peace, we can then become peacemakers. Our internal strife gone, we can impart to others the peace that we now have in us.

The road to peace starts with our reconciliation with God in Step 3 and moves through the housecleaning Steps to our reconciliation with those we have harmed. It is then, we are promised, that "we will comprehend the word serenity and we will know peace" (Big Book, pp. 83–84). We will continue to pray for the serenity to accept, but we will go further. We will ask God to make us channels of his peace, "that where there is discord, we may bring harmony" (12&12, S11, p. 99). We will seek to practice peace in all our affairs.

THE RIGHT USE OF THE WILL

Working Step 3 is a daily endeavor, a matter of following a sustained course of action guided by the principles it sets down. It requires persistent effort and exertion, and like all the Steps, calls upon the virtue of perseverance. This raises the issue of the proper role of the will in the practice of the Steps.

Sometimes we draw the wrong conclusion from two essential facts we learn in AA. Fact one is that willpower is of no use whatsoever in overcoming the obsession to drink: we are powerless over alcohol. Fact two is that many problems besides alcohol will not yield to the force of our will, however strong it may be. When we are driven by willpower and attempt to exercise control over what cannot be controlled, we end up losing control of ourselves and our lives become unmanageable. From this we mistakenly conclude that the will is of little value to recovery.

This view leads some of us into a passive sort of recovery where we tacitly assume that, so long as we don't drink and show up at meetings, we will continue to grow. Rather than seeing Step 3 and the concept of turning our will and our lives over as a call to relinquish power and control, we see it as a reason to abdicate responsibility and abandon all sustained effort at spiritual growth. This is just a backdoor to two-stepping. AA recovery is not magic and it is not religious mysticism. It is not plugging into some mysterious energy and it is not gained by osmosis. It is exacting, God-guided work.

In Step 3 we are called to make a decision, and a decision is of necessity a function of the will. So is executing that decision. Paradoxically though, the decision is to *surrender* our will. In effect, it seems we have to make a decision of the will to yield our will, a decision of the will against itself.

The apparent contradiction arises from a flawed understanding of the problem that the will represents. A similar misunderstanding arises with regards to the self. The two are connected. The self is God's handiwork and as such necessarily good. It is constitutive of the human person and distinguishes us from other animals and the rest of creation. Hence, when we talk about the problem of the self, we are not talking about its *existence*, but about its *perspective*, about the condition into which it has fallen, about self as ego. The self is to be loved, in us and in others. But self as ego, the perspective which claims preference over other selves and subordinates everything to its own self-ish ends, that we are called to surrender totally and unconditionally.

In the same way, our problem with the will is not its use, but its abuse. The will is a good, a distinctly human faculty that is intrinsic to the self as created by God. It is the gift of our Creator, to be used freely in the pursuit of God's purpose for us. Used for our own purpose apart from God, it turns into self-will and is no longer free.

The problem then is not will, but self-will, which is AA's way of referring to the fact that, in the theological terms of C. S. Lewis noted earlier, our will is fallen, cut off from God's, and that we are consequently predisposed to fall short and go wrong. This predisposition manifests itself in our natural tendency to put self before God and above others, which we have identified as the source of our spiritual disease.

The solution as presented by AA is to turn away from self-will and back toward God's will for us. Implementing it begins, as we have been discussing, with that imperceptible displacement of the will known as willingness. This virtue, in its most elementary expression, moves us away from self and toward the decision of Step 3. Further growth in willingness opens us to receive the power by which we can carry it out. Acquiring and developing this willingness is for the alcoholic "an act of his own will," really a series of acts, for "All of the 12 Steps require sustained and personal exertion to conform to their principles and so, we trust, to God's will" (12&12, S3, p. 40).

The will, rightly used, is necessary to the practice of the Steps. In AA we begin to use our will rightly as we try to practice the principles embedded in those Steps. Through this work we seek to align our will with God's will. *"Our whole trouble had been the misuse of willpower. We had tried to bombard our problems with it instead of attempting to bring it into agreement with God's intention for us. To make this increasingly possible is the purpose of A.A.'s Twelve Steps, and Step Three opens the door"* (ibid., italics in the original).

God gave us free will and in the surrender of Step 3 we offer it back to him, to conform it to his own will. We don't seek a strengthening of our individual will in its current condition, for it is bankrupt and bent on self. Nor do we seek to recharge our depleted willpower. We seek instead a redeemed will, a purification, a removal of the impurities of self that adulterate it.

For most people, will is synonymous with power. This is so because, as the faculty central to the self's ability to make decisions and take action, will requires power. Thus it is common to look upon willpower as a good thing.

But our disastrous history of living by the power of our own will as active alcoholics has taught many of us in AA to be wary of this way of looking at will and power. We have come to identify willpower with self-will, with power that is based on self, on ego. We don't seek to reactivate that kind of power, but to relinquish it.

For us, then, willpower is not a vehicle of recovery. In this AA is unique. Programs and therapies outside of the 12 Steps all seem to offer solutions that are based on the will to power. Having more power and control appears to be their answer to every problem. Not so with us. Lack of power is our dilemma, yes. But in another paradox, it is not solved by a reach for power but by its surrender.

The power is God's, as we acknowledge in the Lord's Prayer, which is used to close some meetings. We remain powerless. By his grace our will is transformed even as our self is transformed. We begin to act more and more out of *his* power, not out of that which grows out of our own volition. We find ourselves willing God's will. We do the right thing, even when we don't want to or feel like it, while at the same time the instances of not wanting to or not feeling like it become less and less frequent.

We will continue to be tempted to take our will back, and many impulses will continue to surface that would lead us back to self. But we will become better at detecting these even as they arise, and promptly letting them go. At times we will smile in recognition of those things that once we were, but are no longer. We will be well along the path of a faith that works.

Working the Steps and practicing the principles in all our affairs is how we grow in recovery beyond physical to spiritual and emotional sobriety. We work Step 3 through our practice of the disciplines of surrender and prayer and the virtues of humility, willingness, acceptance, serenity, and faith. Our objective is uniquely spiritual: to turn our will and our lives over to the care of God. We increasingly rely on God and trust him in any and all situations, surrendering the defects of character and emotion that keep him from working in our lives.

"Trust God, clean house, help others," is how we sum up the 12 Steps in the rooms. Trusting God is the essence of faith, the place we come to as we admit our powerlessness, come to believe, and surrender control. It is what enables us to face life on life's terms with equanimity and peace of mind. It is the heart of Step 3, which is in turn the touchstone and spiritual foundation of the remaining Steps.

The surrender Steps lay the groundwork for the housecleaning which begins in earnest with the next set of Steps as we take stock of our character in relation to our fellows, admit our wrongs, prepare spiritually and emotionally to surrender them to God, and humbly ask him to remove them. We will find that as we practice these principles, trust God, and clean house, we will also have started to help others, taking the steps that lead us in our spiritual awakening toward the life of love and service which is the good, the happy, and the fully sober life.

Postscript

Readers who have found this book helpful and who desire to explore some of its ideas further may wish to avail themselves of the extensive resources we have made available online.

The book's website, PracticeThesePrinciplesTheBook.com, offers original articles written by Ray on the Steps and their principles, the emotions, character and its defects, habit, and the concept of a spiritual awakening. These are supplemented by the best quotes on the subject from ancient times to the present as well as by suggested material from AA, other 12-Step fellowships, books, films, and other resources. Additional features include a Big Book Q&A, AA History Timeline, Audios & Videos, Reflections on Recovery, and Ray's Book Reviews. Most of these posts are illustrated with images from AA history.

Readers will also find useful supplementary material on the book's social media platforms. Our Pinterest page features shareable pins illustrating quotes found on the website as well as videos and other material. Because of the nature of this platform, we can do this not only in English, but also in Spanish, French, Italian, Portuguese, and German. Our Facebook page features some of the same English-language material as well as excerpts from the book's website posts. Our YouTube channel carries all the videos referenced on the book's website as well as other videos related to recovery from other perspectives, such as psychology and philosophy. Finally, our Goodreads page features Ray's Recovery Library and other recovery-related books arranged by field (psychology, philosophy, religion, etc.), as well as videos and excerpts from website posts.

As with the book, our primary purpose with these platforms is to carry the AA message. Because of their very broad reach, however, they make it possible for us to carry this message not only to alcoholics and others in recovery but to all those who may be able to benefit from it. The message is that of a spiritual awakening. Its principles are universal and their practice accessible to everyone.

Appendix

The Twelve Steps

1. We admitted we were powerless over alcohol—that our lives had become unmanageable.
2. Came to believe that a Power greater than ourselves could restore us to sanity.
3. Made a decision to turn our will and our lives over to the care of God *as we understood Him.*
4. Made a searching and fearless moral inventory of ourselves.
5. Admitted to God, to ourselves, and to another human being the exact nature of our wrongs.
6. Were entirely ready to have God remove all these defects of character.
7. Humbly asked Him to remove our shortcomings.
8. Made a list of all persons we had harmed, and became willing to make amends to them all.
9. Made direct amends to such people wherever possible, except when to do so would injure them or others.
10. Continued to take personal inventory and when we were wrong promptly admitted it.
11. Sought through prayer and meditation to improve our conscious contact with God *as we understood Him,* praying only for knowledge of His will for us and the power to carry that out.
12. Having had a spiritual awakening as the result of these steps, we tried to carry this message to alcoholics, and to practice these principles in all our affairs.

The Twelve Traditions

1. Our common welfare should come first; personal recovery depends upon A.A. unity.
2. For our group purpose there is but one ultimate authority—a loving God as He may express Himself in our group conscience. Our leaders are but trusted servants; they do not govern.
3. The only requirement for membership is a desire to stop drinking.
4. Each group should be autonomous except in matters affecting other groups or A.A. as a whole.
5. Each group has but one primary purpose—to carry its message to the alcoholic who still suffers.

6. An A.A. group ought never endorse, finance, or lend the A.A. name to any related facility or outside enterprise, lest problems of money, property, and prestige divert us from our primary purpose.

7. Every A.A. group ought to be fully self-supporting, declining outside contributions.

8. Alcoholics Anonymous should remain forever non-professional, but our service centers may employ special workers.

9. A.A., as such, ought never be organized; but we may create service boards or committees directly responsible to those they serve.

10. Alcoholics Anonymous has no opinion on outside issues; hence the A.A. name never ought to be drawn into public controversy.

11. Our public relations policy is based on attraction rather than promotion; we need always maintain personal anonymity at the level of press, radio, and films.

12. Anonymity is the spiritual foundation of all our traditions, ever reminding us to place principles before personalities.

NOTES

CHAPTER 1: THESE PRINCIPLES

1. See *The Language of the Heart* (New York: The AA Grapevine, Inc., 1988), 305.
2. See *Practice These Principles and What Is the Oxford Group* (Center City, MN: Hazelden Publishing, 1997).
3. Page numbers where these and other terms are used in the Big Book and the 12&12 can be found by searching at https://164andmore.com. The Big Book uses pity in the sense of compassion in Step 4, p. 67.
4. See William C. Mattison III, *Introducing Moral Theology: True Happiness and the Virtues* (Grand Rapids, MI: Brazos Press, 2008), Chapter 1, and Julia Annas, *The Morality of Happiness* (Oxford University Press, New York, 1995).
5. Andrew Murray, *Humility: The Journey Toward Holiness* (Bloomington, IN: Bethany House Publishers, 2001), 17.
6. See *The Language of the Heart*, 93.
7. 1 Corinthians 13:13 (NIV).

CHAPTER 2: IN ALL OUR AFFAIRS: EMOTIONAL SOBRIETY

1. Robert C. Roberts, *An Essay in Aid of Moral Psychology* (New York: Cambridge University Press, 2003), 43.
2. Robert C. Roberts, *Spiritual Emotions: A Psychology of Christian Virtues* (Grand Rapids, MI: Wm. B. Eerdmans Publishing Co., 2007), 11.
3. Matthew 6:21 (KJV).
4. 1 Thessalonians 5:18 (Douay-Rheims).
5. *Grapevine,* January 1958; reprinted in *The Language of the Heart*, 237; in *Emotional Sobriety: The Next Frontier* (New York: The AA Grapevine, Inc., 2006), 2; and in *Practice These Principles: Step 4*, 437.

CHAPTER 3: LACK OF POWER: OUR DILEMMA

1. Genesis 1:27, 2:7.
2. Hebrews 11:34 and 2 Corinthians 12:10 (KJV).

CHAPTER 4: THE WILL TO DISBELIEVE

1. Romans 7:19 (KJV).
2. Dinesh D'Souza, *What's So Great About Christianity* (Washington, DC: Regnery Publishing, 2009), 55–56.
3. *The Book That Started It All: The Original Working Manuscript of Alcoholics Anonymous* (Center City, MN: Hazelden Publishing, 2010).

4. Nancy Pearcey, *Total Truth: Liberating Christianity from Its Cultural Captivity* (Wheaton, IL: Crossway Books, 2005), 59.

5. Ibid., 59–60.

6. See Christopher Peterson and Martin E.P. Seligman, *Character Strengths and Virtues: A Handbook and Classification* (New York: Oxford University Press, 2004).

7. Pearcey, 176.

8. Francis S. Collins, *The Language of God: A Scientist Presents Evidence for Belief* (New York: Free Press, 2007), 165.

9. Rodney Stark, *For the Glory of God* (Princeton: Princeton University Press, 2004), 198–199.

10. Ian G. Barbour, *When Science Meets Religion: Enemies, Strangers, or Partners?* (New York: Harper Collins, 2000), 24.

11. Stark, 194.

12. Dinesh D'Souza, *Life After Death* (Washington, DC: Regnery Publishing, 2009), 65.

13. Stark, 197.

14. Elaine Howard Ecklund and others, "Religion among Scientists in International Context: A New Study of Scientists in Eight Regions" (Sage Journals), 2016.

15. Gerald L. Schroeder, *God According to God: A Scientist Discovers We've Been Wrong About God All Along* (New York: Harper Collins, 2009), 219.

16. John Polkinghorne, *Belief in God in an Age of Science* (New Haven: Yale University Press, 2003), 122.

17. Robert J. Spitzer, *New Proofs for the Existence of God: Contributions of Contemporary Physics and Philosophy* (Grand Rapids, MI: Wm. B. Eerdmans Publishing Co., 2010), 17, 48.

18. Ibid., 79.

19. Hebrews 11:1 (KJV).

20. Stephen C. Meyer, *Return of the God Hypothesis: Three Scientific Discoveries That Reveal the Mind Behind the Universe* (New York: Harper One, 2021), 95.

21. Norman L. Geisler and Frank Turek, *I Don't Have Enough Faith to Be an Atheist* (Wheaton, IL: Crossway Books, 2004), 74.

22. Robert Jastrow, *God and the Astronomers*, 2nd Edition (New York: Readers Library, 2000), 14.

23. "A Scientist Caught Between Two Faiths: Interview with Robert Jastrow, *Christianity Today*, August 6, 1982.

24. Meyer, 108.

25. Ibid., 116.

26. Ibid., 115, 117.
27. Hebrews 11:3 (NIV).
28. D'Souza, *What's So Great About Christianity,* 131.
29. Barbour, 30.
30. Meyer, 139.
31. Ibid.
32. Ibid., 141.
33. Eric Metaxas, *Is Atheism Dead?* (Washington, D.C.: Salem Books, 2021), 407.
34. Geisler and Turek, 116.
35. Schroeder, *151.*
36. Ibid.
37. Ibid., 91.
38. Ibid., 226.
39. Psalms 104:24 (NIV).
40. John 1:1-3 (NIV).
41. Barbour, 29.
42. See Antony Flew, *There Is ~~No~~ a God* (New York: Harper One, 2007).
43. Metaxas, 287–302.
44. Jastrow, 105.
45. Geisler & Turek, 120.
46. D'Souza, *What's So Great About Christianity*, 272.
47. Thomas Nagel, *The Last Word* (New York: Oxford University Press, 2001), 130-131.
48. See *Dr. Bob and the Good Oldtimers* (New York: Alcoholics Anonymous World Services, Inc., 2008), 218, and the Sermon on the Mount, Matthew 7:7 (NIV).
49. Bryan Magee, *Ultimate Questions* (Princeton, NJ: Princeton University Press, 2016), 21.
50. Mark 9:24 (NIV).
51. C. S. Lewis, *Mere Christianity* (New York: Macmillan Publishing Co., 1960), 163.
52. Mark 2:17, Luke 5:32.
53. Quoted in *First Things*, December 2018, "The Forgotten Virtue," 33.
54. Timothy Keller, *The Reason for God* (New York: Dutton, Penguin Group, 2008), 53–54.
55. See Ernest Kurtz and Katherine Ketcham, *The Spirituality of Imperfection: Storytelling and the Search for Meaning* (New York: Bantam Books, 2002).

CHAPTER 5: CROSSING THE THRESHOLD

1. Ernest Kurtz, *Not-God* (Center City, MN: Hazelden Publishing, 1991), 70.
2. *Dr. Bob and the Good Oldtimers*, 161.
3. *Alcoholics Anonymous Comes of Age*, 262–263.
4. Ibid., 264.
5. C. S. Lewis, *The Business of Heaven* (New York: Harcourt Brace, 1984), August 1–5.
6. *Alcoholics Anonymous Comes of Age*, 311.
7. G. K. Chesterton, *Orthodoxy: The Romance of Faith* (New York: Doubleday, 1959), 19.

CHAPTER 6: THE TURNING POINT

1. C. S. Lewis, *The Problem of Pain* (New York: McMillan Publishing Co., 1962), 81.
2. Lewis, *Mere Christianity*, 39.
3. Roberts, *Spiritual Emotions*, 71.
4. *Alcoholics Anonymous Comes of Age*, 46.
5. Murray, *Humility*, 16–17.
6. Acts 17:28 (KJV).
7. See C. S. Lewis, *The Business of Heaven*, July 3.
8. Ibid., March 17.
9. See Sam Shoemaker, *Extraordinary Living for Ordinary Men* (Grand Rapids, MI: Zondervan, 1970), 76.
10. Page numbers where these and other terms are used in the Big Book and the 12&12 can be found by searching at https://164andmore.com.
11. *The World's Last Night and Other Essay,* cited in *The Quotable Lewis* (Wheaton, IL: Tyndale House Publishers, 1989), 211.
12. 1 Corinthians 13:12 (KJV).
13. *Catechism of the Catholic Church* (New York: Doubleday, 1995), 49.
14. James S. Spiegel, *How to Be Good in a World Gone Bad: Living a Life of Christian Virtue* (Grand Rapids, MI: Kregel Publications, 2004), 190.

CHAPTER 7: WORKING THE STEPS, PRACTICING THE PRINCIPLES

1. Spiegel, 190.
2. Phil. 2:12–13 (KJV).
3. Lewis, *Mere Christianity*, 115.
4. See *Alcoholics Anonymous Comes of Age*, 196, and *Pass It On* (New York: Alcoholics Anonymous World Services, Inc., 1984), 252.

5. Eileen Flanagan, *The Wisdom to Know the Difference* (New York: Penguin Group, 2009), 6.

6. See Mattison, p.189.

7. Quoted in Karen Casey and Martha Vanceburg, *The Promise of a New Day* (Center City, MN: Hazelden Publishing, 1983), April 26.

8. *Acceptance: The Way to Serenity and Peace of Mind* (St. Meinrad, IN: Abbey Press, 1960), 5.

SUGGESTED READINGS

BASIC AA TEXTS

Alcoholics Anonymous, 4th Edition. New York: Alcoholics Anonymous World Services, Inc. 2002.

Alcoholics Anonymous Comes of Age: A Brief History of A.A. New York: Alcoholics Anonymous World Services, Inc., 1957.

As Bill Sees It. New York: Alcoholics Anonymous World Services, Inc., 1967.

Dr. Bob and the Good Oldtimers. New York: Alcoholics Anonymous World Services, Inc., 2008.

Pass It On: The Story of Bill Wilson and How the A.A. Message Reached the World. New York: Alcoholics Anonymous World Services, Inc., 1984.

The Language of the Heart. New York: The AA Grapevine, Inc., 1988.

Twelve Steps and Twelve Traditions. New York: Alcoholics Anonymous World Services, Inc., 2002.

OTHER AA AND RECOVERY LITERATURE

Practice These Principles and What Is the Oxford Group. Center City, MN: Hazelden Publishing, 1997.

Twenty-Four Hours a Day. Center City, MN: Hazelden Publishing, 1983.

THE VIRTUES

Kreeft, Peter, *Back to Virtue.* San Francisco: Ignatius Press, 1992.

Mattison III, William C., *Introducing Moral Theology: True Happiness and the Virtues.* Grand Rapids, MI: Brazos Press, 2008.

Murray, Andrew, *Humility: The Journey Toward Holiness.* Bloomington, IN: Bethany House Publishers, 2001.

Roberts, Robert C., *Spiritual Emotions: A Psychology of Christian Virtues.* Grand Rapids, MI: Wm. B. Eerdmans Publishing Co., 2007.

Spiegel, James S., *How to Be Good in a World Gone Bad: Living a Life of Christian Virtue.* Grand Rapids, MI: Kregel Publications, 2004.

SPIRITUALITY AND RELIGION

Keller, Timothy, *The Reason for God.* New York: Dutton, Penguin Group, 2008.

Kurtz, Ernest, and Katherine Ketcham, *The Spirituality of Imperfection: Storytelling and the Search for Meaning.* New York: Bantam Books, 2002.

REASON, SCIENCE, AND FAITH

Barbour, Ian G., *When Science Meets Religion: Enemies, Strangers, or Partners?* New York: HarperCollins, 2000.

Berlinski, David, *The Devil's Delusion: Atheism and Its Scientific Pretensions.* New York: Basic Books, 2009.

Collins, Francis, *The Language of God.* New York: Free Press, Simon & Schuster, 2006.

Geisler, Norman L., and Frank Turek, *I Don't Have Enough Faith to Be an Atheist.* Wheaton, IL: Crossway Books, 2004.

McGrath, Alister, *The Twilight of Atheism.* New York: Doubleday, 2006.

Meyer, Stephen C., *Return of the God Hypothesis: Three Scientific Discoveries That Reveal the Mind Behind the Universe.* New York: HarperCollins, 2021.

Morris, Thomas V., Editor, *God and the Philosophers: The Reconciliation of Faith and Reason.* New York: Oxford University Press, 1994.

Polkinghorne, John, *Belief in God in an Age of Science.* New Haven: Yale University Press, 2003.

Schroeder, Gerald L., *God According to God: A Scientist Discovers We've Been Wrong About God All Along.* New York: Harper Collins, 2009.

About the Author

Ray A. is a recovering alcoholic who's been sober in Alcoholics Anonymous since April 26, 1984.

He drank for 25 years and, as with most drunks, alcohol touched every aspect of his life. Early on he earned an undergraduate degree in Romance Languages and a graduate degree in English. As his disease progressed, however, he left a doctoral degree in Comparative Literature unfinished. Alcohol also exacted its toll on his marriage, his family, and a series of promising careers. In midlife, Ray came to AA homeless, alone, and unemployable.

Once in the rooms Ray made progress on many fronts, from personal relations to the establishment of a successful business. By the time of his twelfth sober anniversary, however, he began to suffer an emotional relapse that would worsen over the course of the next six years, result in the collapse of his business, and bring his life crashing down again.

This drawn-out bottom ended in a surrender experience which put Ray on a new path to healing and growth. He was forced to take a hard look at his recovery and find out where things had gone wrong, since he believed he had worked the Steps and done everything the program said to do. In the process, he was also forced to probe into that program and those Steps more deeply than ever.

It was then that he finally began to understand what he had never understood before: the true nature of the principles underlying the 12 Steps and how the practice of those principles can actually bring about the spiritual growth and emotional sobriety that had eluded him all those years and that continues to elude so many recovering alcoholics today.

His progress in this new journey led to the writing of *Practice These Principles*, a work that reflects his experience as well as years of research into the AA, 12-Step, recovery, and related literatures. The first volume discusses Steps 1, 2, and 3 and the second Step 4. Further volumes on the remaining Steps and the 12 Traditions are planned.

INDEX

Made in the USA
Middletown, DE
18 May 2023

30758622R00154